T0305121

Monopoly Policy in the UK

For Jan, Cath and Emma

Monopoly Policy in the UK

Assessing the Evidence

Roger Clarke

Professor of Microeconomics, Cardiff Business School, Cardiff University, UK

Stephen Davies

Professor of Economics, University of East Anglia, UK

Nigel Driffield

Lecturer in Industrial Economics, Cardiff Business School, Cardiff University, UK

Edward Elgar
Cheltenham, UK • Northampton, MA, USA

Published by
Edward Elgar Publishing Limited
The Lypiatts
15 Lansdown Road
Cheltenham
Glos GL50 2JA
UK

Edward Elgar Publishing, Inc.
William Pratt House
9 Dewey Court
Northampton
Massachusetts 01060
USA

Reprinted 2002

A catalogue record for this book
is available from the British Library

Library of Congress Cataloguing in Publication Data

Clarke, Roger, 1949–
    Monopoly policy in the UK: assessing the evidence / Roger Clarke,
Stephen Davies, Nigel Driffield.
    Includes bibliographical references.
    1. Monopolies—Great Britain. 2. Competition—Great Britain.
3. Industrial policy—Great Britain. I. Davies, Stephen, 1948–   .
II. Driffield, Nigel L.   III. Title.
HD2757.2.C55   1998
338.8'2'0941—dc21   97–50054
                                                                          CIP

ISBN 978 1 85898 585 5

Printed and bound in Great Britain by T.J. International Ltd, Padstow

Contents

List of Figures and Tables   vi
Preface   viii

1. Introduction   1

PART I: AN OVERVIEW

2. Review of UK Competition Policy in General   15
3. MMC Investigations of Monopoly: the Population   28
4. Methodology and Selection of Case Studies   51

PART II: THE CASE STUDIES

5. Monopoly Pricing and Price Leadership   61
6. Collusive Practices   82
7. Predatory Pricing (and Price Discrimination)   102
8. Vertical Restraints   116

PART III: CONCLUSIONS

9. An Overall Assessment of the Effectiveness of Policy   175
10. The Case for Reform   190

Appendix: The Population of Cases: 1973–95   198
References   202
Index   207

Figures and Tables

FIGURES

3.1 Distribution of cases by oligopoly type   36
5.1 Average revenue of LRC   68
5.2 Return on capital employed of LRC   69

TABLES

2.1 United Kingdom competition law   17
2.2 The changing pattern of competition policy over time   19
2.3 Coverage of anti-competitive problems   21
3.1 MMC reports on potential monopoly abuse   29
3.2 Industrial distribution of the population of cases   31
3.3 Size of referred markets   33
3.4 Scale and complex monopolies   34
3.5 Classification by type of oligopoly   38
3.6 Industry structure and type of oligopoly   39
3.7 Incidence of monopoly problems   40
3.8 Monopoly problems by type of oligopoly   41
3.9 Types of recommendation   42
3.10 Problems and remedies   43
3.11 Recommendations and industry structure   44
3.12 Time lags (months)   45
4.1 The sample of case studies   55
5.1 Monopoly pricing and price leadership in the population   62
6.1 Collusive practices in the population   84
6.2 Electricity meters, market shares (%)   86
7.1 Discriminatory/predatory pricing in the population   105
8.1 Vertical restraints in the population   123
8.2 Frozen foods, market shares (%)   127
8.3 Postal franking machines, market shares (%)   140

9.1   Brief summary of findings in Part II   178
9.2   Changes in market structure   180
9.3   Is there still cause for concern?   183
10.1 Analysis of population by firm dominance   193
10.2 Analysis of sample by firm dominance   194

Preface

The origins of this book lie in two research projects undertaken for the Office of Fair Trading (OFT) in 1994 and 1995. These projects looked at the effectiveness of remedies introduced following Monopolies and Mergers Commission (MMC) investigations into monopoly abuse. In this work, we undertook a number of case studies of industries investigated by the MMC. In one respect, this took us into territory which was fairly unusual for us. The OFT was keen that our findings should not be based on 'deskwork' alone – they wanted us also to consult directly with the firms and other organisations involved in a number of MMC cases. In the event, we conducted a total of 61 interviews in ten cases and these cases (together with four other cases (see Chapter 4)) form the basis of Part II of this book.

In subsequently converting this research into its present book form, we have made considerable changes. First, in order to respect confidentiality, we have omitted a certain amount of detail from the book. These changes, however, are fairly minor in most cases. Second, we have expanded the material significantly in a number of ways. These include adding a background chapter (Chapter 2) on UK competition policy in general; adding discussion within individual chapters of relevant economic theory; and adding a closing chapter (Chapter 10) on policy reform. Also, in an attempt to fill an important gap in the literature, we have included some discussion of *all* monopoly cases investigated by the MMC between 1973 and 1995. Thus we hope the book will provide a useful reference source for those interested in the control of monopoly abuse in the UK. The book should be of interest in general to three types of audience: the business community and policy makers; undergraduate and postgraduate students of Industrial Organisation, and fellow academic economists.

In undertaking the research and latterly writing the book, we have benefited from the help of a number of people. We would like to thank, in particular, the firms involved in our interviews who were willing to take time to answer our questions and provide us with much valuable information. We would also like to thank the Office of Fair Trading (and, in particular, Dave Elliott, Mike Parr and Peter Bamford) for their advice and support at various stages of our work; Dave Elliott (again) and Mike Utton for their thoughtful comments on draft versions of this book; Melanie Lund for her research assistance on the first project; and Stephen Edwards and Sanji Prasad for setting up the interviews on the second. Finally, we would like to thank Cath Colgan and Penny Smith at the Cardiff Business School for typing and editing the final draft of this book.

Roger Clarke, Steve Davies and Nigel Driffield
Cardiff Business School and University of East Anglia

1. Introduction

This book provides an appraisal of the effectiveness of remedies to monopoly abuse put in place following Monopolies and Merger Commission (MMC) investigations over the period 1973–95.

For those with a sense of history, an appraisal of monopoly policy is quite appropriate as we near the end of the twentieth century. 1998 marks the 50th anniversary of the Monopolies and Mergers Commission[1] and the 25th anniversary of the Fair Trading Act which is still a central part of UK competition legislation. However, there are more important reasons for focusing on monopoly policy. First, privatisation and liberalisation have been a pervasive feature throughout the world for much of the 1980s and 1990s, with the result that state intervention, in the form of ownership and regulation, is now much reduced. Against this background, it is natural to examine the value of another form of intervention: anti-trust policy. Whilst we steer clear of very fundamental issues here – is anti-trust policy necessary at all, or would it be better to leave the market to find its own solutions to competition problems, as and when they arise? – this book does attack, head-on, the more practical question of whether policy, *as it has been practised,* has been 'effective'. Second, for a number of years, policy makers and academics have been discussing the reform of UK competition policy, with particular reference to bringing it closer to European policy. Indeed, at the time of writing, the recently elected Labour government has introduced a new draft competition bill (DTI, 1997a) into Parliament (in August 1997). In the closing chapter of the book, we return to this in the light of our findings. Third, and on a more academic note, this book should help to fill a gap in the existing literature. Only a limited amount of work has been done on the effectiveness of remedies to monopoly abuse in the UK, principally by Shaw and Simpson (1989) in their work on 1959–1973[2] There is clearly a need to examine the effectiveness of more recent policy and this is a key aim in this book.

1.1 OBJECTIVES

In undertaking the research on which this book is based our primary aim was to provide an up-to-date and detailed review of the efficacy of a remedy. We hoped to answer questions such as 'what typically is the effect of a remedy on the state of competition in a given market, following an MMC investigation?', 'are certain types of remedy typically more effective than others?', and 'are effective remedies more likely in certain types of market?'

However, in subsequently writing this book, we have added two further objectives. The first is to report our findings in such a way as to make them intelligible, not only to professional economists, but also to both the general lay reader and the interested undergraduate student. We hope that the individual industry case studies, in which we highlight the opinions of the firms we interviewed, will help to retain a 'real world feel' to our story. So far as the interested student is concerned, we have tried to slant our presentation to illustrate the relevant contemporary theories they are learning in courses on Industrial Organisation and related subjects. Recent years have seen an explosion of theoretical analysis of anti-competitive practices, often based on complex applications of game theory. We have, therefore, included as introductory passages in the case study chapters short summaries of the academic theoretical literature.

Our other objective is to provide a reasonably comprehensive reference source. Although the book is based on a relatively small sample (14) of individual case studies, in order to select that sample we first undertook a comprehensive classification of *all* monopoly investigations undertaken by the MMC between 1973 and 1995. As far as we know, this is the first time any such cataloguing has been attempted, and we believe that the results might be of interest in themselves. With this in mind, we have included summaries (albeit sometimes very brief) of all 61 industries investigated by the MMC over this period, as well as a full tabulation of cases, remedies and market structures in the Appendix of this book.

1.2 AN INTRODUCTORY OUTLINE OF UK MONOPOLY POLICY

In later chapters, we describe the legal and institutional framework of policy in more detail, but a short preliminary sketch will be helpful here before describing the methodology of our research.

UK monopoly policy, as laid down in the 1973 Fair Trading Act (FTA), adopts a cost–benefit approach to monopoly, wherein the Monopolies and Mergers Commission (MMC) undertakes case-by-case investigations of monopolies and considers whether they operate, or can be expected to operate, against the public interest. If the MMC finds evidence that they do (or may) operate against the public interest, it can make recommendations for change. The Secretary of State at the Department of Trade and Industry can then take remedial action either in the form of securing undertakings from the firms involved or through an Order. However, the Secretary of State is not bound by the MMC's recommendations, and can vary them or take no action at all.

Under the FTA, the Secretary of State has wide powers to implement remedies, and these can include *price controls, termination* of anti-competitive practices and *divestment* of assets or shares. In contrast to some other jurisdictions (for example, EU policy; see Chapter 2), however, the exercise of monopoly power is not unlawful and there is no provision in UK law for civil action against a monopoly. Because of this, the effectiveness of policy rests largely on the remedies adopted following an investigation, and these are our main concern in this book.[3]

1.3 BACKGROUND TO THE STUDY

This study derives from two earlier reports[4] undertaken for the Office of Fair Trading (OFT) on the effectiveness of monopoly policy in the UK. In our work, we used a case study approach to look at the effectiveness of policy in a small, but representative, sample of cases. The first investigation (hereafter 'the first report') was confined to desk-study work examining the types of problem encountered and the impact of remedies using a variety of primary and secondary data sources, whilst the second report used interviews with the firms concerned and other interested parties.

In the first report, we selected a sample of ten cases as representative of the population as a whole (see Chapter 4).[5] In the second report, we initially intended to follow up all ten cases in subsequent interviews; however, we found that three of the earliest cases were too distant in time to be able to obtain satisfactory interview evidence. They were, therefore, supplemented by three others (ice cream, foreign package holidays and artificial lower limbs). We also decided to add one other significant case (bus services in the north-east).[6] In total then, we have a sample of 14 case studies. As noted above, we treat them as representative of the population of cases and believe that they provide the basis for a fairly wide examination of the effectiveness of the remedies used over the period 1973–95.

Whilst the initial stimulus for this book derives from our earlier reports, we have extended the work in several ways. First, as already explained, whilst we focus on 14 cases for in-depth analysis we have also included material on *all* cases in the population in order to provide a broader overview of investigations in this area. We have also expanded the work to include a discussion of UK competition policy in general as well as proposals for policy reform (see Chapters 2 and 10). At the time of writing, the new Labour Government has introduced a new competition bill designed to bring UK policy more closely into line with that in the EU and we discuss this briefly also in Chapter 10.

1.4 METHODOLOGY

Our study follows on chronologically from the earlier work of Shaw and Simpson (1986, 1989) on the effectiveness of monopoly policy in 1959–73. They conducted a statistical analysis based on a sample of 28 markets or sub-industries in 19 MMC reports and focused on the impact of MMC investigations on leading firm market shares and profitability. They found, on average, that leading firm market share declined following MMC investigations from about 60 per cent, on average, to 52 per cent over a period of roughly ten years,[7] and that in 22 of the 28 cases leading firms lost market share. However, when Shaw and Simpson compared their results with those for a control group,[8] they found no significant difference in the change in leading firm shares between the two groups. These results suggest (although see our comments below) that MMC intervention had no effect on market shares.

In the case of profitability, they found some evidence that leading firms experienced falls in profitability up to ten years after a report (where profitability was measured relative to average profitability in manufacturing industry as a whole). However, on average, these falls were very small. In seven cases where the MMC had been critical of high profitability, profitability had declined five years later from 192 per cent to 178 per cent of average manufacturing profitability, and to 161 per cent five years further on. Shaw and Simpson also noted that in three cases (Champion (spark plugs), Kodak (cameras) and Proctor and Gamble (washing powders)), profitability remained very high even ten years later. They concluded that 'the Monopolies Commission had only a minor impact on the competitive process' (1989, p. 23).

When designing our own research, we considered undertaking a large scale cross-section statistical analysis similar to that of Shaw and Simpson. However, we rejected this approach for a number of reasons. First, and most obviously, changes in market shares and profitability will reflect many factors, not simply the effects of monopoly policy, and even if those factors can be controlled for statistically, any residual changes may give poor signals of underlying changes in competition. On the first point, market shares and profitability will be sensitive to changes in the level of demand, technical change, changes in costs and so on and it could be misleading to attribute all (or, indeed, most of) these changes to the effects of policy.[9] On the second, changes in a dominant firm's market share and/or profitability could be a misleading indicator of the change in competition. For example, price controls could induce other firms to leave the industry so that the market share of the dominant firm could *increase* despite controls on its price.[10] Or again, in the case of divestment, whilst the market share of the dominant firm might decline, this need not signal tougher competition if the now separate firms continued to act collusively.

Of course, in any analysis in this area the counterfactual assumption is crucial. As Shaw and Simpson (1986, p. 369) point out, even though the declines in leading firm market share in the MMC group and the control group were similar, this *could* still imply that policy was successful – if the plausible counterfactual was that, absent intervention, dominance would increase or at least not fall. The counterfactual problem is especially pronounced in cross-sectional statistical analysis, precisely because one is pulled towards robust generalities, that is, the counterfactual is assumed, in extreme cases, to be the same in all cases. Given the wide range of monopoly problems, market structures and remedies used, we doubt that the search for a robust counterfactual can be justified.

It is for this reason that we have opted for a case study approach in our own work. Moreover, in order to avoid the temptation of approaching each case with our own fixed agenda, we have placed considerable emphasis on seeking the opinion of the main actors involved, through direct interviews. This approach turns out to be rich in the detail uncovered, but it is not without dangers. In particular, we have been anxious to avoid merely producing 14 stand-alone, and largely unconnected, stories. In order to reduce the risk of this, we have structured the cases in such a way as to facilitate comparative analysis. A key element in this has been the classification we have used in identifying broad types of monopoly problem.

1.5 TYPES OF MONOPOLY PROBLEM

As every student is taught, monopolies restrict output and raise prices, leading to an economic welfare loss. Monopolies, however, have much wider effects than this, and, in practice, monopoly pricing is only one (albeit an important one) of several problems that arise. In this book, we distinguish five types of monopoly problem which feature in our cases and we discuss them briefly here.

1.5.1 Monopoly Pricing

Since the conventional arguments about monopoly pricing are well known, we sketch them only briefly here. In standard textbook terms, a monopolist is a firm which controls the supply of some good or service (or, more loosely, dominates such supply) with no close substitutes and no threat of entry. Under these conditions (and absent regulation) the firm can restrict output, raise price and make monopoly profits. Economic theory suggests that this is undesirable for several reasons. First, because monopolists set 'high' prices, consumers (or, more generally, customers) are worse off than they would be in a more competitive market. Second, monopolists set prices above marginal cost and this creates an inefficient allocation of scarce resources. Third, without the pressure of competition, monopolists may also fail to take opportunities to reduce their costs thereby implying less efficient production. And fourth, if they undertake expenditures designed to *acquire* or *maintain* a monopoly position (for example, high advertising) this may also involve a welfare loss.[11]

Of course, there are counter arguments. Monopoly (or, at least, market dominance) may be desirable to gain economies of scale or of scope (although in the context of a natural monopoly, regulation would usually be required). Monopolists may be dynamically efficient and be better able to invent and develop new products and processes. They may also produce better quality products or have lower costs (and hence prices) so that monopoly may simply be the result of greater efficiency, rather than (or as well as (Clarke, Davies and Waterson, 1984)) the result of market power.

An important question in monopoly analysis is why does monopoly power exist at all? One answer is that a monopolist (or a dominant firm) can benefit from or create barriers to entry which allow it both to earn monopoly profits and maintain its dominant position in the long run. Alternatively, following Sutton (1991), the competitive process itself may encourage firms to escalate endogenous sunk costs (such as advertising and/or R&D expenditures) in order to increase consumers' willingness to pay. In this case, there may not be a deliberate strategy to deter new entry – but it could have this effect. Firms may also dominate a market because they have access to scarce resources which enable them to earn monopoly rents (for example through ownership of mineral deposits or key patents).

Or, again, they may be protected by some form of government regulation which restricts entry into the market.[12]

1.5.2 Collusion

In the UK, monopoly policy covers not only monopolies and single dominant firms but also markets which are clearly oligopolistic. This is partly due to the fact that UK policy has quite a low threshold in defining a statutory monopoly (a 25 per cent market share) and, partly, because the MMC can also investigate *complex monopolies* where several firms have a combined market share of 25 per cent. This means that the MMC can look at cases where two (or even three or four) firms dominate a market and engage in collusive behaviour, and also at situations of 'loose oligopoly' where, again, collusion may exist.

In these kinds of cases, the key issue is often whether the firms are able to coordinate their behaviour (that is, tacitly collude)[13] in order to set a monopoly price. Conventional theory suggests certain conditions where this is more likely to happen: in cases where there are only a few sellers in the market; in situations where firms have similar cost and demand conditions, and a similar perspective on the market; in cases where firms can easily monitor their rivals' prices; in situations where demand and supply are fairly stable, and so on.[14] Moreover, recent game theoretic treatments suggest that in an infinitely repeated game, tacit collusion could well be optimal assuming that strong enough punishments can be used and that firm discount rates are not too high.[15] In these kinds of cases, firms may simply decide that they wish to collude rather than compete and hence set a monopoly price.

1.5.3 Predatory Pricing

Predatory pricing is allegedly an important way in which monopolists can exert or defend their monopoly power. Whilst disagreement exists over the precise definition of predation,[16] the general idea is quite straightforward: firms engage in predatory behaviour if they set low prices (or engage in other anti-competitive practices) in the short run in order to *discipline* or *remove* rivals from the market. Predation thus involves two factors: the intent of the monopolist to drive out its rivals and the use of low prices (or other predatory tactics)[17] to do so.

Whilst some writers have criticised the idea that predatory pricing would be a credible strategy,[18] it is now recognised fairly generally that it can be credible under certain conditions. In particular, it is argued that predation can have a *reputation effect* in that dominant firms operating in several markets can set predatory prices in one (or several) markets to gain a reputation for aggressive behaviour which prevents entry taking place in others.[19] Alternatively, if capital markets are imperfect, predation can allow relatively large firms (defined here as firms with access to relatively large amounts of capital) to engage in predatory pricing to drive out their 'smaller' rivals. The point is that small firms are forced to close (or not enter) because they cannot sustain a period of loss-making in the same way that a 'big' firm can.

Predation is a particular problem under existing UK policy because such behaviour is not illegal and there is no right for an affected firm to seek redress through the courts. Moreover, once predation has taken place and, say, a small firm has left the market, an MMC investigation is largely irrelevant to the firm concerned. This is an issue which we discuss further in Chapters 7 and 10 below.[20]

1.5.4 Price Discrimination

It is well recognised in introductory textbooks that linear pricing is only one option available to a monopoly firm. Amongst other things, a monopolist can set (i) a linear price combined with a fixed fee (for example, through a connection charge for electricity or telephone services), (ii) a high and a low tariff (or a series of tariffs) linked to the consumption of a good (for example, electricity tariffs), or (iii) different prices for different segments of the market (for example, standard or concessionary fares on trains or buses). Each type of discrimination has the potential to increase monopoly profits and whilst discrimination is not always against the public interest, it can produce undesirable effects in some circumstances (often when associated with predatory intent) and hence has been the subject of policy concern.

Price discrimination is, in fact, a factor in many markets investigated by the MMC although in relatively few cases is it the *main* cause for concern. The two forms most often encountered are the use of discounts to customers (sometimes linked to exclusive purchasing) and spatial price discrimination.

In the former case, large firms typically give discounts to large customers which are not closely related to differences in the (marginal) costs of supply. In this kind of situation, large customers often exert monopsony power to extract discounts from suppliers (Dobson and Waterson, 1997). Whilst this can be desirable from the consumer's point of view if the benefits are passed on,[21] it is undesirable from the viewpoint of economic efficiency because smaller firms are forced out of the market when from an economic point of view they ought to survive.[22] In the case of spatial price discrimination, a monopolist can take advantage of the fact that markets can be segmented geographically to set discriminatory prices, typically setting a lower price in a market where competition is strong ('to meet the competition') and setting a high price elsewhere.

1.5.5 Vertical Restraints

Vertical restraints have become an increasingly important area of analysis in anti-trust economics and are, in fact, the main problem of interest in just over half of the cases (31 out of 61) considered in this book. Usually, they involve conditions imposed by upstream firms (often manufacturers) on downstream firms (typically, wholesalers or retailers) or customers, designed to extract the *maximum* amount of monopoly profit from supply of a good. Such restraints are varied. At one extreme, an upstream firm may decide that *vertical integration* is the best way to achieve this end and hence control all (or most of the) stages of production, distribution and retailing of a good. Alternatively, it may appoint distributors for its products in different areas and give them monopoly rights to sell those goods in those areas (*exclusive distribution*). Again, an upstream firm may require wholesalers or retailers to distribute or sell only its products and not those of rivals (*exclusive purchasing*).[23] Again, an upstream firm may require downstream firms to buy a range of other goods or services (*tie-in sales* or *full-line forcing*); and it may only allow downstream firms or customers to lease (rather than purchase) products, or impose other conditions on downstream use.[24]

As with price discrimination, the welfare implications of such behaviour are mixed. Most authors argue that vertical restraints (and vertical integration) are likely to be innocuous in competitive markets since customers always have the right to buy elsewhere.[25] But, given horizontal market imperfections, vertical restraints can sometimes be used to *extend* monopoly power and to strengthen and maintain a dominant position. It is well known, for example, that vertical integration can be beneficial in some cases where double marginalisation is involved since it actually leads to lower prices (and higher outputs) than in the non-integrated case (Spengler, 1950). In other cases, however, integration and other vertical restraints can be used for anti-competitive purposes. In the extreme, this may amount to foreclosing rivals entirely from the market, but, more generally, it may take the form of 'softening' competition – either between manufacturers ('inter-brand competition') or between retailers ('intra-brand competition').[26]

1.6 PLAN OF THE BOOK

The remainder of the book is organised in three parts. In Part I, Chapter 2 provides an overview of competition policy in the UK in general, and a comparison with the approaches used in the EU and US. Chapter 3 introduces the full population of monopoly cases investigated by the MMC between 1973–95, and provides some statistical summaries of key features of the population. It describes the structure of the markets investigated, the problems encountered and the remedies used. Chapter 4 outlines the methodology used in our research: the selection of the sample of cases and our use of interviews – the primary source of information in most of our cases.

Part II presents the case studies. These chapters are organised by main type of monopoly problem based on our own assessment of the cases. Chapter 5 covers monopoly pricing (and price leadership); Chapter 6 collusive practices; Chapter 7 predatory pricing (and price discrimination); and Chapter 8 vertical restraints. Each chapter has a similar format, starting with a preliminary theoretical discussion, and an overview of all relevant cases in the population. The bulk of each chapter is a detailed discussion of the main case studies, but we also provide a description of the other cases not selected for detailed analysis.

Part III presents our conclusions. Chapter 9 draws together the material of Part II in order to provide an overall assessment of the effectiveness of remedies introduced following MMC investigations. Finally, Chapter 10 considers possible reform of UK monopoly policy and discusses briefly recent government proposals for reform.

NOTES

1. The Commission was originally established as the Monopolies and Restrictive Practices Commission in 1948. Its name (and responsibilities) were subsequently changed, first in 1956 to the Monopolies Commission, and then in 1973 to its present name.
2. See also the earlier work of Sutherland (1970) and, more recently, Utton (1995).
3. There is a deterrent effect in UK policy in that firms may seek to vary their behaviour in order to avoid an investigation or reinvestigation. This effect is not strong, however, and we discuss a number of cases where reinvestigations have taken place. The actual investigation can also have an effect on behaviour when, for example, a firm reduces price to reduce the chance of criticism in a report, or, again, when firms discontinue some practice which may be frowned on by the MMC. We also discuss one case (artificial lower limbs) where an investigation was useful in highlighting a problem and in providing a 'backstop' should other measures (in this case, a new NHS tendering system) not bring about the changes required.

4. Clarke, Davies, Driffield and Lund (1994) and Clarke, Davies and Driffield (1995).
5. The cases considered in the first report were breakfast cereals, contraceptive sheaths, building bricks, frozen foodstuffs, electricity meters, roadside advertising, films, white salt, postal franking machines and opium derivatives.
6. This is included as representative of a number of bus cases considered by the OFT and MMC in recent years, on which two of the current authors have written earlier (see Jones et al., 1996).
7. Because cases were investigated at different times, the period following a report differed from case to case. In 24 cases the post-report period was between 9 and 13 years, whilst in one case it was 14 years and, in three others, 6 years.
8. This consisted of 19 markets which had been investigated by the National Board for Prices and Income between 1965 and 1970.
9. For example, Shaw and Simpson note in their 1986 study that comparisons could be misleading if there is a tendency for large firms to lose market share ('regression towards the mean') irrespective of any policy intervention.
10. Some evidence of this can be seen in one of our case studies, opium derivatives, where the second ranked firm, Boots, left the market following the introduction of price monitoring. In a further case, white salt, the second ranked firm, ICI, also left the market following the introduction of price controls although, in this case, it sold out to another firm which continued production.
11. For further discussion of these points, see, for example, Tirole (1988, chapter 1).
12. They may also use predatory pricing or vertical restraints to maintain their dominance but these are treated separately below.
13. Explicit collusion is covered by the restrictive trade practices legislation and is therefore not considered in this book. The MMC deals with cases where there is no written agreement but firms may collude tacitly over prices, market shares and so on.
14. See, for example, Scherer and Ross (1990, chapter 7).
15. See Rees (1993b) and Phlips (1995).
16. For recent discussion, see Myers (1994) and Phlips (1995).
17. Other predatory tactics used in some of the bus cases considered by the OFT and MMC include running a bus just ahead of a rival's in order to capture its demand and putting on extra buses not scheduled to run. See Jones et al. (1996) for details.
18. See the early work of McGee (1958) on the Standard Oil (NJ) case. See also McGee (1980) and Phlips (1995).
19. As we will see in Chapter 7, this has been an important feature of the bus industry despite earlier optimism that this might be a contestable market.
20. This issue is well-recognised by the government and forms the basis of the proposal in the new competition bill to allow the DGFT to order a company to desist from some anti-competitive behaviour pending the completion of his report. See Chapter 10 for details.
21. Dobson and Waterson (1997) suggest in their model that it is quite 'likely' that consumers would be *worse off* because of an off-setting effect arising from increased market power at the downstream stage.
22. Clearly, a trade-off is involved here if monopsony power involves lower prices to consumers. We cannot say in general that economic welfare will increase or decrease.
23. We refer to this type of restraint as exclusive purchasing (EXP) rather than exclusive dealing (EXD). EXD is used to mean exclusive distribution in this book.
24. For a recent discussion see Dobson and Waterson (1996).
25. Exclusive purchasing, for example, is regarded by the European Commission as not generally anti-competitive and has a block exemption under Article 86 of the Treaty of Rome. This, however, has recently been relaxed in the ice cream case where it is

suggested that a dominant firm, Unilever, uses freezer exclusivity to block new entry; see Section 8.4 below.

26. For further discussion of these terms see Chapter 8.

PART I

An Overview

2. Review of UK Competition Policy in General

While the main focus of this book is on monopoly policy, this is, of course, only one part of competition policy in the UK. The purpose of this chapter is to place monopoly policy into its broader setting by providing a brief overview of UK competition policy as a whole. Modern UK competition policy derives, initially, from the Monopolies and Restrictive Practices (Inquiry and Control) Act which established the Monopolies and Restrictive Practices Commission in 1948. Since then, there have been a variety of institutional and legal changes, reflecting a widening in the scope of policy, and resulting in a steadily increasing amount of anti-trust activity.

In what follows, we outline UK policy as it currently stands. It is often suggested that the various Acts of Parliament, the institutions and general policy stance, taken together, constitute a singularly British approach to competition policy. In recent years, there have been criticisms of this approach and various proposals for reform. We set out the legal and institutional framework in Section 2.1. Section 2.2 provides a brief statistical look at UK policy. Section 2.3 provides a comparison with EU and US competition policy. And finally, Section 2.4 turns more specifically to UK monopoly policy – the subject of the remainder of the book.

2.1 THE INSTITUTIONAL AND LEGAL FRAMEWORK[1]

The main institutions of UK competition policy are the Office of Fair Trading (OFT), the Monopolies and Mergers Commission (MMC) and the Restrictive Practices Court (RPC). The OFT was set up in 1973 under the Fair Trading Act (FTA) and its role has been to oversee UK competition policy. This involves monitoring industry in the case of monopolies and anti-competitive behaviour, carrying out initial inquiries and calling for in-depth investigations by the MMC. It is headed by the Director General of Fair Trading (DGFT) who also acts as the Registrar of Restrictive Trading

Agreements and brings cases of restrictive agreements before the Restrictive Practices Court.

The MMC is an independent tribunal which is required to investigate specific markets, or the behaviour of companies, or proposed and recently completed mergers and decide whether they operate (or may be expected to operate) against the public interest. In cases where it finds that they do it is able to make recommendations to the Secretary of State at the Department of Trade and Industry (DTI) although the MMC has no power itself to implement policy. The Restrictive Practices Court hears cases brought to it by the OFT and determines whether restrictive agreements operate against the public interest. In this case, the decision of the court determines whether an agreement is banned or not and the firms involved must show that the agreement provides one of several specified benefits (known as 'gateways') and, on balance, that it is in the public interest for it to be allowed.

The legal framework is set out in four main Acts of Parliament (see Table 2.1): the FTA which covers abuse of monopoly power and mergers, the Competition Act which covers anti-competitive practices, the Resale Prices Act which deals with resale price maintenance, and the Restrictive Trade Practices Act which deals with restrictive agreements. A number of more specific pieces of legislation also exist, as shown in Table 2.1. These relate to the privatised industries, public sector organisations and other bodies where the MMC essentially acts as an arbitrator in disputes (for example, between firms and their regulators in privatised industries). Some significant amendments to the FTA and the Competition Act were also introduced in 1994 in the Deregulation and Contracting Out Act. Under this Act, if there is an available and straightforward remedy, acceptable to all parties, then the OFT is able to accept undertakings from firms at an early stage in lieu of a reference to the MMC. The policy is aimed at reducing the number of cases referred to the MMC under the FTA and Competition Act.[2]

A detailed description of the legislation is beyond the scope of this book,[3] but a brief summary of key definitions and procedures is probably helpful at this stage. Under the FTA, the formal definition of a 'monopoly' is that a single firm supplies at least 25 per cent[4] of a market for a particular good or service or that a group of firms (with a combined market share in excess of 25 per cent) behave in such a way as to adversely affect competition (denoted respectively as a 'scale' and a 'complex' monopoly). Monopoly itself is not assumed to be against the public interest but its existence is a *necessary* condition for investigation under the FTA. It is then up to the MMC to judge whether a practice operates against the public interest and to make recommendations to the Secretary of State.

Table 2.1 United Kingdom competition law

Main Acts	Date
Acts Involving the MMC	
1. Fair Trading Act (FTA)	1973
Potential abuse of monopoly power	
Mergers	
General	
Restrictive labour practices	
2. Competition Act (CA)	1980
Competition	
Public sector	
Both are administrative, involving investigation by the OFT, MMC and the Secretary of State. Remedies are secured by voluntary undertakings or orders in exceptional cases.	
Acts Involving the Courts	
3. Restrictive Trade Practices Act (RTPA)	1976
4. Resale Prices Act (RPA)	1976
Both may involve action taken in the courts, there is no role for the MMC and only a limited role for the Secretary of State.	
Acts Relating to the Privatised Industries	
5. Telecommunications Act	1984
6. Gas Act	1986
7. Airports Act	1986
8. Electricity Act	1989
9. Water Industry Act	1991
10. Railways Act	1993
Other Relevant Acts	
F1. Financial Services Act	1986
DGFT monitors Stock Exchange and other professional bodies for restrictions on competition. Reports to the Chancellor of Exchequer.	
12. Companies Act	1989
Reviews bodies regulating auditors. Reports to Secretary of State.	
13. Broadcasting Act	1990
DGFT investigates commercial TV networking and openness of the BBC to independent programme makers.	
14. Courts and Legal Services Act	1990
DGFT monitors legal profession. Advises the Lord Chancellor.	
15. Deregulation and Contracting Out Act	1994
Enables OFT to accept undertakings at an earlier stage under both the FTA and CA.	

The Competition Act is more immediately concerned with anti-competitive behaviour, defined as any practice that has the effect of 'restricting, distorting or preventing competition'. Under this act, the OFT and the MMC can undertake investigations of single firm practices and a full monopoly investigation of the whole market or industry is not required. Mergers are also subject to investigation under the FTA. In this case, proposed (or, in some cases, completed) mergers are investigated by the MMC if they involve assets acquired in excess of £70 million[5] or a share of the market after merger of at least 25 per cent. Restrictive trade practices are defined to include restrictions on prices, market shares, and terms and conditions on which business is conducted and these are brought before the RPC. In practice, the Court has taken a very hard line both on restrictive agreements and on resale price maintenance.[6]

Stepping back from definitional, legal and institutional aspects, it is possible to characterise the general philosophy of UK competition policy in less formal terms. First, it has generally been a story of incremental evolution, with its scope gradually being widened through successive acts. It is essentially flexible, with an in-built ability to evolve to suit changing circumstances; for example, precedent has not, as yet, played an important role, instead there is a tendency to treat each case on its merits. It also has a discernible voluntary flavour: voluntary undertakings are sought from firms found to be 'guilty' of behaviour against the public interest, and only in rare cases of disagreement does the Secretary of State feel obliged to seek an order to secure compliance. General prohibition of certain practices has not occurred (except in the case of resale price maintenance)[7] and fines are only imposed if firms are found guilty of contempt of the Restrictive Practices Court. Institutionally, the MMC and OFT have been maintained as separate bodies so as to maintain the impartiality of the MMC. Whilst it would be wrong to describe the OFT as a 'policeman', its duties necessarily entail some of the features of such a role. Finally, in most instances, the ultimate decision on a case lies not with the anti-trust authorities but instead with a politician (or the RPC).

2.2 A 'POTTED' STATISTICAL HISTORY

The major institutions used to 'judge' the public interest are the MMC and RPC. Since we are primarily interested in the MMC in this book we focus on it, specifically, here. The simplest way of charting the major developments in competition policy over time is to look at the number of reports published by the MMC. Table 2.2 records the number of reports, and their breakdown by type, for five sub-periods within the life of the MMC.

Table 2.2 The changing pattern of competition policy over time

	1950–95	1950–65	1966–72	1973–80	1981–88	1989–95
MMC Reports relating to:						
Monopoly	135	26	19	34	20	36
Mergers	169		16	27	49	77
Competition Act	10				6	4
Public sector	36			2	25	9
Privatised industries	9					9
Others*	12	1	3	2	3	3
Total	371	27	38	65	103	138
Annual average	8.1	1.7	5.4	8.1	12.9	19.7

Note: *Others include two cases under the Broadcasting Act, one on restrictive labour practices and nine general references.

Up to 1965, the Commission averaged rather less than two reports per year, almost exclusively on monopoly. However, with its responsibilities widened to include mergers, its annual output over the following seven years (1966–72) almost tripled. In 1973 the introduction of the FTA further increased the activity of the MMC, which averaged over eight reports per year between 1973 and 1980. The Competition Act, in 1980, was the next major development, and this was obviously a contributory factor in the continued growth in activity between 1981 and 1988. This sub-period also witnessed a large number of investigations into the nationalised industries and other public sector organisations also, in part, allowed under the 1980 act.

Interestingly, whilst the growth in merger reports continued unabated, this particular sub-period saw a definite slowdown in the number of monopoly cases. However, since the late 1980s monopoly references have increased, and have been running at the same annual rate as in the 1970s. Merger reports have also continued to grow rapidly. There were now also nine reports on the newly privatised industries, but, correspondingly, a tailing off of nationalised industry investigations. Also, the Competition Act has failed to generate much activity in recent years, for the MMC at least (although the same is not necessarily true for the OFT).

In summary, since the mid-1960s, there has been an almost uninterrupted expansion in UK competition policy – both in its range and extent (as reflected by MMC activity). Each successive seven to eight year period has witnessed a 50 per cent increase in the number of reports compared to the previous period. The most dramatic expansion has been in merger investigations, but a significant factor since 1980 has been investigation into nationalised and privatised industries, with the mix between the two changing as the privatisation programme progressed. Only the Competition Act has failed to contribute significantly to the overall growth. Monopoly policy, traditionally the main focus of the MMC, has tended to generate a steady stream of reports – typically, rather more than four per year since 1973, apart from a dip in the first part of the 1980s.

2.3 COMPARISON WITH EU AND US POLICY

In this section, we briefly compare UK policy with that in the EU and US.[8] Table 2.3 provides a summary of the main acts in the UK, EU and US and the areas that they cover. EU policy is covered primarily by articles 85 and 86 of the Treaty of Rome although mergers (so-called 'concentrations') are now dealt with under the Merger Regulation 4064/89 which came into force in 1990. US policy is enshrined in a number of acts and amendments over the years beginning with the Sherman Act of 1890.

2.3.1 EU Competition Policy

The main aim of EU competition policy is to promote the fundamental idea of free competition in the single European market. As such, the basis of the policy is firmly rooted in the Treaty of Rome, articles 85 to 94, and, more specifically, articles 85 and 86.

These articles are designed to remove any phenomena likely to act as a restraint on trade and to encourage the unification of markets. It should also be noted in passing, that a large section of EU policy (articles 90 to 94) relates to action by governments. These articles are designed to increase competition by preventing preferential treatment of nationalised firms, public bodies and so on and therefore lie outside the scope of the present book.

EU competition policy is implemented by the European Commission (the 'Commission') and, in particular, the Competition Commissioner who heads the Directorate General DG IV. DG IV has powers to investigate competition cases which may infringe articles 85 and 86 and can impose fines and require that firms desist from anti-competitive agreements or practices. Similarly, in the case of mergers, it can investigate cases and rule that a merger should not go ahead or be modified in some way. Competition decisions are, however, taken by the Commissioners as a whole and, as we note below, this can cause conflict within the Commission.

Table 2.3 Coverage of anti-competitive problems

	UK	EU	US
1. Monopoly pricing	FTA	Art. 86	Sherman Act (1890)
2. Mergers	FTA	Art. 86	Clayton Act (1914)
		Merger regulation	Celler/Kefauver Act (1950) Merger guidelines
3. Restrictive agreements/collusion	RTPA FTA	Art. 85	Sherman Act
4. Predatory pricing	FTA CA	Art. 86	Sherman Act Robinson–Patman Act (1936)
5. Discriminatory pricing	FTA CA	Art. 86	Clayton Act Robinson–Patman Act
6. Vertical restraints	FTA CA RPA	Art. 85	Sherman Act Clayton Act State laws

KEY: FTA – Fair Trading Act; RTPA – Restrictive Trade Practices Act; CA – Competition Act and RPA – Resale Prices Act.

Article 85 of the Treaty prohibits 'all agreements between undertakings, decisions of associations of undertakings and concerted practices which may affect trade between Member States and which have as their object or effect the prevention, restriction or distortion of competition within the common market' (article 85(1)). Further, in article 85(2), 'any agreements or decisions prohibited pursuant to this Article ...[are declared] automatically void'. Article 85(3) provides for exemptions from the article as, for example, in agreements dealing with research and development which have no major anti-competitive effect and provide off-setting benefits.

Article 85 is used to deal with cartels (and other concerted practices) and vertical restraints. As far as cartels are concerned, the Commission has taken a strong line against price-fixing, sharing markets, and so on and can impose fines of up to 10 per cent of the turnover of a firm. Moreover, because such agreements are void under article 85(2), they cannot be enforced through the courts whilst private parties can sue the firms involved. In other areas, such as informal agreements and vertical restraints, the law is less clear-cut[9] although, in a number of cases, block exemptions (and, in some cases, individual exemptions) have been granted.[10] In cases where the Commission rules that a violation of article 85 (or 86) has occurred, the firms concerned can appeal and this appeal is currently heard (since the early 1990s) in the European Court of First Instance.

Article 86 deals with abuse of a dominant position and, hence, is similar in intent to the FTA. There are, however, important differences. Whilst article 86 prohibits the abuse of market power by *one or more* firms; in practice, the policy has focused almost exclusively on dominant firms (where dominance is often held to imply at least a 40 per cent market share).[11] This contrasts with the FTA where several firms with market shares greater than 25 per cent ('scale monopolies') can be investigated, as well as groups of firms which *together* have a share greater than 25 per cent ('complex monopolies'). In addition, whilst article 86 discusses (amongst other things) 'high' prices as a form of monopoly abuse; in practice, DG IV does not use price controls to counter such abuse. One reason is that DG IV has insufficient resources to implement such a policy, although (according to Korah, 1994, p. 3) the main reason is that it would conflict with the liberal spirit in which the EU was created. In contrast to the UK, the main weapon against monopoly abuse has been the use of fines.[12]

Since 1990 the Commission has also been able to investigate mergers with a significant European dimension under the Merger Regulation 4064/89. Under this policy, the Commission carries out investigations on whether mergers are compatible or incompatible with the Common Market and, if found incompatible, may require that off-setting conditions are met or that the merger be banned. In practice, the former approach has mainly been used. In 1990–3, for example, there were eight cases in which off-setting conditions were required compared to only one case

(Aerospatialle/Alenia/de Havilland, 1991) in which a merger was banned (Clarke and Driffield, 1995).

Another feature of EU policy is the conflict that sometimes arises between competition and industrial policy. The brief of DG III, and the Industry Commissioner, is broadly to promote efficiency and cooperation between member states. It has long been EU policy to foster links between firms from different member states, encouraging joint ventures and cooperation in R&D and elsewhere. The analogy with Japanese industrial policy under the Ministry of International Trade and Industry (MITI) is clear. However, DG IV has tended to take the view that such cooperation is likely to lead to a reduction in competition. This has served to highlight a further distinction between the UK and what is designed to be a supra-national policy. While it is impossible to view any competition authority as free of political interference, the EU has the added complication of national interest. Any major decision of a Commissioner requires the approval of the Commission as a whole and this has led to much frustration for successive Competition Commissioners. A good example of this is the 1994 case of the proposed merger of the French, German and Italian steel firms: Vallourec, Mannesman and Dalmine. The Competition Commissioner opposed this merger on the grounds that the resulting company would have a virtual monopoly in several key markets; however, this was overturned by the Commissioners as a whole. It is perhaps significant that the major competitor to these companies was Swedish, and that DG III was allegedly in support of the venture since this was precisely the kind of agreement that EU industrial policy was seeking to encourage.[13]

A number of other member states of the EU (including Italy, Belgium, Spain, Ireland and Portugal) have adapted or adopted laws modelled on articles 85 and 86. The German and French systems have also more in common with EU policy than does the UK, especially as a result of important amendments (in 1986 in France and 1989 in Germany).

2.3.2 US Competition Policy

In contrast to UK (and EU) policy, US policy relies much more heavily on the courts, where both criminal and civil actions are mounted in anti-trust cases. Under section 1 of the Sherman Act, horizontal and vertical price fixing are illegal *per se* and the act is applied to various other cases of concerted action found to have anti-competitive effects such as tie-in sales and exclusive dealing. Section 2 deals with monopolisation of an industry which is also prohibited, although in this case a 'rule of reason' is applied. This section makes illegal anti-competitive conduct such as predatory pricing which is deemed to maintain or enhance a monopoly position. The Robinson–Patman Act deals with price discrimination (although it has rarely been used in recent years) while exclusive dealing and tie-in sales are also dealt with under section 3 of the Clayton Act.

In contrast to the UK, US policy incorporates significant penalties for firms found to be transgressing anti-trust laws. Under the Sherman Act, for example, firms can be fined up to $10 million (individuals up to $350,000) and a prison sentence of up to three years can be imposed. Civil actions can also be brought by the Department of Justice, and private individuals can obtain damages for losses sustained at three times the value of the injuries incurred. In the US, the Federal Trade Commission also investigates cases, although in this case an administrative rather than a legal approach is used. In this respect, US policy is similar to policy in the EU, in that administrative decisions are made subject to federal judicial review. In the US, however, FTC remedies are essentially civil in nature and do not carry fines.[14]

2.4 POLICY ON ABUSE OF MARKET POWER

Against this background, we now return more specifically to that part of UK policy which is the particular concern of this book. As we have seen, current policy on abuse of market power in the UK takes the form of two acts: the 1973 FTA and the 1980 Competition Act (with the addition of the provisions of the Deregulation and Contracting Out Act of 1994). The Competition Act enables the OFT and MMC to investigate specific cases of anti-competitive behaviour and, if necessary, accept undertakings for the termination of practices. The FTA, in contrast, enables the MMC to look at particular industries in detail and to decide whether the leading firms in those industries act (or may be expected to act) against the public interest. It is this latter act which is our primary concern in this book.[15]

Under the FTA, the DGFT refers cases of possible monopoly abuse to the MMC.[16] The MMC then decides whether a monopoly exists as defined by the law, and, if it does, whether the monopoly acts, or may be expected to act, against the public interest. If it does find such evidence, it can make recommendations to the Secretary of State, although it has no powers itself to implement any change. The Secretary of State then decides what action to take and, typically, instructs the OFT to seek undertakings from the firms concerned. In some cases, however, firms are unwilling to give undertakings and the Secretary of State may, then, make an Order against the firms concerned.

As noted in Section 2.1, the FTA defines two types of monopoly: 'scale' and 'complex' monopolies. A scale monopoly exists if a leading firm has a 25 per cent market share, whilst a complex monopoly exists where a group firms, jointly, have a 25 per cent market share and act in such a way as to restrict or distort competition. These thresholds are clearly quite low and this provides considerable flexibility in the law. For example, a number of cases where there was concern over a monopoly (for example, the 1989 beer case or the 1990 petrol case) involved no single firm with more than a 25 per cent market share but were, nevertheless, investigated under the complex monopoly provisions. Moreover, in contrast to EU law, cases where similarly-sized firms dominate a market (for example, films (1994)) have also been investigated. This is an important factor in considering reform of UK policy (which we discuss in Chapter 10).

If a monopoly exists, the MMC is required to assess whether it operates, or may be expected to operate, against the public interest. Whilst the FTA lays down several criteria (in particular, the importance of maintaining competition and of promoting the interests of consumers) which the MMC should consider, in practice the MMC considers all matters which it deems to be relevant in a particular case. If it finds evidence that firms are operating against the public interest, it can make recommendations to the Secretary of State. The Secretary of State is, however, not bound by the recommendations and can vary them or not implement them at all.

Under UK law, the Secretary of State has wide powers to seek to remedy a case of monopoly abuse: he may require that undertakings be sought to *terminate* a particular practice, introduce *price controls* to curb monopoly prices or seek to break up a firm or require it to sell some of its assets, that is, *divestment*. He can also issue an Order against the firms concerned if they fail to give satisfactory undertakings. As we will see in Part II, by far the most frequently used remedy is termination, which has been used in over 70 per cent of cases in which a remedy was sought. Whilst less common, both price control and divestment have played a significant role in a number of cases. Divestment was used, for example, in the 1989 beer case where the dominant firms in the brewing industry were required to sell off some of their tied public houses. Price control has also been used in a number of high profile cases, including breakfast cereals (1973), contraceptive sheaths (1973, 1982, 1994) and white salt (1986).

At the time of writing, there has been considerable speculation over possible reform of competition policy in the UK and the new Labour government has recently introduced a new competition bill into Parliament. Whilst this bill deals primarily with reform of restrictive trade practices legislation, it also proposes reform of UK monopoly policy; in both cases to bring UK policy more into line with the EU. We discuss these possible reforms of UK policy briefly in Chapter 10.

2.5 SUMMARY

Monopoly policy in the UK, in roughly its present form, dates back to 1948. The central institution is the Monopolies and Mergers Commission, and it is the MMC's reports on specific cases which form the core material of this book. This chapter has described the legal background and included a brief comparison with policy in the EU and the US. We have seen that, since the Fair Trading Act of 1973, the MMC has averaged slightly more than four monopoly reports per year over most of the period. Whilst competition policy, in general, has gradually widened over the last 30 years and monopoly reports are now only part (about 25 per cent) of the output of the Commission, they continue to represent an integral and high-profile dimension of its activity. In the next chapter we concentrate in more detail on the population of monopoly reports since the introduction of the FTA in 1973.

NOTES

1. This section draws in part on Davies (1996).
2. In fact, the acceptance of undertakings 'in lieu' was first introduced in the Companies Act of 1989, but was limited to structural remedies. It was extended to include behavioural remedies in the 1994 Act.
3. Utton (1995, especially chapter 3) includes a longer description of the detail of UK competition legislation and an interesting comparison with the US and EU.
4. As explained in the OFT's current information booklet on 'Mergers', the market share threshold is not necessarily based on the relevant *economic* market. To reflect this, the test now uses the words 'the share of supply of...' (a reasonable description of the goods/services); that is, it is a legal not an economic test.
5. Increased from £30 million in February 1994.
6. The two major cases in which RPM was initially allowed by the RPC were books and medicaments. The net book agreement has, however, recently been struck down (in March 1997) and the DGFT is (at time of writing) applying to the Court for the medicaments exemption to be removed.
7. The Resale Prices Act prohibits collective resale price maintenance *per se*. Individual RPM is also prohibited but subject to exemptions under the RPA.
8. For more detail see Goyder (1993) and Korah (1994) on EU policy, and Scherer and Ross (1990) for the US.
9. The recently published EC Green Paper on Vertical Restraints (1997) has amongst other things, questioned the current treatment of vertical restraints under article 85.
10. Currently, exclusive distribution and exclusive purchasing agreements, as well as agreements licensing intellectual property rights, have block exemption under EU law.

These and other exemptions have been implemented in order to enable the Commission (with limited resources) to deal with other 'more important' cases.
11. The 40 per cent market share criterion is not laid down in EU law (in contrast to the 25 per cent market share in the FTA) but is often used in practice (see Green Paper, 1992, para. 4.9). There are problems in the definition of dominance in EU law – the ability to behave independently of others in the market. 'Market power' can be extended to include more than one firm only if the firms are linked, in some way, such as by an agreement to cooperate on R&D.
12. Fines are not available under existing UK law, although they are proposed in the new UK competition bill. See Chapter 10 for details.
13. *Financial Times*, 26 January 1994.
14. The FTC can apply for preliminary injunctive relief pending a full investigation. A similar measure is proposed in the new competition bill (see Chapter 10).
15. For a fuller discussion of the operation of the Competition Act see Utton (1994).
16. The Secretary of State also has powers to make general references to the MMC but has only used these once (in the case of gas, 1993). He also has the power to veto OFT references to the MMC but, again, has only used this once, in the Competition Act reference of bus services in the Isle of Arran. Our thanks to David Elliott for pointing this out.

3. MMC Investigations of Monopoly: the Population

This chapter now focuses more precisely on that part of UK policy concerned with monopoly, and the abuse of monopoly power. It provides a factual and definitional background to the case studies considered in Part II of the book, introduces our terminology and classificatory schemes and establishes a profile of the full population of MMC investigations. We also use the chapter to identify some general features of the population (for example, the connection between industry structure and type of monopoly problem) which are pursued further in the case study chapters.

Section 3.1 identifies the full population of monopoly reports, and describes some of the characteristics of the firms and industries involved. Section 3.2 highlights a key feature of industrial structure, namely seller concentration, and derives a classification scheme which is used throughout the book. This is also compared to the legal definitions of: 'scale' and 'complex' monopoly. Section 3.3 introduces a typology for classifying the potential monopoly problems identified in the MMC reports. Section 3.4 classifies the recommendations made by the MMC and the undertakings subsequently secured from the firms concerned. Section 3.5 briefly identifies some changes that are apparent over the period, and Section 3.6 draws some conclusions. The Appendix at the end of the book includes a full list of the population, plus the various measures used in this book.

3.1 DEFINING THE POPULATION

As noted in Chapter 2, since its creation, the MMC has produced 135 reports investigating monopoly, that is roughly three per year (Table 3.1(a)).[1] The Fair Trading Act (1973) was something of a watershed; in the 23 years prior to the FTA, the MMC averaged about two reports per year, but this annual rate more than doubled between 1973 and 1980. Although the annual average fell back between 1981 and 1988,[2] it has risen sharply again in recent years, and between 1989 and 1995, the Commission has been producing more than five monopoly reports on average per year.

Table 3.1 MMC reports on potential monopoly abuse

(a) Entire history of MMC: 1950–95

Period	Total	Annual Average
1950–1995	135	2.9
of which:		
1950–1972	45	2.0
1973–1980	34	4.3
1981–1988	20	2.5
1989–1995	36	5.1

(b) Breakdown for 1973–95

Total reports	90
minus investigations of professional bodies	17
Population of interest here	73
minus follow up reports	12
Number of cases	61

For the purpose of this book, we have narrowed this population in two ways. First, we consider only reports published from 1973 onwards, that is during the second half of the MMC's existence. This is partly because 1973 marks the beginning of 'modern' (indeed, current) policy, as prescribed in the FTA, but also because it coincides with the end point of the earlier study by Shaw and Simpson (1986, 1989).[3] Second, we also exclude 17 reports during the 1973–95 period which investigated various practices in a number of the professions.   Whilst not uninteresting in their own right, these investigations were typically concerned with the rules and practices of professional bodies, rather than individual firms. They tend to raise rather different issues to those that are our main concern here.

With these exclusions, there is a revised population of 73 reports (Table 3.1(b)) which form the basis of this study. Twelve of these reports are, in fact, reinvestigations of industries already covered in earlier reports,[4] and so the final population relates to 61 separate cases. Since there has been no previous documentation of this particular population of industries as a whole, the remainder of this section outlines briefly its main characteristics.

3.1.1 The Industries

The most striking feature of the industrial breakdown of this population is that manufacturing accounts for a disproportionately large share of cases. Manufacturing in the UK accounts for less than one quarter of GDP, yet 70 per cent of all cases originate from this sector (Table 3.2(a)). This can be explained, in part, by the typically higher levels of concentration which one expects to find in manufacturing as opposed to services (although this is only an expectation since 'hard' data on concentration in many service industries is still remarkably scarce). However, recent decades have seen conspicuous examples of rapid increases in concentration in some service sectors (for example, in distribution, some privatised transport industries, auditing, banking, and so on) Whilst it is true that, more recently, more service cases have been looked at by the MMC, this has not had a large impact on the overall figures presented here.

A somewhat similar picture emerges within manufacturing, with some sectors more likely than others to have been investigated (Table 3.2(b)). Most notably, there have been six cases involving building materials (that is, 14 per cent of the manufacturing total) which accounts for only 4 per cent of total manufacturing activity; and food, drink and tobacco, chemicals, and engineering and vehicles are also over-represented, whilst paper, printing and publishing and other industries are under-represented. Again, the obvious explanation might be that the former sectors are more likely to include highly concentrated industries, and to some extent this is true. Superficially, these sectors defy any obvious or simple encompassing description (they include both consumer and producer goods industries; some offer highly differentiated, and some largely homogeneous, products; and some are relatively R&D intensive whilst others are more obviously 'traditional').

But, there are some common features. First, most industries in building materials and food, drink and tobacco face relatively light degrees of import competition, and this is also so for consumer good industries in chemicals (for example, soaps and detergents, pharmaceuticals, toilet preparations, paint) but not all engineering industries. Second, they include many natural monopolies and oligopolies: in building materials this results from quite pronounced production scale economies coupled with the limited size of local or regional markets; in many food, drink and tobacco and some chemicals and engineering industries, it results more from endogenous sunk costs (notably advertising but also R&D) which are driven upwards inexorably over time by competition between large, often multinational, firms (Sutton, 1991). In both cases, domestic entry is difficult, and, when combined with limited import competition, there is clear potential for monopoly abuse. In other words, it is unsurprising that these particular sectors have been investigated over the years. On the other hand, there are some other sectors which share the same characteristics, but which have been less often the focus of MMC attention. These include certain types of transport good industries, consumer electrical goods and some metal manufacture.

Table 3.2 Industrial distribution of the population of cases

(a) Share of cases by broad sector of the economy

	Reports	
	No.	%
Extraction of oil and gas (2)	2	3.3
Manufacturing industries (23)	43	70.5
Transport (8)	5	8.2
Services and other sectors (67)	11	18.0
Total	61	100.0

Note: The bracketed figure after each sector denotes its share of GDP in 1990.

(b) Share of manufacturing cases by sector within manufacturing

	Reports	
	No.	%
Metals and metal products (9)	4	9.3
Building materials (4)	6	14.0
Chemicals (10)	6	14.0
Engineering and vehicles (24)	13	30.2
Food, drink and tobacco (12)	9	21.0
Paper, printing and publishing (11)	2	4.6
Others (30)	3	7.0
Total	43	100.0

Note: The bracketed figure after each sector denotes its share of manufacturing net output in 1990.

3.1.2 The Markets

Of course, the industry categories used in Table 3.2 are too aggregated to do more than identify the broad pattern of industries involved. The very nature of the typical MMC report means that the *markets* investigated within these industries are usually very much more disaggregated than the three, or even four, digit industry levels of comparisons such as this.

Turning to specific markets investigated, the question of *market size* is of central importance from both a normative and a positive point of view. It can be argued that, because anti-trust activity is itself costly for all parties, it should be targeted on cases where the potential for welfare gain is likely to be substantial, and this will depend, in large part, on the size of the market concerned. Equally, in terms of positive analysis, small market size will inevitably constrain the range of feasible market structures, and, thus, conduct and the potential for effective intervention.

With this in mind, we have derived estimates of *total market size* for as many as possible of the referred products in the 61 cases. Table 3.3 presents the results using figures reported in the individual MMC reports, normalised to 1990 prices. Discounting the 11 cases for which the MMC reports offered no guide to the value of market sales,[5] it is clear that a large proportion of cases are really quite small: more than one quarter had total sales less than £50 million, and three quarters had sales less than £500 million in 1990 prices. In some of these cases, at least, one suspects that any welfare gain from the removal of monopoly abuse may have been relatively small – certainly when compared to high turnover products such as petrol or cars.

On the other hand, precisely because of the limited sizes of many of these markets, they may well tend to be natural oligopolies, with an increased likelihood of anti-competitive behaviour and limits on the range of effective remedial weapons that can be used. Looked at from the firms' point of view, a small market may also be one to which they feel no particular affinity. In the case of large conglomerates, an adverse MMC ruling may simply encourage them to exit from the industry. These issues are pursued in later chapters.

3.1.3 The Firms

The effectiveness of any anti-trust remedy must depend in part on the *ex-post* behaviour of the firm(s) concerned, as well as upon the remedy itself. In turn, this behaviour might depend upon certain characteristics of the firm (for example, its aggregate size, ownership, diversification, and so on), and on how significant the referred product is within the firm's overall product range.

Table 3.3 Size of referred markets

Sales Range*	No. of cases
1 – 50	14
51 – 100	5
101 – 200	7
201 – 500	11
501 – 1000	2
1001 – 5000	6
> 5000	5
unknown	11
Total	61

Note: * in £million in 1990 prices.

We have gathered a limited amount of background information on as many as possible of the firms involved – 56 firms drawn from 39 cases.[6] Generally speaking, the firms tended to be large, diversified and often multinational. We estimate that about half of the sample were amongst the giants of UK industry, in that they appeared within the *Times* top 500 in the year of the appropriate report; indeed, almost one third of firms were in the top 100. We also found that 70 per cent had significant multinational operations, and 25 per cent of these firms were subsidiaries of foreign-owned multinationals.

But perhaps the most important statistic relates to the significance of the referred product to the investigated firm. We estimate that, for the average firm, the referred market accounted for 35 per cent of its sales in the UK. However, there is considerable variation about this mean. Whilst there were a significant number of firms for whom the referred products were relatively unimportant in this sense – these tend to be large conglomerate, often multinational, firms – for about 20 per cent of the firms, the referred products were their main source of turnover; and for 10 per cent their sole source. It seems likely, therefore, that the importance of an MMC investigation may be viewed very differently depending on the type of firm involved.

3.2 INDUSTRY STRUCTURE AND CONCENTRATION

By definition, every case in this population qualifies as a 'monopoly situation' in the legal sense; and we have a clear definition of what this means in the Fair Trading Act (1973, paras 6 and 7) – in terms of 'scale' and 'complex' monopolies (see Chapter 2).

We apply these definitions here to distinguish four types of industry structure (Table 3.4). First, there are those industries in which the MMC report identified just a single scale monopoly: this happened in 40 per cent of cases, and, loosely speaking, we would expect these to be industries in which there was a single dominant firm, including, at the extreme, literal monopoly. Second, in a further ten cases, a complex monopoly was found alongside a scale monopoly: here, the implication is less obvious, although this might reflect a more significant presence for the other non-dominant firms. Third, the 15 cases in which the industry includes two or more scale monopolies (in some of which there were also complex monopolies) are more likely to indicate oligopolistic situations, with more equally-sized rivals. Finally, there were 11 industries in which there was only a complex monopoly, these must be *relatively* unconcentrated, with the potential for abuse of market power dependent on the combined behaviour of the leading firms.

Table 3.4 Scale and complex monopolies

	Number of cases involving:
1 SCALE only	25
1 SCALE and COMPLEX	10
Multi-SCALE	
(including also COMPLEX)	15
COMPLEX only	11
Total	61

However, these classifications are of limited value for analytical purposes, given the relatively low 25 per cent yardstick used in the FTA definitions. Clearly, this leaves open the possibility of a wide range of different industrial structures in each of the four categories just identified, and since oligopoly theory suggests that conduct may vary significantly between those different structures, we believe that there is some value in developing a classificatory scheme, which goes beyond the FTA definitions.

Most theory[7] suggests that two dimensions of the firm size distribution may be relevant in identifying the nature of competition amongst the leaders in any given industry:

- their combined share of the market, that is *market concentration*;
- their relative sizes within the group, that is *size inequalities.*

In loose terms, monopoly/oligopoly power is more likely, the higher is concentration; but whether that power is reflected in, say, price leadership as opposed to collusion, will depend on the relative sizes of the leading firms.

We therefore employ a classification scheme which recognises these two dimensions by using the three firm concentration ratio (CR3) alongside a measure of inequality (I). As always, when using a K firm concentration ratio, the choice of value for K is largely arbitrary; here, we select K = 3 for two reasons. First, most previous studies suggest that the value of the more familiar five firm ratio (and, indeed, most other standard concentration indices) is typically dominated by the shares of the largest three firms.[8] Second, MMC reports only infrequently record the shares of firms outside the top three (if there are any). Our measure of inequality is based on the market share of the leading firm (MS1) relative to the combined shares of the next two firms (MS2 + MS3). The formal definitions are:

$$CR3 = MS1 + MS2 + MS3 \qquad (3.1)$$

$$I = MS1/(MS2 + MS3) \qquad (3.2)$$

Thus CR3 may vary between 0 and 100, usually nearer the upper limit in this set of industries, of course. I may vary between a lower bound of 0.5, as in the case of a *symmetric* triopoly (that is, three equal-sized leaders), to infinity for a literal monopoly.

The cases have been split into four groups, using a critical value for each index: CR3 = 75 per cent and I = 1.5. The choice of these particular values is largely arbitrary, but they do split the population into two more or less equal halves by each index. Moreover, when combined, they permit easy interpretation, as illustrated in Figure 3.1.[9] Industries lying in the 'A' segment of the diagram (CR3 > 75 per cent and I ≥ 1.5) are very highly concentrated, with the leading firm in a dominant position (it is easily shown that these values imply a market share for the largest firm of at least 45 per cent). For this reason, 'A' cases are labelled *dominant firm*.

Industries in the 'B' segment (CR3 > 75 per cent and I < 1.5) are also very highly concentrated, but with more significant competitors for the leader. By construction, the second firm must have a share no less than 15 per cent, rising to 33.3 per cent as symmetry increases.

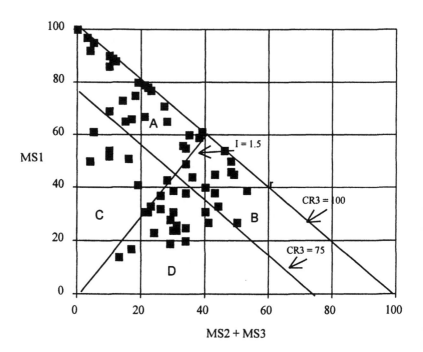

Figure 3.1 Distribution of cases by oligopoly type

Special cases will include (i) symmetric triopoly, in which the three firms will each have a market share of no less than one quarter, and as much as one third, and (ii) roughly equal duopolies. The 'B' segment is therefore characterised as *dominant group* (with potentially collusive connotations). Segments 'C' and 'D' are obviously somewhat less concentrated. Nevertheless, 'C' (CR3 < 75 per cent and I ≥ 1.5) will still include industries in which the leader dominates at least part of the market, and there are likely to be few other firms of significant size – the second largest firm can never exceed a market share of 30 per cent. Therefore, 'C' is labelled *partial dominance*. The 'D' segment (CR3 < 75 per cent and I < 1.5) will include rather more fragmented structures, without a dominant firm – we call this residual area *loose oligopoly*.[10]

Unsurprisingly, the 'A' segment is the most densely populated in the present sample (Table 3.5). It is also the most concentrated: the average three firm concentration ratio is 95 per cent. The 23 industries concerned include three literal monopolies (shown in the extreme left-hand corner of Figure 3.1). In only five cases do the second and third largest firms together account for more than 30 per cent of the market, and, in 12 cases, there are no firms, apart from the top three in the market, as defined by the MMC (these, therefore, lie exactly on the CR3 = 100 per cent line). The 11 industries in the 'B' segment also all have very high concentration, on average CR3 is 86 per cent, but here the second and third firms constitute significantly greater competition for the leader; in most cases, their joint share comes close to that of the leader and in six cases it exceeds it. The 'partial dominance' 'C' segment, includes six industries: the share of the market leader always lies in the range 40–65 per cent and in only one case does the second largest firm have a share in excess of 11 per cent. Thus, the term 'dominance' does remain appropriate. But mean CR3 is much lower (65 per cent) than for the A group, and in all cases, CR3 lies between 60 per cent and 71 per cent, indicating much larger shares for non-top three firms – hence the 'partial'. The most striking feature of the 18 industries in the 'loose oligopoly' 'D' segment is the much more modest shares of the number one firms – never higher than 38 per cent and only in excess of 30 per cent in seven cases. Similarly, concentration is more modest, on average 55 per cent and typically in the range 53–59 per cent and exceeding 60 per cent in only four cases.

Table 3.6 compares our classification scheme and the FTA terminology. There is a reasonably close concordance: (i) nearly all (17 of 23) dominant firm cases (A) involve just a single scale monopoly, (ii) similarly, most (9 of 11) dominant groups (B) are found when there are multiple scale monopolies, and (iii) all 11 cases where there is no scale monopoly are loose oligopolies (D). However, there remains a significant minority of 24 cases not covered by this general concordance. For example, a single scale monopoly does not necessarily imply very high concentration (14 of the single scale cases appear in the C and D segments), and, although the absence of a scale monopoly is sufficient for an industry to be classified as loose oligopoly, it is not necessary. Ten D segment industries do involve at least one scale monopoly. Therefore, we conclude that the nature of monopoly identified in the MMC reports is insufficient to distinguish finely between the structures of different industries, and we tend to rely on our own classification scheme below.

Table 3.5 Classification by type of oligopoly

Type	CR3	Relative sizes	No.	Type	Mean CR3 (%)
A	> 75%	MS1 ≥ 1.5(MS2+MS3)	23	Dominant Firm	95
B	> 75%	MS1 < 1.5(MS2+MS3)	11	Dominant Group	86
C	75% >	MS1 ≥ 1.5(MS2+MS3)	6	Partial Dominance	65
D	75% >	MS1 < 1.5(MS2+MS3)	18	Loose Oligopoly	55
Market shares unavailable			3		–
Total			61		78

Note: Individual market shares are typically given in the MMC reports but there are some exceptions: (1) for three cases (greyhound racing, specialised advertising and electrical contracting) there were no useful market share data in either the report or any other source of which we are aware; (2) for four (wire and fibre ropes, primary batteries, domestic gas appliances and marine radio) more than one market was involved and firms' shares across markets were amalgamated into single figures; and (3) for 11 others, the shares of the second and/or third placed firms were unavailable. In these cases, we have usually made informed guesses.

38

Table 3.6 Industry structure and type of oligopoly

	A	B	C	D	Total
1 SCALE only	17	1	5	2	25
1*SCALE+COMPLEX	2	1	1	6	10
Multi-SCALE	4	9	0	2	15
COMPLEX only	0	0	0	11	11
Total	23	11	6	21	61

Note: Hereafter, the three unclassified cases in Table 3.5 are assumed to be in the D concentration class.

3.3 NATURE OF MONOPOLY PROBLEMS DETECTED BY THE MMC

In recent years, Industrial Organisation economists have examined an increasingly wide range of potentially anti-competitive practices using a game theoretic perspective. Many of those practices might be expected to surface in a sample of industries characterised by the structures just described, but for present classification purposes, we start by distinguishing just two broad groups: price-related problems and vertical restraints.

(i) Pricing Problems

These will include, most obviously traditional monopoly pricing (that is, pricing 'too high'), but also include price leadership (from a position of market dominance), price discrimination, predatory pricing and collusive pricing. Needless to say, these terms and practices often overlap; for example, price discrimination may be associated with predatory behaviour, or price leadership.

(ii) Vertical Restraints

The academic literature on vertical restraints includes a wide spectrum of different practices, which are not always described consistently or unambiguously. These include exclusive dealing, exclusive territories, most favoured customer practices, tying, full-line forcing, resale price maintenance, refusal to sell or implicit foreclosure and systems and product compatibility. Unfortunately, it is sometimes difficult to apply this nomenclature unambiguously to the multitude of practices, alleged and real, as described in the MMC reports. In later case study chapters, we will need to be more precise, but at this stage, we opt merely for a two-way distinction, differentiating those cases where *exclusivity* in some form or another is present, as opposed to all other vertical restraints.

Table 3.7 records our reading of the 'main' problem[11] in each of the 61 cases. As can be seen, there is an almost exact 50:50 split between pricing and vertical problems. Within pricing, straightforward monopoly pricing and/or price leadership is the most frequent category, price discrimination and/or predatory pricing also often surface either as a main problem (and often in a more secondary role) and collusion is the least frequent. Within vertical restraints, exclusive practices occur in just over half the cases.

Table 3.7 Incidence of monopoly problems

Abbreviation	Nature of problem	Frequency
MP	Monopoly pricing and/or price leadership	13
DP/PRED	Discriminatory and/or predatory pricing	10
C	Collusive behaviour	7
EX	Exclusivity	15
VR	Other vertical restraints	13
EX/VR	Exclusivity and other vertical restraints	3
Total		61

Note: These figures refer only to the major problem identified in each case. For vertical restraints, 15 cases involved either exclusive purchasing and/or exclusive distribution (3 cases involved both), 13 cases involved other vertical restraints and 3 cases involved both exclusivity *and* other vertical restraints.

An obvious question is whether the incidence of certain types of problem varies systematically between different industry structures. The answer is a qualified yes (Table 3.8). As expected, monopoly pricing and price leadership are more prevalent where there is a dominant firm (segments A and, less so, C); collusive practices are more common in segments B and D, in which firms are more equally sized. On the other hand, discriminatory and predatory pricing occur more evenly across structural sectors, except in loose oligopoly. Exclusive practices are most likely to be found in the D segment although they also appear in segments A and B, whilst other vertical restraints occur most frequently in loose oligopoly or the dominant firm group A. This last result indicates that some dominant firms may use vertical restraints to support their dominant position; and some evidence of this is shown in Chapter 8 below.

Nevertheless, only four cells in the cross-tabulation are entirely empty, and this establishes that there is by no means a one-to-one concordance between types of problem and types of structure. This may imply that a given problem may require a different remedy depending on the structure from which it is seen to arise.

Table 3.8 Monopoly problems by type of oligopoly

Problem	A	B	C	D	Total
	Structural segment				
Monopoly pricing/price leadership	9	0	2	2	13
Discriminatory/predatory pricing	4	3	3	0	10
Collusive behaviour	1	4	0	2	7
Exclusive practices	2	3	0	10	15
Other vertical restraints	7	1	1	7	16
Total	23	11	6	21	61

Note: Cases involving both exclusivity and other vertical restraints are classified in the latter category in this table.

3.4 RECOMMENDATIONS AND UNDERTAKINGS

We next turn to the recommendations made in the MMC reports and the remedies put in place. Under the FTA, the Secretary of State is not required to accept the recommendations made by the MMC and can choose to vary them or not implement them at all.[12] In most cases, however, the Secretary of State accepts the recommendations (or a variation of them) and asks the DGFT to seek undertakings from the firms involved. Whilst this process is straightforward, it is often quite lengthy (see below). In some cases, firms seek to weaken the undertakings and may adopt a largely non-cooperative stance. In such cases, the Secretary of State is empowered to make an order to require firms to adopt the remedies proposed and this has happened in six cases: car parts (1982), films (1983), foreign package holidays (1986), specialised advertising (1988), credit card services (1989) and beer (1989). In one case, films (1983), negotiations went on for six years before an order was made.

The main focus of our study is the undertakings *actually* negotiated by the OFT, as set out in a section 88 letter under the 1973 Act and any orders actually imposed. Both are now published annually in the OFT's *Register of Undertakings and Orders* (see Office of Fair Trading (1996)).

3.4.1 Defining Types of Remedy

We have identified four broad types of remedy which have been applied:

PC: price control, under which referred firms must limit the rate of increase (or, in some cases, lower the level of) price.

PM: price monitoring, where the OFT monitors the firm(s)' prices (with the implication that further intervention may be necessary).

D: divestment, whereby the firm(s) is required to split up by selling off its subsidiaries or parts,[13] and

T: termination, where firms are required to discontinue certain practices deemed to be anti-competitive. These can be pricing practices, such as discriminatory or predatory pricing, but, more often, they are exclusive practices and other vertical restraints. Particularly in the latter cases, termination often requires that contracts be changed or abandoned.

Table 3.9 Types of recommendation

Abbreviation	Nature of recommendation	Frequency
T	Termination of practice/agreement	30
PC	Price controls	5
PM	Price monitoring	5
D	Divestment	5
None		19
Total		64

Note: The frequencies sum to more than 61 because three cases (breakfast cereals, primary batteries and contraceptive sheaths) were subject to elements of both price monitoring (PM) and price control (PC) at different stages. In this table they are counted twice.

Table 3.9 shows the frequencies with which these remedies have been applied. As can be seen, termination has been the most frequent, being used in almost half of the cases (30), whilst price control/monitoring (7) and divestment (5) have been applied much less frequently.

3.4.2 The Probability that no Remedy is Required

Table 3.9 also shows that in 19 cases no remedies were required, and in almost all of these the MMC concluded that there was no evidence of any practice against the public interest.[14] Over this period, therefore, the probability that the MMC will make no adverse finding (31 per cent) is roughly one third.

Table 3.10 Problems and remedies

Remedy			Problem			
	MP	DP/PRED	C	EX	VR	Total
T	3	8	2	11	6	30
PC	4	0	1	0	0	5
PM	4	0	1	0	0	5
D	1	0	1	0	3	5
None	4	2	2	4	7	19
Total	16	10	7	15	16	64

Note: see Table 3.9.

Key: MP = monopoly pricing/price leadership; DP/PRED = discriminatory or predatory pricing; C = collusive practices; EX = exclusivity and VR = other vertical restraints.

Table 3.10 disaggregates the remedy frequencies according to type of problem. This shows that the probability of no adverse finding is slightly higher for vertical problems (11/31 = 35 per cent) than for pricing problems (8/30 = 27 per cent). However, further disaggregation reveals that this difference is accounted for entirely by a higher probability of no adverse finding for 'other vertical restraints' (7/16 = 44 per cent). This category apart, for all three pricing problems and exclusivity, the probability lies within a narrow range of 20–29 per cent.

3.4.3 Remedies: Problems and Structure

Table 3.10 also examines whether, when the different types of remedies *have* been put in place, they have been more frequently applied to some types of problem than others.

As can be seen, monopoly pricing and price leadership have attracted the full range of remedies (although, as one might expect, termination was used relatively less frequently); collusive practices have also attracted all types of remedy. On the other hand, only termination has been applied as a remedy for discriminatory and predatory pricing. Price-type remedies are obviously inappropriate for vertical practices: in nearly all vertical cases termination was the chosen option, although in three cases involving other vertical restraints, divestment was used. (This finding is explored in detail in Chapter 8.)

Table 3.11 Recommendations and industry structure

Remedy	Industry Structure				
	A	B	C	D	Total
T	9	7	5	9	30
PC & PM	6	1	0	0	7
D	3	0	0	2	5
None	5	3	1	10	19
Total	23	11	6	21	61

Table 3.11 disaggregates the frequencies, alternatively, across the four types of market structure. Here the most striking finding is that the probability of *no remedy* is significantly greater in unconcentrated loose oligopoly industries (D), with nearly half of all cases being given a 'clean bill of health'. This compares with figures of 22 per cent, 27 per cent and 17 per cent for structures A, B and C respectively, and suggests that high levels of concentration (with or without dominance) are a useful first indicator of abuse of market power; as indeed traditional theory would lead us to believe.[15] The results also show that termination has been widely used in all four market structures, although relatively more in C; and, as might be expected, price control/monitoring has been confined almost exclusively to the dominant firm sector A.[16] Divestment has been used in three category (A) cases (domestic gas appliances (1980), artificial lower limbs (1989) and razors and razor blades (1991)). Perhaps surprisingly, it has also been used in two loose oligopoly cases, (D), each involving elements of *vertical disintegration.*[17]

3.4.4 The Time Lag between Referral and Remedy

It is sometimes argued that what firms fear most about an MMC investigation is the uncertainty and inconvenience caused by the sheer length of time before a final outcome is agreed. It is also possible that a lengthy time lag makes it more likely that referred firms will engage in strategic behaviour with respect to the regulator. More generally, the relevance and effectiveness of the remedies themselves may be blunted by lengthy lags between referral and report and undertakings.

Table 3.12 Time lags (months)

Months	Referral to report	Number of cases Report to undertaking/order	Referral to undertaking/order
1 – 12	17	17	0
13 – 18	17	7	3
19 – 24	12	5	3
25 – 36	21	4	10
37 – 48	5	1	8
48 –	1	3	13
Total	73	37	37
Mean lag	22	19	43

Note: The number of cases shown for referral to report is higher than for report to undertaking for three reasons: not all cases lead to undertakings, for some early cases records are incomplete, and for some recent cases undertakings were still being negotiated at the time of writing.

The first column of Table 3.12 shows the time lags involved between referral and report[18] across the 73 reports. The average time between referral and report is just less than two years, and most cases are bunched quite closely around this mean; there is a 70 per cent probability that any case will involve a time lag between one and three years. However, reports were produced within a year in 17 cases, whilst six cases involved more than three years. There is also often a considerable delay between publication of the report and the eventual undertakings being given (or orders being made). Part of this delay arises as the Secretary of State decides what remedies to seek, and part arises in the negotiation process.

The second column of the table gives a breakdown of the total delay between report and undertakings. As can be seen, the average delay at this stage is 19 months, although this figure is influenced by four 'outliers' exceeding three years. For this reason, the median, which is just over 12 months, is perhaps more representative. If the two lags are consolidated for those cases resulting in an undertaking, the mean overall time taken from the date of referral to the remedy being put in place is more than three and a half years. Similarly the median exceeds three years. Thus, it appears that fears of delay are often well-founded, and this might be considered a weakness of UK monopoly policy.[19]

3.5 CHANGES OVER TIME

One potential drawback in pitching the time period covered by this book over a relatively long period is that we will fail to identify significant changes in policy *within* the period. Whilst this is probably inevitable, and the relatively small size of population prevents us from undertaking a detailed time series analysis, in this section we point to a number of discernible differences in the pattern over time. The first we have already remarked upon in Section 3.1: whilst the MMC has asked to report on a fairly steady stream of cases throughout the period – typically, about three per year – there was a discernible dip between 1981 and 1988.[20] Second, the emphasis on manufacturing (also noted earlier in the chapter) lessened somewhat after 1980: since then, only 64 per cent of cases have come from that sector, as opposed to 87 per cent for 1973–80. Third, there has been a continued decline in the proportion of cases involving just a single scale monopoly (52 per cent for 1973–80; 40 per cent for 1981–8; and 33 per cent for 1989–95) whilst complex monopoly has become more frequent, and, typically, the industries investigated have become somewhat less concentrated.

Not unrelatedly, vertical problems have also become increasingly important over time (30 per cent in 1973–80; rising to 60 per cent for 1981–88; and 60 per cent for 1989–95.) There were no cases involving collusion in the last sub-period. Correspondingly, the MMC has become increasingly less likely to recommend price control or monitoring (22 per cent of cases for 1973–80; 10 per cent for 1981–88; and only 3 per cent for 1989–95). Termination has become more frequently used as a remedy, but even more significantly, the probability that a case results in no remedies has risen noticeably in the 1990s (26 per cent between 1973–80; 30 per cent between 1981–8; and 47 per cent between 1989–95). Finally, there has been a reduction in the time lags typically involved. Reports were produced noticeably faster in the later sub-periods (the mean lag for 1973–80 was 30 months, falling to 24 months for 1981–88, and further to 13 months for 1989–95 – notably, only one report has involved more than two years since 1989). This suggests that the MMC has reacted to earlier criticisms over the length of its investigations. Similarly, the mean lag between report and undertakings being secured fell from 27 to 25 to 15 months respectively in the three sub-periods.

3.6 CONCLUSIONS

The main purpose of this chapter has been to set the scene for the detailed case studies discussed in the rest of the book. We have identified a population of 73 MMC reports over the period 1973–95; this comprises all cases where the OFT has referred a monopoly in which the firm(s) concerned have the potential for abuse of market power. Since some firms have been investigated more than once, these reports refer to 61 different cases; and, hereafter, this is defined as the population.

Although the incidence of reports has inevitably varied from year to year, one can discern a distinct medium-term pattern, with a decline in activity during most of the 1980s, followed by an increase in the late 1980s and 1990s – during the last seven years, the MMC has averaged more than five monopoly reports per year. Two other general features of the population are noteworthy: (a) a disproportionate emphasis on the manufacturing sector, and (b) a relatively high incidence of very small markets. Although the former tendency has weakened slightly in recent years, the latter, given the cost of an MMC investigation, gives food for thought that welfare gains are likely to be limited in small markets – even if the monopoly abuse is rectified.[21]

Most importantly for present purposes, we have identified a number of features in the population as a whole which provide a background for the detailed case studies which are to follow. For ease of cross-reference, we number these as follows.

(i) Market Structure

All cases relate to 'monopoly' by definition. However 'monopoly' is widely defined in the FTA to encompass a variety of different market structures. Using our own typology, in preference to the 'scale' and 'complex' monopoly definitions in the legislation, we have characterised somewhat more than a third of the industries (23) as having a single 'dominant firm' (with a typical CR3 of 95 per cent) and somewhat less than a third as 'loose oligopolies' (being relatively unconcentrated with a mean CR3 of only 55 per cent, and having no obvious market leader). The remainder have either a 'partially dominant' leader (mean CR3 of 65 per cent) or a 'dominant (potentially collusive) group' (with mean CR3 of 86 per cent).

(ii) Types of Monopoly Problem

Vertical restraints (broadly defined) are the main monopoly problem in almost exactly half of the cases, and, while they occur under all types of market structure, they are most common in relatively less concentrated 'loose oligopolies'. Pricing problems have been categorised, in order of frequency, as monopoly pricing/price leadership (unsurprisingly, most common where there is a dominant firm); discriminatory and/or predatory pricing (most common in concentrated industries, usually with large leaders); and collusive practices (usually where there is a dominant group). The mix between vertical and pricing cases has increasingly shifted towards the former in more recent years.

(iii) The Chances of Adverse Findings

In roughly one third of all cases, firms have not been required to give any undertakings following an MMC Report. The chances that no remedy will be required are highest (a) for loose oligopolies (48 per cent), and (b) where the potential problem is vertical (other than exclusivity) (44 per cent).

(iv) Types of Remedy

In those cases where a remedy was put in place, the most frequently used was termination of practices. Price control and/or monitoring is the main alternative, but this has been far less common in recent years. In five cases only has divestment been used, although in some of these cases, this has led to substantial market change.

In the next chapter, we describe how we have selected a sample of cases from this population for further detailed investigation so as to be representative of the population as just described.

NOTES

1. Monopoly reports are always signalled in the report's title by the words 'Report on the supply of...'.
2. Bearing in mind that investigations typically lasted about 2 years at that time, the 1981–88 period corresponds roughly to most of Mrs Thatcher's premiership. The slackest years were 1982–85 during which only five reports were published.
3. Moreover, it is doubtful whether a new examination of cases more than 25 years ago would add much to Shaw and Simpson's analysis: data availability would be an obvious problem, and it is improbable that we would have found sufficient interviewees with long enough memories to make an interview approach worthwhile.
4. See Appendix for details. Films, beer and petrol had also been investigated in the earlier 1950–73 period but are not counted as reinvestigations for our purposes.
5. The predominance of small markets in the table would probably be increased still further were data available on these cases. They include industries such as greyhound racing,

specialised advertising, electrical contracting and caravan sites in Northern Ireland – all of which would appear to involve very small markets.

6. We have combined the firm-level data in the MMC reports with data from the OFT and other sources (such as company reports and business directories) in constructing this database. Details are available in our first OFT report (Clarke et al., 1994).

7. See, for example, Davies et al. (1989, Chapter 4), Tirole (1988, pp. 221–3) or Carlton and Perloff (1994, Chapter 9).

8. See, for example, Hart and Clarke (1980), Davies et al. (1989).

9. The construction of the diagram is probably fairly obvious. The two grades for concentration, 'very high' and 'high', are represented by the diagonal wedges (sloping downward from left to right in the figure). But, within each wedge, industries are classified by the extent to which the leading firm dominates: dominant leaders are portrayed by points lying above the ray with slope 1.5 from the origin.

10. This is similar to Utton's (1986) classification scheme. However, he uses the market shares of only the two largest firms and identifies just three types of structure: 'dominant firm', 'concentrated' and 'loose oligopoly'. The first corresponds roughly to our 'dominant firm', the second to our 'dominant group' and the third is a catch-all group for the rest of the industries in his sample.

11. Some cases exhibit more than one problem. In particular, price discrimination often coincides with vertical restraints of some sort, and exclusive practices often coincide with tying arrangements. We have also widened price collusion to include certain other types of collusive behaviour, including general information sharing agreements.

12. For example in artificial lower limbs (1989), the Secretary of State decided that subsequent structural changes in the industry made intervention no longer necessary. Again, in opium derivatives (1989), price control was recommended but the undertaking sought only required price monitoring.

13. This also includes selling off a beneficial interest in another firm (for example, equity or debt), as in the razors and razor blades (1991) case.

14. In one exceptional case, contact lens solution (1993), a number of features were found to operate against the public interest, but the MMC merely recommended changes in the licensing system for producers and retailers. No undertakings were required, although price control was mentioned as a possible backup option.

15. In some of the D category cases, the MMC looked at just one or two particular practices and found them not to be against the public interest, thereby requiring no remedy. This does not weaken the point, however, that no remedy cases are much more prevalent in the D category.

16. The one exception to this is white salt (1986). In this case, two firms, British Salt and ICI, dominated the market and price control was placed on the more efficient firm, British Salt.

17. The cases are roadside advertising (1981) and beer (1989). The first involved the establishment of a joint selling agency for poster companies and the second ownership and control of tied public houses.

18. Throughout, we date reports by publication and not their submission to the DTI.

19. In the case of predation in particular, firms can be forced out of the market even before the MMC reports (or, indeed, before it starts its investigation: see the case of buses in the north-east (1995) in Chapter 7).

20. This dip was associated with a rise in MMC activity in other areas; notably in section 11 cases (under the 1980 Competition Act) involving efficiency audit references of nationalised industries.

21. There are two points here: namely, the size of any welfare gain arising from an investigation and the costs of the investigation itself both to the government and the firms

involved. On the latter point, we accept that smaller cases are less costly, although they may still involve significant costs for the firms involved. For a discussion of this issue with a different viewpoint see Morrison et al. (1996).

4. Methodology and Selection of Case Studies

In the early stages of this research, we considered the possibility of undertaking a large scale cross-section statistical analysis of all 61 cases. In the event we rejected this methodology, and opted instead for in-depth case studies of a sample drawn from the population. The reasons for this are discussed in Section 4.1. Basically, they involve problems of interpretation of statistical results given the diversity of cases in the population. Section 4.2 explains how we selected the specific case studies, and assesses the representativeness of the resulting sample. Section 4.3 explains, in broad terms, how the case studies were conducted and Section 4.4 draws some conclusions.

4.1 CROSS-INDUSTRY ECONOMETRICS OR CASE STUDIES?

The main purpose of this book is to assess the effectiveness of remedies to monopoly abuse put in place following MMC investigations. In principle, this should be, at least partly, revealed by comparing the pre- and post-report behaviour and performance of the firms concerned. Whilst behaviour is not always directly observable, one might argue that it is reflected in the firms' performance, and, perhaps, in changes in industry structure. If so, one way of conducting an appraisal would be to compare pre- and post-report data across the population of reports on (a) market shares and concentration, and (b) prices and profitability. In essence, Shaw and Simpson (1986, 1989) used this methodology in their study of the period up to 1973, and Utton (1986) employed a similar approach in his study of dominant firms.

However, the limitations of such an approach are fairly obvious. In particular, there is what one might call the *comparator (or counterfactual) problem*, and ambiguities of *interpretation and causality*. The comparator problem arises because profits, prices, and so on will be determined by many factors other than the remedies implemented following MMC investigations. For example, profits and other firm level indicators are typically sensitive to the business cycle and to random exogenous shocks, whilst dominant market shares have an almost inbuilt tendency to decline rather than increase.[1] Partial solutions to this problem are possible, and have been used in previous studies – for instance, prices and profits can be normalised, and measured relative to appropriate aggregate price or profit indices, and control variables might be added to capture the influences of other determinants of profits and market shares.

However, even more sophisticated statistical analysis cannot hope to avoid difficulties concerned with *interpretation and causality*. To see the nature of this problem, consider the interpretation to be placed on changes in market shares *after* MMC reports. As an example, consider a firm which agrees to discontinue a vertical restraint as a result of an MMC investigation. Should its market share decline as a consequence? Not necessarily, for a number of reasons. First, the MMC may have been wrong – the 'restraint' may not have been anti-competitive at all, in which case its removal will not affect competition. Second, the MMC may have been right, but the firm is still able to maintain its dominance *ex-post*, by erecting alternative barriers. Third, the firm may be able to maintain its market share by increasing efficiency and fighting off any potential competitors. Crucially, each explanation has different welfare implications concerning the value of competition policy.

Next, consider a firm which is compelled to lower price or limit its rate of increase. In this case, it is difficult to see what subsequent changes in market share would reveal. To the extent that the firm is constrained to charge a lower price than it would wish, this can only reduce the chance of new entry or encroachment by an existing smaller rival – market share remains unchanged. On the other hand, if the regulation is non-binding and the firm is able to keep prices, or their rate of increase, high, this may still have no market share effect if entry is blockaded.

Might price/profits data before and after the event tell us more? Perhaps, although they are more prone to the comparator problem. More crucially, however, we encounter the classic market power versus efficiency debate (see, for example, Demsetz, 1973; Clarke, Davies and Waterson, 1984). Often, one can argue in favour of vertical restraints in terms of their efficiency-enhancing effects. In many instances, a vertical restraint is quasi-integration which can be justified because it economises on transactions costs of using the market (see Chapter 8). Consider then a hypothetical case where the MMC 'gets it wrong' and recommends the withdrawal of a practice which the firm pursues for innocent efficiency purposes. In this case, the removal of the restraint will increase the firm's costs and profits will fall. Depending on the extent of its market power, it may be able to raise price to compensate partially for this. So, the MMC gets it wrong, profits fall and prices rise!

For these and similar reasons, a broad brush econometric comparison across the population as a whole of firms' prices, profits and/or market shares could lead to misleading results. In principle, econometric panel techniques distinguishing sub-samples (for example, by the nature of problems and remedies) might be used in order to recover direct estimates of behaviour, but an early feasibility study of the data convinced us that usable comparable time series information would be available for only a small minority of firms and industries in this population.

In the event, therefore, we opted for a more qualitative case study approach. The main problem with case studies, of course, is that small samples may not be representative of the population as a whole, and it is essential to select a sample which is 'representative' whilst sufficiently diverse to permit comparisons between cases. To meet this point, we took considerable care in selecting cases which were as representative of the population as possible and these are discussed in Section 4.2.[2]

In an attempt to minimise the risk of being overwhelmed by details of individual cases, or of over-generalising from a small sample, we have structured the analysis as follows. In a first stage, described in Chapters 5–8, we group together the case studies according to the broad monopoly problems involved. For each problem, we discuss the relevant cases in detail, and then widen the net to consider also other, non-sample cases, more briefly. In this way we hope to widen our understanding of the full range of issues involved for any *type of monopoly problem*. In the second stage, described in Chapter 9, we draw the threads of this analysis together, and consider the effectiveness of *the different remedies used*. This chapter also looks at the wider issue of the overall effectiveness of policy and the inter-play with other changes in the markets which also took place.

4.2 SAMPLE SELECTION AND REPRESENTATIVENESS OF THE SAMPLE

Our structured approach to comparative case studies means that it would be unwise to select a sample at random, and we have deliberately chosen a sample to be representative of the population in three dimensions: industry structure, monopoly problem and remedy used. We selected 14 cases and these are shown in Table 4.1.

As can be seen, the cases are drawn fairly evenly from each of the three sub-periods identified earlier in Table 3.1. Also in line with the population, there is a heavy incidence of manufacturing cases: 10 out of 14 cases (71 per cent) is virtually identical to the population proportion, 70 per cent (see Table 3.2). The 'main problems' identified are: six vertical restraints, three monopoly pricing/price leadership, two price discrimination/predatory pricing and three collusive practices. This is fairly representative of the population proportions, shown in Table 3.7, except that collusive practices are over-represented by one, at the expense of vertical restraints. The remedies include eight terminations, four price controls/price monitoring and two divestments. Compared to the population proportions (excluding cases where no undertakings were required), this is an under-representation of terminations (by two cases) and a corresponding over-representation of price control/price monitoring (see Table 3.9). The distribution of market structures is also roughly representative. The sample includes four dominant firms (in our nomenclature, category A); five dominant groups, (B), one partially dominant firm, (C), and four loose oligopolies, (D). Category B is over-represented by two in this case (see Table 3.5) but again the difference is not great.

Table 4.1 also indicates the ten cases in which interviews were conducted. Initially, we had selected a sample of ten cases in stage 1 of our work (Clarke, Davies, Driffield and Lund, 1994) which we examined using information obtained from OFT files plus various published sources such as trade directories, industry reports and so on. In the second stage, we conducted interviews with the main parties involved, either the principals (that is, firms investigated), their rivals, their customers, or other interested parties. In this part of the work, we realised at an early stage that we would be unable to obtain suitable information on the earliest cases, simply because few people contacted had any knowledge of the cases going back 20 years (or more). We therefore opted to replace three of the earliest cases (breakfast cereals, building bricks and frozen foodstuffs) with three more recent ones (ice cream, foreign package holidays and artificial lower limbs), paying attention again to the representativeness of the cases. Finally, we added one further case, bus services in the north-east, as representative of a number of bus cases investigated by the OFT and MMC in the past ten years, and about which we had a detailed knowledge from another research project on which two of the authors had been recently engaged.[3]

Table 4.1 The sample of case studies

Case	Date of Report	Structure	Scale/Complex	Problem	Remedy
Breakfast cereals	1973	A	S	MP	PC/PM
Contraceptive sheaths*	1975/82/94	A	S	MP	PC/PM
Building bricks	1976	C	S	DP/PRED	T
Frozen foodstuffs	1976	D	S	EXP	T
Ice cream*	1979/94	B	2S,C	EXP/(TIE)	T
Electricity meters*	1979	B	S,C	C	T
Roadside advertising*	1981	D	S,2C	C	D
Films*	1983/94	D	4S,C	EXD/(TIE)	T
Postal franking machines*	1986	A	2S	TIE	T
White salt*	1986	B	2S	C	PC
Foreign package holidays*	1986	D	C	RPM/(EXD)	T
Opium derivatives*	1989	A	S	MP	PM
Artificial lower limbs*	1989	B	2S	VI/MP	(D)
Buses in the north-east	1995	B	2S	PRED	T

Note: Interview cases are denoted *

Key: MP = monopoly pricing or price leadership; DP/PRED = discriminatory or predatory pricing; C = collusive practices; EXP = exclusive purchasing (exclusive dealing); TIE = tie-in sales; RPM = resale price maintenance; EXD = exclusive distribution; VI = vertical integration. Bracketed items are less important problems.

55

The upshot is that we have a sample of 14 industries (23 per cent of the population as a whole) which we examined in depth, ten of which involved direct interviewing and four where deskwork only was used. Together, they account for 18 reports over the period 1973–95, and they represent exactly one third of all 42 cases which actually ended up with undertakings (or orders) being secured.

4.3 CONDUCT OF THE SURVEY

As already noted, we undertook interviews in ten of the cases shown in Table 4.1. Details of the survey method are described in full in our second report (Clarke, Davies and Driffield, 1995) and we make only brief comments here.

Our aim in the interviews was to obtain as much useful information as possible on the effectiveness of the remedies in the selected cases. To this end we used a semi-structured questionnaire (which differed slightly depending on whether a principal (i.e. a referred firm), rival or customer was involved). The interviews focused on the background to the case but, more importantly, on what had happened following the implementation of the remedy and the effectiveness of the remedy itself. In many cases, the interviewees were very forthcoming and we were able to build up a very comprehensive picture of what had happened in each particular case. In particular, in a number of cases we did not stick rigidly to the questionnaire but adapted our questions to focus on the important factors involved in that case.

In all we conducted 61 interviews, almost half of which (30) were direct ('face-to-face') interviews and the remainder were by telephone. In each case, we sought to identify the main participants in the investigation and, if possible, we interviewed these 'face-to-face'. We also sought a wider range of opinion in our telephone interviews. In total, we interviewed 18 principals, 17 rivals, 16 customers and ten other parties spread fairly evenly over the different cases.[4] Generally speaking, we believe we have a good cross-section of views in each of the cases. We also received correspondence from a number of individuals and organisations who were willing to provide information but did not feel they had enough to say to warrant a full interview. Several respondents (including one principal) also gave us interviews 'off the record' which were of considerable help in understanding some of the cases.

4.4 CONCLUSIONS

The second part of the book focuses, in particular, on the 14 case studies just identified. Together, they account for a third of all the cases investigated by the MMC between 1973 and 1995 which resulted in remedies (that is, where some monopoly abuse had been detected). The sample has been constructed to be broadly representative of the population as a whole with respect to type of monopoly problem, type of remedy and industry structure.

NOTES

1. There is a general tendency for very dominant firms to lose market share over time as a matter of course. In a stochastic world, any variate which is bounded from above by 1 (or 100 per cent) and which is subject to an element of 'chance' is more likely to decline if it starts from a value near that upper limit (see, for example, Davies and Geroski, 1997).
2. In one case, however, an element of 'double-counting' may be involved, in that we deliberately selected ice cream in our second report to replace an old case, frozen foods, where a similar problem of manufacturer/retailer exclusivity in food was involved.
3. See Jones et al. (1996).
4. In most cases we were able to interview most of the principals involved. In two cases, white salt (1986) and films (1983, 1994), we were only successful in interviewing one and two principals respectively.

PART II

The Case Studies

.

5. Monopoly Pricing and Price Leadership

5.1 THEORETICAL PERSPECTIVES

Ask the informed lay person for an interpretation of 'monopoly abuse', and (s)he will probably describe the case of a single seller exploiting its unique position in the market by selling to consumers at a price which is 'too high'. Even good undergraduate economics students, who have nevertheless not taken a specialist option in Industrial Organisation, would probably answer in similar terms.[1] In fact, examples of classic textbook abuse of this sort are relatively rare amongst the population of MMC reports studied in this book – especially in more recent years. The typical case does not involve a single firm selling direct to final consumers at a 'high' price. Rather, most cases which come before the MMC involve anti-competitive behaviour by one firm, or a group of firms, at the expense of their rivals. Only infrequently do 'final' consumers feature directly in the story; more commonly, the focus is on contractual relationships between firms.

In a recent publication, the Office of Fair Trading (1995) makes this distinction by referring to two types of behaviour: 'exploitation of monopoly power' and 'anti-competitive behaviour'. Its definition of the former is an adequate introduction to the subject matter of this chapter:

> 'the exploitation of market power at the expense of customers is most likely to take the form of charging excessive prices or making excessive profits or both. A scale monopolist can exploit its market power in this way only if it does not face effective competition, either because of circumstances in the industry – it may be a natural monopoly – or because the company itself is protected by entry barriers of some form'. (1995, p. 14)

Since textbook monopoly theory *is* well known, this will suffice for present purposes with two additional remarks. First, the role of entry barriers (or barriers to contestability, see Baumol et al. 1982; Baumol, 1982) is clearly crucial. Given the potential for free entry, either from domestic firms or from imports, anti-trust intervention is unnecessary. Second, we should not confine this chapter merely to cases of *literal* monopoly: there will also be cases where the market includes other small firms, but where there is still a single dominant firm which possesses some advantage (perhaps lower costs or accumulated brand loyalty) which effectively reduces its smaller rivals to the role of followers.

5.2 OVERVIEW OF CASES IN THE POPULATION

There are, in our view, 13 cases in the population (just over 20 per cent) in which the main problem investigated by the MMC was monopoly pricing or price leadership (see Table 5.1). Of these, eleven cases involved market structures in which there was a single, clearly identified, leading firm: nine were of the 'dominant firm' type (type 'A' in our classification) and two were slightly less concentrated, but still with a clear market leader (type 'C').[2] In chronological terms, all but two cases were clustered in two short

Table 5.1 Monopoly pricing and price leadership in the population

Case	Oligopoly type	Remedy
Breakfast cereals (1973)	A	PC/PM
Librium and valium (1973)	A	PC
Wire and fibre ropes (1973)	C	T
Primary batteries (1974)	A	PC/PM
Contraceptive sheaths (1975, 1982, 1994)	A	PC/PM
Insulated wires and cables (1979)	D	None
Pest control (1988)	C	T
Opium derivatives (1989)	A	PM
Coffee (1991)	A	None
Razors and razor blades (1991)	A	D
Cross Solent ferries (1992)	A	None
Matches and disposable lighters (1992)	A	T
Compact discs (1994)	D	None

Note: Detailed case studies are shown in bold. Artificial lower limbs (1989) might also be included in this list but because we judge the vertical aspects of the case to be more important it is discussed instead in Chapter 8.

time periods – five between 1973 and 1975[3] and six between 1988 and 1992. Interestingly, all of the first five attracted an adverse finding – usually resulting in price control or monitoring. On the other hand, three of the five most recent cases did not lead to an undertaking. This last group contains, in particular, compact discs where many people felt the MMC 'got it wrong' – an issue which we mention briefly in Section 5.6.

The three cases selected for further investigation are breakfast cereals, contraceptive sheaths and opium derivatives. Each involved an obvious market leader (segment A in our classification) and resulted either in price control or price monitoring.

5.3 BREAKFAST CEREALS (1973)[4]

This case focused on the pricing policies of Kellogg which was the dominant supplier of ready-to-eat (RTE) breakfast cereals in the UK, with a market share of 55 per cent in 1971. Kellogg was a highly profitable company with an estimated rate of return on capital of about 70 per cent on average, on an historic cost basis, between 1962–66; although this fell to about 46 per cent on average between 1967–71. In spite of some significantly sized competitors,[5] the MMC concluded that Kellogg acted as a price leader, and that it had, in earlier years, set monopoly prices. Kellogg's position of market power was created and maintained by its high level of advertising, and, to a lesser extent, by brand proliferation.[6]

In its report, the Commission did not find that Kellogg's *current* profits were 'too high' but argued that the potential for monopoly pricing in the future did still exist. It, therefore, recommended that Kellogg's profits should be kept under review and that it be required to seek government approval for further price increases. An undertaking to this effect was signed in 1973. At the same time, Kellogg was also subject to price controls by the Price Commission[7] which sought to keep price increases in line with increases in costs. From 1976, these latter controls were relaxed, although the Price Commission itself was not abolished until 1979. However, in 1980, after a review, the OFT decided to remove price controls, replacing them simply with a requirement of notification of price changes. Finally, after considerable pressure from the company, price notification itself was also dropped in 1988.

In evaluating this case, albeit many years later, certain features are incontrovertible. Certainly, Kellogg had been a dominant firm for many years, and, at varying times, earned high monopoly profits. Faced with this the MMC chose to implement price controls which, together with the controls operated by the Price Commission,[8] significantly reduced Kellogg's prices and profits after 1973. Evidence from the OFT's files suggests that price controls were effective in this period. As a particular example, Kellogg applied to the Price Commission in 1973 to increase its prices by 17.8 per cent (following a large increase in grain prices) but, under pressure from the government, limited its increase to just 9.8 per cent. Partly as a result, its rate of return (on an historic cost basis) fell to just 15 per cent in 1973. Whilst in later years it was more successful in obtaining price increases (especially after 1976 when the Price Commission relaxed its controls), we believe that the constraint was still binding. This is reflected in Kellogg's low level of profitability in the period as a whole:[9] between 1973–79, its average rate of return on an historic cost basis had fallen to just 22 per cent.

One other emergent feature of the market (which may have persuaded the OFT to remove the price controls) was the growth of supermarket own-brands. In 1971 these accounted for just 4 per cent of retail sales but, by the early 1980s, this had risen to 17 per cent. Own-brands typically enjoy a specific advantage, in that they do not require heavy advertising expenditures because they benefit from the brand name of the supermarkets themselves. Whilst much of their growth was at the expense of other major producers (Weetabix and Nabisco), Kellogg also lost market share. This was particularly so after Kellogg raised its prices in the early 1980s, following the removal of price controls. Kellogg's response was to escalate its advertising expenditure to very high levels in the second half of the 1980s, thereby winning back market share. Partly as a result of this, its profitability was lower in the latter part of the 1980s than it had been before the MMC report, but its market share (at about 50 per cent of retail sales) was not much below what it had been in 1971.

In this case the question arises as to whether price controls should have been lifted in 1980, and whether price notification should have been removed in 1988. In answer to the first question, it could be argued that growth of own-brands had introduced more competition into the market and weakened Kellogg's market power. However, Kellogg has been able to maintain its dominance since by increased advertising and has increased its profitability to levels which are higher than under the price control.[10]

On the second question, it is clear from circumstantial evidence that Kellogg lobbied strongly especially after 1986, for the removal of price notification. This raises the general issue of sustained pressure from a regulated firm and how 'the regulator' should respond. In this particular case, the OFT took the view that it could continue to monitor Kellogg under its general powers under the FTA, and, because of this, the requirement for price notification was dropped in 1988. We have no evidence, one way or the other, on whether Kellogg's pricing has remained a matter of (informal) interest to the OFT.

Our conclusions in this case, therefore, are that price control had an effect in reducing Kellogg's prices and profits in the 1970s. However, after the removal of the control in 1980, Kellogg was able to increase its prices and, through advertising, largely re-establish its market share. Clearly, there has been growth in supermarket own-brands and this must have served as a source of competitive discipline on Kellogg. Certainly, although its profits have recovered somewhat compared to the period of price control, they are still not at the very high levels observed in the 1960s. Since the emergence of own-brands was obviously not a consequence of the remedy, the most favourable interpretation would be that price control served as a useful short-run constraint on market power, until the market itself produced effective competition. A less favourable conclusion would be since Kellogg still dominates the market, that price control had a merely transitory dampening effect, without fundamentally changing the competitive process.

5.4 CONTRACEPTIVE SHEATHS (1975, 1982, 1994)

5.4.1 Case summary

All three investigations into the contraceptive sheaths (condoms) industry centred on the dominant position of the London Rubber Company (LRC, owned by London International) which makes Durex and other leading brands. Historically, its dominant role was even more pronounced than Kellogg's,[11] but, in more recent years, there has been significant entry which has accompanied substantial growth in market demand.

In its first report, the MMC found that LRC had a significant monopoly and that it was exploiting its position to a considerable degree. In particular, it argued that there were 'excess profits' (an average rate of return on capital of at least 77 per cent in 1969–73), and that LRC used price discrimination, both to deter new competition and to exploit sectors of the market where demand was particularly price inelastic. The MMC recommended that LRC's average revenue (that is, its weighted average price) should be reduced by 40 per cent.

However, the government did not adopt this radical recommendation and, instead, a series of maximum prices were put in place. These had a much smaller effect on average revenue than the MMC had intended, reducing it by about 1.8 per cent in nominal terms in 1975–77 (see the 1982 report). Although LRC's profitability fell dramatically at the time of the investigation, it later recovered, rising to about 46 per cent by 1982.

Largely as a result of pressure from LRC itself, a second investigation took place in 1980–82. Again, the MMC concluded that LRC had a scale monopoly, with over 90 per cent of the market, although it acknowledged that condoms now accounted for a much smaller share of overall contraceptive sales. The MMC again recommended price control, such that LRC's average revenue should not be allowed to rise by more than 1.5 percentage points below a special index designed to capture costs of production of condoms.[12] In this case, however, substantial negotiations took place between the government and LRC with lengthy delays in implementation of this remedy.[13] It was finally put into effect in 1988.

In the second half of the 1980s, a significant exogenous shock was emerging – the AIDS epidemic. This resulted in both a change in the image of the product and a massive growth in demand. Two consequences should be noted. First, there was a significant increase in advertising expenditures. Traditionally, there had been little advertising of condoms, but this changed with the emergence of AIDS. LRC began to undertake what it calls 'public information' advertising and, amongst other things, in 1990, advertising for condoms was allowed on television before 9.00 p.m. By 1990, LRC's advertising had risen to 7 per cent of sales from just 0.8 per cent in 1986. LRC's sales volume also grew by 35 per cent from 1982–93 compared to a decline of 13 per cent from 1974–82.[14]

Second, new entry occurred, notably by Mates, Jiffi, and, more recently, Femidom. Mates, in particular, made significant inroads into the market towards the end of the 1980s, achieving a market share of 21 per cent by 1991, and being particularly prevalent in the vending machine sector. However, the growth of Mates was halted and reversed after 1992 as it became increasingly unprofitable, and tended to follow LRC's prices (see the 1994 report). Hence, it is by no means certain that the entrant was providing an effective competitive constraint on LRC at this time.

The case was referred to the MMC for a third time (at the request of LRC) in 1992. The company argued against continued price control, partly on the grounds of equity (it was not controlled in this way in any other country) and partly because it claimed that the controls were deterring entry. Whilst the evidence on the latter is by no means clear, the potential effect of price controls on entry is undoubtedly the central issue in this case. Clearly, price control may deter entry and, paradoxically, maintain concentration at a higher level than would otherwise occur. If so, there may be a consequent loss in consumer surplus, both from an (arguably) higher price, and reduced competition on quality and introduction of new products. In the event, the MMC took a sympathetic line in its last report, recommending that price controls be lifted, bearing in mind the increased presence of other firms. However, as something of a side issue, the MMC noted that LRC was employing an anti-competitive practice in signing solus ties (that is, exclusive purchasing contracts) with retailers, the effect of which was to reduce competition at the retail stage. It recommended that this practice should cease and an undertaking to this effect was given in 1994.

5.4.2 Interviews

The consensus of opinion expressed in our interviews was that both the 1975 and 1982 reports had placed binding constraints on the profitability of LRC, although several respondents felt that these were not as tight as they should have been. Also the removal of the restrictions in 1994 was deemed (by some) to be inappropriate.

Certainly, while the undertakings agreed following the 1975 report were weaker than the MMC had recommended, the quantitative evidence suggests that they had a major effect on LRC's profitability in the short term. Although average revenues declined by less than 2 per cent between 1975–77, LRC's profitability fell dramatically from about 80 per cent in 1974 to less than 20 per cent between 1977–79 (1982 report). Interestingly, LRC's pressure for a new investigation in the early 1980s came at a time when its profitability was recovering strongly – a point which counted against it in the 1982 report.

Evidence published in the 1994 report shows that price control continued to have an effect in the 1980s.[15] Average revenue data (Figure 5.1) show that LRC's prices must have risen broadly in line with the cost index suggested by the MMC although there was a price over-shoot in 1983 and an under-shoot from 1987–89 (the latter probably being influenced by the entry of Mates). Thus, real prices were more or less constant (and may even have decreased) over the period. Figures for profitability (Figure 5.2) are less clear-cut, with a considerable increase in profitability between 1983–86 and then a sharp fall between 1986–90. It seems likely that the increase in profitability was associated with the growth of the market due to the AIDS scare, whilst the fall was associated with new entry by Mates. Data for advertising expenditures show that there was a dramatic increase in industry advertising in 1987, which then levelled off at a reduced, but nevertheless, much higher level than previously. It seems likely that this expenditure (plus some loss of market share) were the main reasons for the observed fall in LRC's profitability.

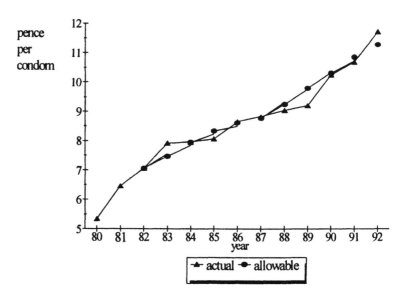

Source: 1994 Report.

Figure 5.1 Average revenue of LRC

Most interview respondents felt that LRC was acting as a monopoly in the early 1980s and that an MMC investigation had been appropriate. They also agreed that the measure adopted (price control) had an effect – a point emphasised by the customers in our sample. As one respondent put it 'LRC had about 97 per cent of the market in 1982 and was able to charge the price it chose'. Hence, most felt there was a clear need for action and the recommendations were justified.

However, a number of firms qualified this response. First, it was argued that, by setting price controls, the MMC effectively prevented new entry to the market and thereby helped to maintain LRC's monopoly position. Whatever the strength of this argument, with hindsight it should be remembered that at the time of the first report, the MMC was dealing with a dominant firm in a small, declining industry in which prospects for entry seemed small. Hence, price control seemed the most appropriate action at the time. Subsequently, of course, the industry became much larger and price control could have prevented new entry.

Of course, this is a counterfactual issue. Nevertheless, several firms argued that price controls had effectively kept out a number of Japanese and

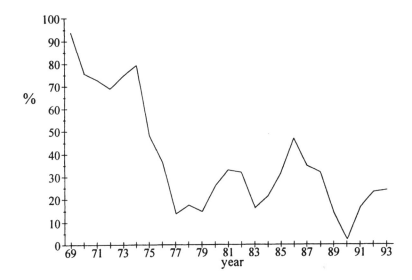

Source: 1994 Report

Figure 5.2 Return on capital employed of LRC

South East Asian firms who had successfully entered other markets in Europe (notably Spain and Italy) in the 1980s, selling high quality condoms. On the other hand, others commented that, even with the removal of price controls in 1994, they did not expect Japanese and South East Asian firms to enter the UK market because LRC's brand leadership was so strong.

Second, not all respondents felt that price controls had been effective in the 1980s. It was argued by several that the MMC had made a crucial mistake in linking LRC's average revenue *as a whole* to the cost index. They suggested that LRC was able to 'play the index' by cross-subsidisation (that is, price discrimination). In particular, LRC had lowered its prices to the NHS (and the Ministry of Defence) in order to deter entry into these sectors, whilst cross-subsidising this from higher retail and vending machine prices. Hence, it was argued that competition would have been better served had price control been applied separately to each of the three sectors (NHS, retail and vending machine). From a theoretical point of view, this is a case where the remedy itself may have caused a distortion (Nuttall and Vickers, 1996) which LRC was able to use to its own advantage.

Third, part of LRC's response to the price control had been to franchise its vending machine business, enabling it to withdraw from the vending stage whilst still controlling wholesale prices. It was explained to us that the company had thereby 'squeezed' their franchisees who were forced to pay high prices for LRC's products. In other words, franchisees were caught between the price control (which was set at the retail level) and the price charged by LRC. Of course, it is unlikely that franchisees would consistently accept subnormal returns in the long term, so the force of this argument would appear to be that independents could operate at lower cost than LRC and this generated extra profits (which accrued to LRC). Interestingly, this is a similar type of response to that following the 1989 beer case, where leading brewers raised tenants' rents in order to recover any monopoly rents that the latter might earn.

On the crucial role of new entry, opinions were mixed. As mentioned earlier, the most significant entry was by Mates, set up by Richard Branson, which supplied condoms produced by Ansell's, an Australian company (and a subsidiary of Pacific Dunlop).[16] Mates has been able to sell its condoms, in particular, through Boots (the dominant retailer) and this has enabled it to gain considerable market share, currently estimated at about 15–20 per cent. In addition, Jiffy entered (and is also sold by Boots), as did Healthline Products.[17] Boots also sell Femidom which is seen as a competitor to condoms.

In fact, as early as 1988, LRC had begun to argue that the entry had changed the market dramatically and that there was no further need for price control. As mentioned above, this led to the 1994 report in which the price control was dropped. There were mixed views about the 1994 decision. Several customers argued that LRC was still the dominant firm in 1994 and that there was no reason to believe that it would limit its price increases voluntarily should the price control be removed. The view of this group was that removing price control would lead to significantly higher prices (which they claim has subsequently occurred). One respondent told us that condom prices had been rising by between 5 per cent and 12 per cent each quarter since the report was published, although rises to the NHS had been somewhat less (about 6 per cent). Surprisingly, several respondents felt that the intention of the most recent investigation had been to look further at

LRC's abuse of market power and did not seem to realise that it was actually pressure by LRC which had brought the report about. For these firms, LRC is still a monopolist whose prices should be controlled.

On the other hand, other respondents argued that the market had changed since 1982 and that price control was no longer needed. One firm suggested that competition should be left to the market and that this should also have happened in 1982. Several others argued that, even if higher prices did result from the decision, this would encourage new entry and hence lower prices in the long run.

We have some reservations about these arguments. First, several respondents told us that competition in this market is largely via brand image and perceived quality, not price, and that LRC acts as price leader (with the dominant brand). Hence, it is not clear that competition will develop amongst incumbent firms. Second, these respondents also said that they did not expect significant new entry due to LRC's dominant brand, and so price competition from this source was also unlikely. It remains to be seen whether higher prices will attract new entry (for example, by Japanese firms) or whether these arguments will prevail.

Turning to the solus ties with retailers (highlighted by the MMC in its 1994 report), LRC argued, during the investigation, that these ties had in fact been requested by retailers and were not suggested by itself. However, several of our interviewees explained that LRC had tried to persuade retailers to remove their products from their shelves, and that this was an anti-competitive policy which needed to be stopped.

Several other points which arose in the interviews can also be mentioned briefly. First, we were told that retailers (and, in particular, Boots) have considerable buying power in this market, and this enabled them to extract significantly lower prices from the manufacturers. One respondent argued that Boots uses its monopsony power to increase its profit margins on condoms (rather than passing the benefits on to customers) and that these margins were currently about 115 per cent. Whilst we are unable to corroborate this estimate, it is clear that Boots has been able to play off different suppliers against each other in order to obtain lower prices. Boots apparently considers stocking any brand which satisfies the appropriate BS or EU standard and it is likely that it will continue to benefit from this approach.

Second, several firms mentioned the question of the kite mark (British Standard BS3704) for condoms and one suggested that it may act as a barrier to entry. However, views about this were mixed, and several other respondents argued that the standard was reasonable and did not act as a barrier.[18] It should be noted that a new European standard (EN 600) was adopted at the end of 1995 and that this may affect competition in the UK. In particular, it could be that adoption of the standard will encourage Japanese firms (who already meet the standard) to enter the UK market, although at time of writing, no such development has occurred.

Finally, several firms noted that new polyurethane condoms would shortly appear on the market, offering important new qualities. However, our respondents felt that this would not undermine LRC's dominance since it had already invested heavily in the new product itself. Moreover, other firms such as Healthline, would be unlikely to follow this route.

5.4.3 Conclusions

In this case, we have found that price control did have a significant effect in reducing monopoly prices and profits over a considerable period. The main development in this market has been the growth in demand associated with the AIDS scare in the 1980s which, in turn, has facilitated advertising and significant new entry. This entry has clearly persuaded the MMC that price control is no longer necessary. However, LRC has a strong brand name and has been able largely to maintain its dominant market share and we suspect that this will continue. It remains to be seen whether the potential for monopoly abuse has really changed significantly since the 1970s. Certainly, a number of our interviewees doubted that this is the case.

5.5 OPIUM DERIVATIVES (1989)

5.5.1 Case Summary

In this case, the MMC investigated MacFarlan Smith Ltd (MSL) – a subsidiary of Glaxo – which at the time of the report supplied 88 per cent of the market for opium derivatives in the UK. Opium derivatives are intermediate goods produced from opium poppies which are then sold on to drug companies for use in making pain-killing drugs (for example, codeine, but also much more powerful drugs such as diamorphine). The market is very small with total sales of only £7 million at the time of the investigation and this was undoubtedly a factor in the near monopoly structure observed.[19]   Significantly, imports were banned by the Home Office because of the security risks associated with this potentially dangerous product. Hence, MSL was largely protected from the threat of competition and this enabled it to set (alleged) monopoly prices in the UK.

In its report, the MMC concluded that the monopoly operated against the public interest and that MSL had set monopoly prices and earned monopoly profits. It also concluded that MSL had used price discrimination by offering discounts to larger companies to the disadvantage of smaller firms. It concluded that, in the longer term, these problems could be overcome by liberalising trade in opium derivatives within the Common Market and recommended that the Home Office should work towards this goal. In the shorter term, however, it recommended that MSL should publish a maximum price list for its products and that it be subject to price control for a period of three years.

In the event, the remedy was much weaker than this and merely required MSL to publish maximum prices and report any changes in its prices to the OFT (that is, price monitoring). However, the company decided to meet the conditions of the price control voluntarily in 1989–92. Undoubtedly, this was because it was anxious to avoid a possible second investigation which would have involved it in further costs and (possibly) the introduction of price controls at a later stage. In 1992, however, it felt it should no longer be bound by the controls, which it argued were irrelevant to the market anyway as it then stood.

Two subsequent developments should be noted. First, Glaxo divested itself of a number of its subsidiaries in the early 1990s, including MSL, which was subject to a management buyout in 1990. The company has since obtained a listing on the Alternative Investment Market (AIM), in March 1995 (with initial capital of £48 million). Second, Boots (the only other significant producer) ceased production of codeine phosphate in 1990 mainly because it felt that it could not justify further investment in this field. Boots now purchases opium derivatives from MSL.

5.5.2 Interviews

Clearly, the Commission felt that the best answer to the monopoly problem in this market was to encourage trade in opium derivatives within the EU. In the interim, however, notification of maximum prices was the measure implemented and we consider the effect of this first.

The period following the investigation was quite difficult for MSL, not least because its principal customer, Evans Medical (now Medeva, but also part of Glaxo at the time), suspended its purchases of opium derivatives soon after the report (due to high existing stock levels). This, and other factors, led MSL to make negative profits in both 1989 and 1990. Given the firm's monopoly position, it might have raised its prices to improve its profitability but, as noted above, it chose to follow the price control. We were told that the initial investigation had been extremely expensive for the company,[20] and that it was very concerned that a second investigation might take place. The short run effect of the investigation, therefore, was probably that prices were lower than they otherwise might have been, at least in the period 1989-92.

At the present time, MSL is the sole producer of opium derivatives in the UK and there are no imports. However, when we explored this issue in our interviews, it was pointed out that MSL did, in fact, face competition at the downstream stage. This is because several drug companies had switched production from the UK to Ireland in the second half of the 1980s, thereby obtaining opium derivatives at lower prices on the international market. This then had had the effect of reducing demand for MSL's products in the UK, with the result that differentials between UK and international prices had fallen in recent years. This effect should not be underestimated because without it, MSL could, in principle (and without MMC intervention), have set very much higher prices in the UK − a classic case of an upstream firm (potentially) extracting all monopoly profits from downstream firms. Constraints do, therefore, exist on MSL's monopoly power, although in more recent years, with the recovery of international prices, these have been reduced.

Several respondents noted that, whilst differentials between UK and international prices had fallen in the early 1990s, a significant differential still exists. One customer commented that MSL had reduced its prices at the end of 1991, but, in its view, prices were still considerably higher than those in Europe, especially in France. Another argued that, whilst prices were lower after the investigation, the change was not dramatic and may have occurred anyway because of falling raw material prices. These comments suggest that, although there was an effect on prices in the short term, the effect may not have been that strong.

Turning to the MMC's recommendations on imports, the story is quite complicated and we only summarize it briefly here. First, the Home Office has made some attempt to discuss trade in opium derivatives within the EU, but has met with little success. The Home Office told us that it had approached the European Commission and a working party had been set up, but in the end this had come to nothing. It also approached several European countries directly (notably France and Spain) but again·met with no success. Of course, the sticking point for the Home Office, and *a fortiori* MSL, is that trade should take place multilaterally. We were told that unilateral free trade could lead to dumping in the UK (for example, by East

European countries). On the other hand, multilateral trade would probably benefit MSL given that it is a low cost producer.

The Home Office has also been engaged in lengthy court proceedings which may (eventually) have some bearing on this case. These centre on an attempt by a company called Generics UK to import diamorphine from Holland into the UK. At the time of writing, this case has recently received preliminary judgement in the European Court which appears to support Generics' case (subject to some provisos) and this may mean that, eventually, imports will be allowed. However, it seems unlikely that the government would support such a move without obtaining reciprocal arrangements from other European countries and this suggests that the case may go on for some time yet.

One other point of more general interest is the size of the market. Opium derivatives is a good example of a case in which a very small market is involved and this clearly limits the scope for welfare gains. In fact, the price of opium derivatives is only a very small fraction (about 5 per cent) of the final price of the finished drugs, and it would make little difference to consumers, in particular, if prices were, say, twice as high. Whilst we accept the view of the OFT that it is important to act on customer complaints, even though markets involved may be small, it is clear that in this case any likely gains to final consumers were very small. By a similar argument, since there is greater value added at the downstream stage, there may be more prospect of welfare gains by cutting prices at that stage. In fact, this point is very apposite because a combination of entry of new drug companies, and a new tendering system introduced by the NHS, has led to dramatic falls in prices of opium-based drugs over the last few years.[21] We would argue that the scope for welfare gains should be a significant factor in deciding cases for investigation by the MMC.

5.5.3 Conclusions

The findings in this case are that the investigation and monitoring of pricing did have an effect in lowering prices for opium derivatives from 1989–92. This was particularly so in that MSL chose to follow the price guidelines in this period in order to avoid a possible further investigation. In the longer term, competition in this industry would best be served by opening up the European market to freer trade, although at the moment MSL remains a monopoly supplier in the UK.

Finally, we noted that this is a very small market and this has limited the likely benefit to consumers of the investigation. New entry at the downstream stage, however, combined with the introduction of a new tendering system by the NHS, has produced substantial falls in prices at the downstream stage.

5.6 OTHER CASES

Turning more briefly to the ten other cases in Table 5.1, the most obvious feature is the greater likelihood of an adverse MMC finding in the early cases as opposed to those in more recent years. In librium and valium (1973), the monopoly supplier of these drugs, Hoffman-La Roche, was found to have charged excessively high prices. Its monopoly power derived from a combination of patent protection and the popularity of the (new) drugs at the time. In what looks, by today's standards, a draconian judgement, the MMC recommended price cuts of over 50 per cent and a repayment of some monopoly profits to the NHS. Similarly, in the following year, in the batteries (1974) case, Mallory (Duracell) and Ever Ready, the two dominant producers of batteries, were also found to have charged excessive prices. Again, part of the MMC's recommendations involved price cuts, although it appears that the eventual undertakings merely required Mallory not to increase its prices faster than costs, and Ever Ready's price was to be monitored. The two firms were released from these undertakings in 1988.

The third case in the early years, wire and fibre ropes (1973), was rather different. Here, the dominant firm, British Ropes, played the role of price leader, with a fringe of small competitors. The MMC took a softer line in this case, apparently because of a declining market, the existence of excess capacity and cheap imports. Nevertheless, it judged that competition in the domestic market could be made more effective by requiring the termination of information exchange. The information in question referred to the discounts firms gave to customers, and this appears to have been used by the dominant firm as a device to maintain its leadership. These undertakings still appear in the OFT's Register of Undertakings.

In the pest control (1988) case, attention focused on Rentokil, which controlled over 60 per cent of the market and was the only nationwide supplier of pest control services. Rentokil, on the strength of its national brand name, was able to set monopoly prices and earn monopoly profits. In addition, it had followed a policy of acquiring moderate-sized competitors in order to prevent the growth of national competitors, and of selectively cutting prices in areas where competition was strong. Surprisingly, the MMC argued that entry barriers were low in this case and, hence, new entry (under the right conditions) would be sufficient to allow competition to develop. It, therefore, proposed that Rentokil give an undertaking to notify the OFT of any new acquisitions, and that it provide potential customers with a breakdown of costs associated with its services.[22] The implication is that, with greater information, customers are more likely to be able to shop around for a better buy. Whether this sort of remedy will be more successful than direct price regulation depends crucially on whether the MMC's judgement of minimal entry barriers is correct. An alternative view is that Rentokil's national brand name creates an endogenous sunk cost which gives it a natural monopoly in what is a relatively small market. In one other case, insulated wires and cables (1979), a monopoly was found in favour of BICC (and its subsidiaries) with a market share of 37 per cent in 1974. Again there were concerns that BICC might be abusing its market power but, in the event, no recommendations were made.

Of the more recent cases, three are of particular interest. First, razors and razor blades (1991) is one of the very few cases where divestment was used. This case focused on a proposed buyout of the consumer products division of a company called Stora Kopparbergs Bergslag (Stora) which included Wilkinson Sword, the number two supplier of razors and razor blades in the UK, with a market share of 20 per cent. The problem arose because the buyout vehicle, a company called Swedish Match NV, had strong financial links with Gillette, the world leader in razors and razor blades. Gillette had 60 per cent of the UK market. In its report, the MMC concluded that these links were too strong to allow Wilkinson Sword to compete independently of Gillette. It, therefore, recommended that Gillette divest its equity and creditor interest in Swedish Match, and, pending this, waive its pre-emption and conversion rights and options.

Another significant case is compact discs (1994).[23] Here it was alleged that CDs were over-priced in the UK and that record companies and record retailers were exploiting their monopoly power.[24] In particular, it was argued that the high price of popular CDs retailing at as much as £14.99 bore no relation to their cost of production and was typically much higher than in the US, the implication being that the record companies were 'creaming off' profits from the CD-buying public. However, the MMC concluded that this was not so and that CDs was a very competitive market, and that there was no evidence that prices were 'too high' nor that the majors were making monopoly returns. The report does, however, raise some doubts. In particular, it noted that major companies set uniform prices in wholesaling (for example, for full price compact discs) and that a standard mark-up is also typically applied at the retail stage. In the recent electrical products case,[25] in contrast, similar evidence was interpreted as suggesting tacit collusion between producers and between retailers, but for CDs the MMC did not conclude that this was the case.

In matches and disposable lighters (1992) the MMC was concerned with the dominant position of Bryant and May which had 78 per cent of retail sales of matches in the UK and was also the largest supplier of disposable lighters. The MMC concluded that the company had been making excessive profits on its sales of matches contrary to the public interest and recommended that price controls be introduced. These controls were, in fact, imposed although they were later removed due to changed market conditions.

Two other cases led to no recommendations. In soluble coffee (1991), Nestlé had a scale monopoly of 56 per cent of the UK market. The MMC found in this case that Nestlé earned significantly higher profits than its rivals but concluded that this was due to its superior performance, both in the face of competition and despite the pressure of strong retail customers. It also suggested there were no barriers to entry in this case, and hence, no recommendations were made. In Cross Solent Ferries (1992), Wightlink (owned by Sea Containers) had 77 per cent of the relevant market in 1991. Again, the MMC found no cause for concern and no recommendations were made.

5.7 CONCLUSIONS

Not surprisingly, price control (and/or monitoring) has been the most commonly used remedy in cases where firms are found to be setting monopoly prices or acting as a price leader. Typically, this has been in market structures where there is a single dominant firm, and this is certainly true for the three main case studies described in this chapter. Over   the period as a whole, there seems to have been a softening of the MMC's attitude to this type of problem, in that recent referrals of this type have been less likely to attract adverse findings than earlier cases (see Table 5.1). Also, the stringency of price intervention seems to have lessened, with the price cuts and indexation of earlier years being replaced more recently with at most price monitoring.

The three cases we have selected for special attention share some common features. In each case, we conclude that the price remedy did have an effect in the short run, but we have doubts as to its longer term impact. Also in two cases (breakfast cereals and contraceptive sheaths), new entry has played a role in the discussion, although it should be stressed that in no case was entry the consequence of the remedy. In contraceptive sheaths, a genuinely exogenous shift in demand (caused by the AIDS epidemic) helped to transform the markets and this more than anything, facilitated the growth of a few new entrants. In breakfast cereals, the growth of supermarket own-brands made inroads into Kellogg's market share. In both cases, arguably, this entry persuaded the OFT to lift the price controls. Yet we are doubtful whether the dominant market positions of either LRC or Kellogg are much changed since the time of the investigations. Both retain dominant market shares, and both are (reputedly) still price leaders. In the third case, opium derivatives, no significant entry has occurred, primarily because of import restrictions which are outside the control of either the MMC or the OFT.

This raises the central issue of anti-trust intervention in natural monopolies/oligopolies. In opium derivatives, this is largely the result of a very small market size but for breakfast cereals and (increasingly in recent years) contraceptive sheaths, it is more a consequence of endogenous sunk costs – market growth can no longer be relied upon to attract new entry if incumbents escalate their endogenous costs in order to increase consumers' willingness to pay. Under these circumstances, the case for price control – seem as a short-term measure to serve as a holding operation, until the market generates its own solution (entry) – is debatable, to say the least.

Finally, two other points can be briefly made. The first concerns the ongoing dialogue between the regulated and regulator which inevitably accompanies any long-run remedy such as price control. In both contraceptive sheaths and breakfast cereals, there was continuing (and presumably costly) lobbying by the referred firm to have the controls removed. For both cases, this was successful although only after considerable time (and two further reports) in contraceptive sheaths. At the least, this underlines the need to have well-defined rules of the game when dealing with a dominant firm.

The second concerns the use of other remedies to monopoly pricing. In fact on this question we must remain agnostic. Each of the four other cases where either termination or divestment was used involved fairly minor remedies or were too idiosyncratic to support any robust general conclusions.

NOTES

1. Perhaps they would answer with greater sophistication, pointing to welfare triangles, and qualifying their conclusions by explaining that price discrimination may muddy the welfare implications somewhat.

2. The other two cases (compact discs and insulated wires and cables) are somewhat anomalous definitionally and we return to them briefly in Section 5.6 below.
3. Although one of these cases, contraceptive sheaths, was re-investigated twice in later years.
4. This is one of the earlier cases where interviews were not used.
5. Weetabix had a market share of 22 per cent and Nabisco (which produced Shredded Wheat) had a market share of 12 per cent in 1971. Smaller competitors included Quaker Oats and Viota (which produced own-brand cornflakes), each with about 4 per cent of the market.
6. The breakfast cereal market is well documented already in the academic literature, being cited as a classic example of brand proliferation (Schmalensee, 1978), and of endogenous sunk costs (Sutton, 1991).
7. The Price Commission was set up in a direct attempt to control inflation by limiting the rate at which firms could raise prices. Not surprisingly, it was abolished by the Thatcher Government when it came to power in 1979.
8. It is a moot point whether the OFT price controls added anything extra to the controls implemented by the Price Commission. Certainly, in the early part of the period, the Price Commission took the lead in controlling Kellogg's prices. On balance, however, we believe that the OFT controls did constrain Kellogg's prices, at least after 1976.
9. Kellogg was also squeezed by rising grain prices in the 1970s and, to some extent, by growth of own-brands (see below). Price controls, however, were clearly the major constraint on its ability to raise prices in the 1970s.
10. In 1994, Kellogg's market share by weight was 48 per cent compared to 17 per cent for supermarket own-brands, and its market share by value (56 per cent) was little different to what it had been in 1973 (see Keynote Market Report, *Breakfast Cereals*, 1995). According to Keynote, own-brand performance is poor in this sector, mainly because of the very high level advertising expenditure by the market leaders – particularly Kellogg (ibid., p. 12). Kellogg's rate of return was, on average, 25.6 per cent in 1989–94.
11. LRC's market share was 90 per cent in 1975.
12. This remedy was the first example as far as we are aware of an 'index-x' formula used in an MMC case.
13. This is one of the four outlier cases mentioned in Section 3.4.4 where the delay from report to undertaking exceeded three years.
14. According to a Mintel report on the industry, 85 per cent of users now use sheaths as protection against AIDS.
15. Note that because the undertakings were not signed until 1988, LRC was still operating under the 1975 price control for much of the 1980s.
16. Branson sold Mates (in 1988) and it is now 100 per cent owned by Ansells.
17. Healthline products diversified into the market from making surgical gloves. Unlike LRC, Mates and Jiffy it does not have a kite mark (and associated British Standard) and is not stocked by Boots. It is also unable to compete for NHS contracts and so sells mainly to the vending machine sector.
18. One firm also suggested that there was some collusion between LRC and the British Standards Institute in setting and testing standards. We found no independent evidence, however, to corroborate this.
19. The only other significant producer was Boots, with 11 per cent of the market, but mainly producing for its own use.
20. MSL made a charge for the direct costs of the investigation in its 1989 accounts which accounted for about half of its recorded losses in that year.
21. New entrants at the downstream stage were Napp Pharmaceuticals and CP Pharmaceuticals (both buying from MSL) who now form a triopoly with Medeva (Evans

Medical). The Department of Health told us that in some cases price reductions have exceeded 40 per cent since 1992.

22. It should be noted that this is costly for independents to do, and, it could be argued, creates a further barrier to entry in this case.

23. This is the 'outside' case mentioned most by respondents in our interviews. The general view was that the MMC had clearly 'got it wrong' in this case.

24. The 'majors' were five multinational companies (EMI, Polygram, Sony, Warner and BMG) which together accounted for 70 per cent of the UK market. There was also a scale monopoly in retailing, where W.H. Smith (with its subsidiary, Our Price) controlled 27 per cent of the market.

25. MMC report Nos 402–3, *Domestic Electrical Goods, Parts I and II*, London: HMSO, (Cmnd 3675–6, 1997).

6. Collusive Practices

6.1 THEORETICAL PERSPECTIVES

Collusion is most obviously covered within UK competition policy by the Restrictive Trade Practices (RTP) legislation, which is not the direct concern of this book. However, we know from oligopoly theory that collusion can take many forms, and that cartels and other more or less explicit price-fixing arrangements are merely the most extreme form. Indeed, nowadays, they are unusual, precisely because they are either illegal, or at least, prone to anti-trust intervention via the RTP legislation.

It seems likely that, in a population of 'monopoly' cases such as the present one, we would encounter other, less formal or tacitly collusive practices. In fact, there turn out to be relatively few cases where collusion is the main focus of the MMC investigation, and most of these are not very recent.[1] Nevertheless, the few examples that we have found prove to be very illuminating – not only for the main purpose in this book, evaluating the effectiveness of MMC remedies, but also, more generally, in furthering our understanding of the form that collusive practices may take in the real world.

In contrast to most other areas of monopoly abuse (notably, vertical restraints), there is general agreement amongst most academic economists that collusion is usually welfare-reducing,[2] and deserving of the hostile treatment it receives in most countries' legislation. Collusion leads to prices which are 'too high' and, in the absence of price discrimination, quantity is 'too low', and there may also be other more dynamic losses if collusion is stable and reduces the pressure to reduce costs and to innovate.

On the other hand, some argue that, although collusion may be generally undesirable, it will also be fairly uncommon. Not only is it subject to the RTP legislation in its more explicit forms, but also it is inherently unstable (and therefore unlikely) because there is always an incentive for individual members of a collusive agreement to renege. However, this need not be so if firms are able to employ devices designed to facilitate and subsequently

82

sustain collusion. The most obvious of these is the creation of forums for exchanging information (for example, trade associations, information sharing agreements, and, arguably, collaborative R&D ventures). Less obviously, firms may partake of practices or contracts which conspicuously pre-commit themselves to collusive behaviour or to punish any firm reneging. These include 'meet the competition', 'most favoured customer' and 'loyalty clause' policies. By meeting the competition, the firm makes price-cutting for rivals less attractive, whilst most favoured customer clauses in effect establish a price floor for later sales, and loyalty bonuses reduce the price elasticity of demand of existing customers.[3]

The task of any anti-trust agency in detecting and then remedying collusion is likely to be demanding. By its nature, tacit collusion is very hard to prove, especially where firms produce a homogeneous good, and face similar demand and cost conditions (see Porter and Zona, 1993). Information sharing agreements may be justified by the parties by pointing to efficiency-enhancing motives (for example, avoiding duplication in certain transport sectors, or sharing research results in technological agreements). Similarly, 'meet the competition' pricing policies are arguably important to firms competing in cut-throat retail markets.

Equally, the most likely remedies are fraught with difficulties: direct intervention on price (or some other policy variable) may merely serve to ossify parallel pricing; insisting that information sharing be discontinued may simply drive the practice underground; and termination of meet the competition clauses and so on may be unpopular with customers who are unaware of the underlying strategic motives. Superficially, dismantling entry barriers may be the most effective long-term solution, but even this may be impracticable where the number of effective competitors is limited by the size of the market.

For these reasons, some commentators doubt the intrinsic efficacy of monopoly policy in this area. Kuhn et al. (1992, p. 10) suggest that 'generally it does not seem practical to use competition policy to constrain tacit collusion directly'. More optimistically, Rees (1993a, p. 38) argues that targeted investigations of the MMC type may be quite effective in specific cases, 'I would contend that it is a major strength of the British legislation that the MMC *did not have to decide* whether the firms had "really colluded"'.[4]

One final introductory point worth underlining is that mergers are often seen as a substitute for collusion. There have been many historical instances where, when firms are prevented from colluding, they turn to merger as an alternative method of avoiding competition. This is a feature of one of our detailed case studies (roadside advertising), where a number of mergers were instituted following the remedy, resulting in further MMC intervention.

6.2 OVERVIEW OF CASES IN THE POPULATION

Table 6.1 shows that the population includes seven cases in which potentially collusive practices were the main focus of MMC attention.[5] Not surprisingly, they include four markets involving dominant groups, category B in our classification, and, in four cases, a classical duopoly was effectively involved.[6] Two other cases, ceramic sanitaryware and roadside advertising, involved loose oligopoly, category D: in ceramic sanitaryware, there was evidence of parallel pricing whilst in roadside advertising, a group of ten leading firms formed a joint selling agency. Although there are only seven cases they illustrate the variety of forms that collusion can take, including tacit collusion, joint selling arrangements and information sharing agreements. They have also attracted a variety of different remedies from the MMC – in fact, the full gamut of remedies, including termination, price control, price monitoring and divestment. It is interesting, therefore, to see how effective these remedies have been against the different types of collusion involved. To anticipate, we find that different remedies can be effective in different cases, for example, divestment in roadside advertising and price control in white salt.

Table 6.1 Collusive practices in the population

Case	Oligopoly type	Remedy
Cross-Channel car ferries (1974, 1989)	B	T
Cat and dog foods (1977)	B	None
Ceramic sanitaryware (1978)	D	None
Electricity meters (1979)	B	T
Tampons (1980, 1986)	A	PM
Roadside advertising (1981)	D	D
White salt (1986)	B	PC

Note: Case studies are shown in bold. Some other cases (for example, petrol) involve potentially collusive elements, but we assess the main problem to be other than collusion, and they are, therefore, discussed in other chapters.

6.3 ELECTRICITY METERS (1979)

6.3.1 Case Summary

In this case, four almost equal-sized firms (Landis and Gyr (L&G), Sangamo Weston (SW), GEC Measurements (GEC) and Ferranti) controlled the supply of electricity meters in the UK. The case centred on the fact that these suppliers (through their trade association) had operated a *price notification agreement* since 1971 under which each firm was required to circulate to the others details of any price changes it made, no earlier than one day before, and no later than three days after, its issue to customers. Another key feature of the case was the attitude of the buyers of meters, the Area Electricity Boards (AEBs). These took a very ambivalent attitude to the prices of meters, being more concerned to maintain quality than to secure a lower price. This created a rather relaxed relationship between the big four producers and the AEBs with no real competition taking place.[7] Moreover, there were virtually no imports because of the typically different designs and standards of foreign meters which were not in general acceptable to the AEBs.

The report includes evidence of a close alignment of prices in this market over a considerable period of time. In addition, the companies admitted that the lack of price competition was due to their belief that price cuts would not permanently increase market shares but just lead to lower prices and lower profits. Given that the product was largely homogeneous, this anticipation was probably correct, and is reminiscent of textbook descriptions of tacit collusion in a homogeneous good industry. But, as noted above, the attitude of the AEBs was also crucial – fearing that price competition might lead to a reduction in product quality, and viewing price as a signal of quality, they did not typically apply pressure to cut prices.[8]

In its report, the Commission recommended that the price notification agreement should be terminated. In addition, it suggested that the AEBs should reconsider their purchasing policies to put more pressure on prices; that they introduce greater coordination in meter specification; and that they introduce meter testing in suppliers' factories, in order to avoid unnecessary duplication of work when testing deliveries of meters. Assurances to these effects were subsequently given. The AEBs also agreed that each board would decide independently with each supplier the quantities of meters to be supplied and their prices on an annual basis.

This market was relatively small at the time of the report (with total sales of just £20 million in 1977 prices). More recently, it has grown in size and, by 1990, total sales had risen to roughly £70 million – a dramatic increase, even allowing for inflation. The main reason for this was an important change in technology (the replacement of old electro-mechanical meters with new electronic ones), which has roughly doubled the unit price, and created a much larger market when measured by value. There has also been some new entry[9] into the industry (in part, linked to the new technology), although the original leading firms continue to dominate the market.

Table 6.2 shows the market shares of the leading firms in 1977 and 1990. Clearly, SW has grown significantly since the report, largely at the expense of GEC. These changes in market share appear to be due to the technological change noted above and the speed with which firms have adopted the new technology. As a group, however, these four firms clearly continue to dominate the market with a combined share of 98 per cent of sales in 1990.

Table 6.2 Electricity meters, market shares (%)

	1977	1990*
Landis and Gyr (L&G)	27.1	20
Sangamo Weston (SW)	25.0	43
GEC	24.6	15
Ferranti	22.3	20

Note: *1990 estimates by the Electricity Council for the home market by volume.

6.3.2 Interviews

In general, the evidence collected in the interviews suggests that the remedy had little effect. One reason for this (suggested by one of the principal firms) was that the big four suppliers each had close geographical ties with the AEBs, and that these were largely unaffected by the undertakings. L&G, for example, had a strong presence in the London area which continued after the MMC investigation, although it later moved to Scotland to develop its customer base there.

Most customers felt that competition had not been affected by the remedy and that things went on very much as before. One firm suggested that the big four probably continued notification of prices after 1979, even though no *formal* price notification agreement was in place. This respondent also suggested that there had been little in the way of genuine price competition in the market in the 1980s and it was only much more recently that true competition had developed. As one would expect, the respondent could not provide any evidence that price notification had continued and hence this view should be treated with care.[10]

One interviewee, however, took a different line, suggesting that quality was traditionally a key feature of competition in the meters market, and complaining that the report had led to an over-emphasis on price at the expense of quality. This had resulted, he claimed, in newer meters which were less robust and which required more maintenance than previously. This interviewee also argued that the investigation was inappropriate in the first place because customers had always been able to negotiate discounts with suppliers, and actual prices were lower than the monopoly level implied by list prices.

In the longer term, there have been two significant developments in this market, neither of which could have been anticipated at the time of the report. The first is technological innovation. In the mid-1980s, electronic meters were developed and these are now replacing the older electro-mechanical ones which had remained largely unchanged for a hundred years. An important initial step in this development was the introduction of card prepayment meters based on an idea patented by a new firm, Ampy, in 1986. Initially, GEC developed prepayment meters using the Ampy patent, although, more recently, Ampy has started production itself. Electronic meters, whilst more expensive to produce, offer new features (such as remote meter reading) which are clearly of major importance. Because of this all the major producers (as well as new entrants such as Polymeters) have now switched almost entirely to production of the new meters.[11] In addition to remote reading, electronic meters will allow customers to buy electricity from alternative suppliers (not simply the Regional Electricity Company (REC) operating in their area). This technology forms the basis of the proposed liberalisation of the domestic market for electricity due to take place in 1998.[12] At the present time, the industry is awaiting details of the proposed changes, and the design and specification of meters that will be required, and, perhaps not surprisingly, demand has been very low in the last few years.

Opinions were divided on how industry structure will evolve in the light of this developing new technology. One firm suggested that possibly two of the existing big four firms would leave the industry whilst other firms more heavily involved in the new technology (such as Ampy) would gain market share. Others, however, anticipated that the leading producers would continue to dominate by developing their product range to incorporate the new technology. As noted above, demand for meters is very low at the time of writing mainly because customers are not ordering meters which might become obsolete after 1998. Significant growth in the market can be expected then, however, assuming that the liberalisation goes ahead.

The second major development is the privatisation of the twelve Regional Electricity Companies (RECs) in 1990. Whilst one interviewee (a customer) suggested to us that there had been some attempt by his company to introduce multi-sourcing of meters prior to 1990, the major drive in this direction (both for his company and for others) had come after privatisation. He suggested that, by adopting a more commercial stance, his firm had been able to reduce the cost of meters by as much as 40 per cent in the last four years. This was partly due to the low level of demand for meters, but also by shopping around, significant savings had been made. Implicitly, of course, this also suggests that high margins had continued to exist prior to 1990. Not surprisingly, all meter manufacturers we spoke to believed there was intense (even cut-throat) competition at the present time which was likely to continue for the foreseeable future.

Finally, it is possible that import competition may become more important in the future following the recent Public Utility Procurement Directive by the European Commission.[13]   Under this directive, EU producers of meters will be able to bid for contracts with the RECs on equal terms with domestic firms, and, in principle, UK firms will be able to do the same in EU markets. As was pointed out to us, however, a number of EU electricity companies have signed long-term contracts with their domestic suppliers of meters (just before the directive came into effect) and this is likely to restrict the ability of UK firms to compete at least in the short term.

6.3.3 Conclusions

There is little evidence in this case that competition increased following the 1979 report, or that the AEBs sought to encourage more competition. Rather, we believe, that competition post-1979 was very similar to that which had existed before and that the fairly cosy relationship between the big four suppliers and the AEBs continued.   More recently, new developments have taken place in this market which have encouraged more competition; most notably the privatisation of the RECs in 1990, which has introduced more commercialism into buying decisions and much lower prices.   However, these (and other) developments have occurred independently of the remedy, which, in our view, had little effect in the ten years following the report.

6.4 ROADSIDE ADVERTISING SERVICES (1981)

6.4.1 Case Summary

Firms in the roadside advertising industry supply space (panels) on poster sites, usually situated by the roadside, to advertising agencies or other intermediaries who act on the behalf of their clients. The majority of these sites are not owned by the roadside advertising firms themselves; rather, they hold them under rights acquired from site-owners, who are often local authorities or property companies. This case revolved around British Posters Ltd (BP), which was a company formed as a joint-selling agency by a number of the leading suppliers of roadside advertising.[14] Prior to the formation of BP, many poster firms were organised on a regional basis, and it was set up largely as a means for supplying national packages of sites to the agencies, in line with the development of national TV advertising.[15] At the time of the report, the ten members of BP accounted for 82 per cent of the market; the two leading firms were Mills and Allen Ltd (MA) and London & Provincial Posters Ltd (LPP), with market shares of 30 per cent and 27 per cent respectively. The case therefore involved scale and complex monopolies, both in respect of the leading firms and BP itself.

This case raises a number of vertical, as well as horizontal, issues.[16] For example, there is an important monopsony element (the two trade associations in the industry both had codes of conduct which prevented members from negotiating with landowners for a site whilst another member was still resident); and the MMC also highlighted an instance of attempted foreclosure in 1976, where the members of BP had sought not to supply panels to Independent Poster Sales Ltd, the only major poster sales group not part of BP. However, we concentrate here on what we take to be the central issue: the MMC concluded that BP had become the dominant supplier of short-term campaign packages, bringing about a uniform pricing strategy which had led to 'high' prices and profits in the industry. The MMC recommended that BP should be dissolved as the best means of dealing with this problem. In addition, its members were required to give undertakings to provide the OFT with details of any subsequent joint-selling arrangements entered into.

Much of the interest in this case derives from the unusual structural 'solution' proposed by the MMC. This led to dramatic subsequent developments in industry structure, and these are best described within the account of our interviews with the various interested parties.

6.4.2 Interviews

It is clear from the interviews that this remedy caused considerable problems for the roadside advertisers themselves. Several interviewees commented that, whilst they believed that BP had probably gone too far in exerting its monopoly power, they had not expected the MMC to propose such a radical solution. The decision obviously caught some firms by surprise and led to considerable uncertainty in the market. The early 1980s were a period of deep recession which would have affected the firms anyway, but in the view of several firms the dissolution of BP aggravated this considerably and led to severe (even 'dire') consequences in the industry. In the absence of a joint-selling organisation, member firms were thrown back on their own resources to try to meet the demands of their customers for national advertising campaigns, and the largely regional structure of the industry made this very difficult. It was argued that significant business was lost at this time (as advertisers turned to other media) and this contributed to the poor sales and profit record of the industry in the early 1980s. We were told that uncertainty continued in the market up until 1984 when, with the upturn of the economy as a whole, the industry started to recover.

There was general agreement in the interviews that the break-up of BP created a vacuum in the industry in respect of organising national poster campaigns, and this contributed to two significant subsequent changes in industry structure: (a) the rise of the 'outdoor specialists', and (b) major restructuring of the roadside advertisers themselves, in part through merger.

As already noted, the members of BP accounted for about 80 per cent of the supply of posters, of which about 30 per cent was sold directly through BP. In addition, some sales were organised on the other side of the market by 'outdoor specialists'. With the break-up of BP, there was a need to organise national poster campaigns and the outdoor specialists moved into this gap. Interviewees argued (persuasively, in our opinion) that this would not have happened in the absence of the report and so it can be regarded as a direct consequence of the MMC intervention. The main role of these specialists is to act as intermediaries between poster suppliers and advertising agencies, and to put together packages of poster services for their customers. By the mid-1980s, eight or nine major specialists had emerged, largely replacing the role that British Posters had played. Some consolidation has since taken place, partly through merger, reducing the number of majors to four or five firms[17] (with perhaps ten smaller firms). The majors are also now closely allied to the major advertising companies although in some cases the link is at arm's length.

Our respondents were divided in their opinions on how this has affected competition. Several argued that it created too much market power on the buying side of the market and that this enabled the specialists to 'squeeze' higher commissions out of suppliers. They argued that the specialists earned monopolistic commissions, suggesting that, typically, a 5 per cent premium is paid to specialists on top of the 15 per cent commission paid to advertising agencies for other forms of advertising; moreover, smaller firms were often required to pay a further 2–5 per cent commission for bulk orders. The smaller firms, in particular, argued that these commissions were excessive and amounted to monopoly rents paid to the specialists. On the other hand, other respondents felt there was sufficient competition between the specialists to enable the roadside advertisers (if necessary) to trade one off against another and secure competitive rates. One suggested that countervailing power is a feature of the market, with major suppliers and major specialists facing each other and bargaining over commissions charged. However, this respondent (and others) admitted that smaller firms were less well-placed to counter the outdoor specialists and this gave rise to possible abuse of market power.

Turning to the restructuring of the roadside advertisers themselves, there have been a number of mergers, and also MMC and OFT investigations, since 1981. Two important mergers were investigated by the MMC.[18] The first, in 1987, concerned a merger between MA (by that time, a wholly-owned subsidiary of MAI) and London and Continental Advertising Holdings (LACH), which had previously acquired LPP (the number two firm in 1981). LACH had run into financial difficulties immediately after its acquisition of LPP and this apparently motivated MA's bid. The outcome of the investigation was that the merger was allowed to stand (it had previously gone ahead in January 1987), but MA was required to sell off some of its sites (about 2,000 48-sheet panels)[19] in order to bring its market share below 25 per cent in certain TV regions (London, Southern, North-West and South-West) and to pre-merger levels in others.

The second investigation (1991) also involved Mills and Allen (by this time a wholly-owned subsidiary of the French group, Avenir) and Brunton Curtis Outside Advertising, whose Dolphin brand name had 5.3 per cent of the market. In this case, the Commission expressed concern over the share of the national market which would be controlled by the merged firms in the 48–sheet and larger poster size market (about 34 per cent), and it recommended that all 48 and larger panels acquired from Brunton Curtis be divested so that there would be no increase in concentration in this part of the market.

Thus the MMC's stance was to allow mergers, whilst restraining their concentrating effects. A number of the firms argued, however, that these, and other, mergers were motivated by the need to supply national packages to advertisers and to achieve the advantages of scale. They commented that the effect of this MMC policy had been to limit their growth and otherwise restrict competition. Two other examples were also frequently cited to us. In the first, More O'Ferrall had bid for London Transport Advertising (in 1994), but this was referred to the MMC and the bid was subsequently dropped. Similar approaches made by MA and British Transport Advertising were also dropped on advice given by the OFT.[20] The result was that LTA was eventually sold to Transport Displays Advertising (TDA), the largest transport advertising company in the US. The second case concerned a proposed merger between British Transport Advertising (BTA) and Maiden Outdoor Advertising which was allowed to go through in September 1995. In this case, the bus advertising interests of Maiden were sold to TDA in November 1995.

The general opinion expressed to us was that there is a genuine conflict between the advantages of larger scale and the exercise of market power that this facilitates. It is quite clear that entry on a small scale is very easy, as witnessed by the many small contractors actually in the market. At the same time, however, it was argued that a critical size is needed to compete as a major in the market both nationally and, more generally, in the EU. Several respondents argued that the OFT and MMC had failed to take adequate account of this and this has hampered firm growth in the market. On the other hand, the various MMC cases have stopped the build-up of a truly dominant firm (or firms) in this case and hence possible exercise of monopoly power.

The upshot of the various changes in industry structure is that, of the ten members of BP in 1981, five smaller firms no longer exist (some were acquired) and one other remains very small. The four majors (MA, More O'Ferrall Adshel, Maiden Outdoor Advertising and BTA), together with a fifth firm, Allam & Co., are the main contractors at the present time. MA had about 27 per cent of the market in 1991, More O'Ferrall 20 per cent, Maiden 14 per cent and Allam 9 per cent (1991 report). According to our calculations, the implied three firm concentration ratio (61 per cent) is almost identical to the 1981 level, with the identity of the number one firm unchanged. However, this conceals considerable underlying turbulence, and the variety of different strategies employed by the majors. Thus, More O'Ferrall has grown mainly internally (through its development of bus shelter sites) whilst MA has been more heavily involved in mergers. Maiden (the third placed firm) is currently seeking to merge with BTA, which would put it on more equal market share terms with the other two leading firms.

One final point made by several firms should be mentioned because it concerns a theme which recurs in many MMC monopoly reports. This is the claim made by several firms that the competition authorities failed to use an appropriate market definition. One argument here was that the appropriate market should include *all* advertising media (that is, TV, press, radio, cinema and roadside advertising) and that roadside advertising is only a very small part (about 5 per cent) of the market as a whole. This kind of argument is met frequently in MMC investigations although in this case it did not hold much sway.[21]

6.4.3 Conclusions

This case displays a number of features of more general interest. First, it is a rare instance of divestment as a remedy. Significantly, (at least some of) the majors reacted to the remedy by attempting to re-establish market dominance through intensive and continued merger activity. As noted above, this was, in part, due to the need to supply roadside advertising for national advertising campaigns. Second, to the extent that the divestment *did* precipitate the enhanced market power of the outdoor specialists, one might argue that it has partly relocated the monopoly problem in the vertical chain.

We believe that OFT and MMC intervention (in the 1981 and other reports) has had the effect of limiting the growth of truly dominant firms, and probably, thereby protecting competition. At the present time, a bilateral oligopoly structure exists between the suppliers and the specialists which does allow some competition between the larger firms. Small suppliers of advertising space, however, are at a disadvantage relative to specialist firms, and the latter are able to exert some monopoly power against them.

6.5 WHITE SALT (1986)

6.5.1 Case Summary

In this case there was a duopoly, with one low cost producer, British Salt (part of Staveley Industries) with a market share of 50 per cent and one high cost producer, ICI, with 45 per cent. The main customers are chemical companies who use salt or brine in their chemical processes, councils who use salt on the roads, the catering industry and final consumers (table salt). Demand tends to be stable and certain; and since there are relatively high entry barriers (including limited, and geographically concentrated, mineral deposits), this industry satisfies most of the conditions usually identified as facilitating collusion.

The MMC found that the two firms had set almost identical prices over a 13-year period. Typically, when one firm changed its price, the other followed suit within a matter of weeks; indeed, they notified each other of impending price changes. They justified this by explaining that they each bought (usually small) quantities of salt from the other, and that it was normal practice to notify customers of forthcoming changes in price. The MMC concluded that there was sufficient evidence of tacit collusion between the two firms leading to 'high' monopoly prices. To remedy this, it recommended that price control be introduced on the lower cost firm, British Salt. This case is interesting in that it is the only instance in our population in which price controls were recommended by the MMC in a market where there was more than one dominant firm.

Undertakings were given by British Salt (BS) in March 1988 not to raise prices by more than 1 per cent below an appropriate index based on costs, and this restriction was set to continue for a period of five years. These undertakings were reviewed by the OFT in 1992. It found that, over the five years, BS had raised its average price by less than the permissible cost index,[22] so that, in this sense, price control had not bitten. Nevertheless, given that BS's rate of return between 1986–91 was still high (at about 11.5 per cent compared to 12.9 per cent between 1980–84), the firm was still found to be earning high profits in a relatively low risk market. Revised undertakings were therefore negotiated under which prices would now be allowed to rise by no more than 2 per cent below the index of costs. This restriction is set to continue until 1997 when a further review will take place.

In the period after the report, ICI, the high cost firm, decided to leave the market. ICI's profits from salt had been declining over a number of years with a rate of return of 9 per cent in 1979 down to just 1 per cent in 1984, and in 1989 it decided to close one of its plants. Given the nature of the product, ICI was forced to match BS's price cuts and this further weakened its profitability. Faced with the alternative of putting in large quantities of investment to improve its productivity, ICI chose instead to sell its business to a US firm, the Salt Union, in 1992. This company has since put in new investment and is now more competitive with BS.

This case raises a number of issues of direct interest to the game theoretic analysis of collusion. Indeed, Rees (1993b) used the data in the MMC report to test supergame theory, and judged that the Abreu/Lambson model of collusion most closely explained the facts in the salt case. His conclusion was that collusion was the natural outcome of the structure of the industry and that the MMC was right in suggesting that the duopolists 'acted to restrain competition'.

Turning to the remedy itself, it is possible that the introduction of price control could change the payoffs in a duopoly game so that it is now in the interests of the lower cost firm to remove its rival from the market rather than seek to keep prices 'high'.[23] If this is the case, then the effect of regulation in a duopolistic market could be to create a monopoly, with an increased need for price control in the longer run.

6.5.2 Interviews

A number of firms that we interviewed in this case thought that the MMC investigation was justified and that the remedy adopted was appropriate. In addition, several respondents thought that they had benefited directly from the original price control and that they were likely to benefit further from the more recent one.

All firms interviewed thought that there had been an increase in competition since the time of the report and this was linked, in particular, to increased imports, and the potential for further imports should prices rise higher. However, they also thought that price control had benefited some firms. One large customer explained that, in its case, prices paid were much lower than those set under the price control, and they attributed this to their own industrial strength and their ability to play off suppliers against each other. Given this, the firm was able to obtain prices from both BS and SU which were well below the level of import prices and they, therefore, bought most or all of their salt from these two firms. In their view, however, smaller customers would have been paying much higher prices for salt than large firms (that is, there was significant price discrimination in the market) and for these the price controls were important.

This was also the view of other customers. One firm argued that the price control was a useful lever to bargain with BS and SU and because of this it was able to obtain prices (in some cases) at a discount to the index price.[24] Several firms argued that by multi-sourcing they were able to play different suppliers off against each other and thereby obtain a lower price. Whilst it could be argued that this effect is not directly attributable to the price control itself, it does seem that buyers became more eager to multi-source following the report, and that the report did raise awareness of the high prices charged by BS.

It seems likely that competition will increase in this market in the future. Demand for salt for catering and retail purposes has been declining for a number of years as consumers become more aware of the health hazards involved. In addition, imports are a growing threat to UK producers; in particular, those from Eastern Europe and Israel. It is important to recognise, however, that BS is still in a dominant position in the UK market[25] and that it continues to make reasonable profits in what is essentially a low risk industry. Hence, there are good reasons for retaining the price controls at the present time.

One other point raised in the interviews concerns the likely effect of SU's acquisition of ICI's business. Whilst the Salt Union was not involved in the recent revision of price control on BS, this is, of course, directly relevant to its own prices and profits. In its view, competition is currently intense and it does not expect that this will change in the near future. As far as we were able to assess, therefore, it seems that entry of the SU will not bring about any major changes in the market in the short run. Whether it will in the long run remains to be seen.

6.5.3 Conclusions

The introduction of price control in this market has had an effect in lowering prices; in particular, to smaller customers. However, BS remains the dominant firm and is earning significant profits given the low risk nature of the business. There are forces at work tending to increase competition; in particular, increased imports (and a, possibly, more competitive second ranked firm) and these may mean that, in time, sufficient competition will develop to enable the price controls to be removed – although this remains uncertain at the present time.

6.6 OTHER CASES

We now look more briefly at the other cases involving potential collusion. The Cross-Channel ferries (1974) case, is in some ways similar to electricity meters, in that there were also four main firms and an information sharing agreement. However, in this case, only two were major players – European Ferries and the British Railways Board, with market shares of 45 per cent and 35 per cent respectively. The historical source of this structure lies with the nationalised nature of the railways, and possibly to a lesser extent, with the natural capacity constraints imposed by ports and shipping lanes. In any event, the crucial element of behaviour was a significant set of information agreements made under the so-called 'Harmonisation Conference'.

The leading firms claimed that the Harmonisation Conference, although possibly limiting price competition, had no damaging anti-competitive effects, and that the pooling arrangements served mainly to facilitate the inter-availability of tickets and the coordination of regular sailing schedules. However, the MMC found that, although the general monopoly situation was not a cause for concern *per se*, the Harmonisation Conference was. It recommended termination of the agreements under which the car ferry companies collectively set fares and against further pooling agreements without government approval. Undertakings to this effect were given by the leading firms.

In 1989 a further investigation took place where again the ferry companies sought to coordinate sailings and set fares, in this case in preparation for the opening of the Channel Tunnel in 1993/4. The MMC again concluded that there was no justification for such pooling and the proposed agreement was not allowed.

As with roadside advertising, there were a number of mergers (realised and aborted) in the following years (involving Stena-Sealink, P&O, British Ferries and Hoverspeed), reinforcing the view that merger is often a predictable consequence of the removal of a collusive agreement. Significantly, at the time of writing, a further merger is planned by the leading firms (P&O and Stena Lines) both of whom have suffered heavy losses following the opening of the Channel Tunnel.[26] This proposal was referred to the MMC in November 1996 and at the time of writing the final outcome is still pending. Interestingly, the Secretary of State released the firms from their undertakings in July 1996 in recognition of the difficulties they were experiencing in competition with the Channel Tunnel, but it is not clear at the present time exactly how matters will be resolved.

Tampons (1980) is another duopoly case: Tampax had about 60 per cent of the market and Southalls the remainder. The MMC conceded that 'prices were under little competitive pressure' in this industry; however, it did not recommend a price cut or control, believing that proposed new entry by a US company, Playtex, could affect competition significantly. It therefore recommended that the DGFT keep prices, profits, and so on under review for a period of two years. In its subsequent report in 1986, it noted that Playtex had entered in 1980 but had then exited in 1981,[27] and that the leading firms continued to dominate (with a combined market share of 97 per cent). Perhaps surprisingly, however, it reiterated that entry was relatively easy, and that it would eventually reduce the market power of the dominant firms. It therefore recommended no further action.

In the other two cases in which potentially collusive behaviour was investigated, no recommendations were made. Cat and dog foods (1977) was another duopoly, involving Pedigree Petfoods (Mars) and Spillers Foods with 49 per cent and 31 per cent of the market respectively. The MMC examined: (i) the high level of advertising, (ii) discounting to distributors, and (iii) the proliferation of product varieties. It also investigated price movements and found some evidence that Pedigree acted as a price leader. However, Spillers (the weaker of the two firms, judged by its low rate of return) claimed that the presence of Pedigree acted as a constraining influence – without which it would probably wish to raise its price. The MMC found no evidence of anti-competitive behaviour and recognised that high profits earned by Pedigree resulted largely from its superior efficiency. It therefore made no recommendations for change.[28] In ceramic sanitaryware (1978), Armitage Shanks benefited from a scale monopoly, and the similarity of its prices and those of other producers suggested possible tacit collusion. Indeed, an export agreement, by which all exporters agreed a minimum export price, also qualified the industry for referral as a complex monopoly. However, the MMC also made no recommendations in this case.

6.7 CONCLUSIONS

There are only seven cases in the population in which collusion was the main problem, and six of these appeared within a short period (1974–81). Of course, the scarcity of cases is unsurprising since most practices involving *explicit* collusion are covered by the Restrictive Trade Practices Act. The cases covered here have involved less explicit collusion such as possible tacit collusion over price (for example, white salt, tampons), a price notification agreement (electricity meters), more explicit information sharing (Cross-Channel ferries) and the establishment of a national selling cartel (roadside advertising). Although most of these industries have duopolistic or other symmetric oligopoly structures, interestingly, different remedies were applied in different cases: termination of practices (ferries and meters), divestment (roadside advertising) and price monitoring/price control (salt and tampons).

Our investigations suggest that the remedies have met with mixed success. On the positive side, the imaginative use of price control in the salt case appears to have constrained price increases, particularly to smaller customers, and may be partly responsible for a takeover, and subsequent modernisation, of the number two firm. Divestment in roadside advertising had dramatic effects in the short run, and this can be interpreted as beneficial for competition. However, the longer-term effects have extended to a sustained period of subsequent consolidation (via mergers), and, arguably, a transfer of market power away from the roadside advertisers in favour of the 'outdoor specialists'. Termination of information sharing appears to have been quite ineffective in electricity meters, and it is only with the later (and unconnected) ownership changes on the customer side (via privatisation) that price competition appears to have intensified in recent years. One other non-case study industry, Cross-Channel ferries, provides further evidence on the consequences of discontinuing an information sharing agreement: these include a long period of lobbying by the referred firms and a number of mergers (actual or proposed), as in roadside advertising.

NOTES

1. But collusion also features less directly in other cases discussed in other chapters, for example, RPM in Chapter 8 and basing point pricing in Chapter 7.
2. See Vickers (1996) for a recent exploration of the possibility that collusion might be efficiency enhancing.
3. See Salop (1986), Banarjee and Summers (1987), Caminal and Matutes (1990), Klemperer (1992), Cooper (1986) and Padilla (1991).
4. However, both US and EU case law on 'conscious parallelism' and 'concerted practices' suggest that 'tacit collusion' can be confronted, albeit imperfectly.
5. At least one other case, compact discs (1994), might have been classified to this group, although on balance we have chosen to view it as a monopoly pricing case (see Section 5.6).
6. These cases were Cross-Channel ferries, cat and dog foods, tampons and white salt. The tampons case is classified to the A class because the leading firm had a substantially larger market share (61 per cent) than the second ranked firm (39 per cent). There were four dominant firms in the meters case.
7. One smaller firm, Dennis Ferranti Meters Ltd (unconnected with Ferranti), did consistently undersell the big four, and its membership of the Association was only intermittent. However, it was paid £40,000 in 1974 to stop producing – the payment being divided equally between the big four firms.
8. As nationalised monopolies they probably had little incentive to adopt an aggressive purchasing policy. Also, meter purchasing had long been the prerogative of engineers rather than accountants (or economists) in the AEBs and price was often viewed as of secondary importance to the specification and build quality of the meters bought.
9. Entrants in the 1980s included Polymeters, Ampy and Thorn; however, all have remained relatively small.

10. The problem, of course, is that it is very difficult to find evidence of tacit coordination. In the respondent's view, however, there was no evidence that the big four would offer lower prices to undercut each other in the 1980s.

11. GEC was the only firm which continued to produce electro-mechanical meters in the UK at the time of our interviews whilst Landis and Gyr import theirs from Greece.

12. In its original form, it was suggested that a completely free market would be created in electricity supply for domestic customers (*The Competitive Electricity Market from 1998*, OFFER, January 1995). More recently, however, it has been suggested that such a scheme would be too complicated and a system based on bands of customer usage ('customer profiling') is to be introduced.

13. European Union Directive (90/531/EEC) which came into effect on 1 January 1993.

14. British Posters was a limited company controlled by its members.

15. Clearly, the issue of economising on transaction costs was important here.

16. To that extent, our inclusion of it in the present chapter is fairly arbitrary – it might equally have been included in Chapter 8.

17. The major outdoor specialists in 1991 were Portland Outdoor Advertising, Harrison Salinson, Concord & Posterlink, Poster Publicity and International Poster Management.

18. MMC, *MAI plc and London and Continental Advertising Holdings plc*, 1987 and MMC, *Avenir Havas Media SA and Brunton Curtis Outdoor Advertising Ltd.*, 1991 (hereafter the 1987 and 1991 Reports). The OFT has also been involved in other cases on the supply side: notably those involving London Transport Advertising in 1994 and British Transport Advertising in 1995. It was also involved in the proposed merger of Portland Outdoor Advertising and Concord & Posterlink (both outdoor specialists) where it expressed its opposition to the merger, which did not go ahead.

19. These are the larger panels often seen at the roadside.

20. The *Financial Times*, 20 July 1994.

21. It was also argued that the MMC had looked at narrower markets in other ways (for example, by distinguishing different sheet sizes, different regions, and even stationary and moving advertising).

22. The average price of salt increased by 15 per cent between 1988–93 compared to about 30 per cent allowable under the index.

23. This, of course, depends on a variety of factors including costs of entry and exit, the time frame being considered and so on. The intuition is that the higher cost firm, already weakened, may more easily succumb to predatory action. As noted above, BS increased price in the period by less than allowable under the cost index so that one might think that it was attempting to remove its higher cost rival. Our reading of the case, however, is that import competition combined with the need to discount heavily to large chemical companies underlies this result, and that predation was not involved.

24. This was possible because it was able to obtain information on the index from the OFT and then use this to calculate the price rise allowable under the undertaking(s). Whilst the undertakings relate to *average* prices, the firm was able to use the average to argue that its own price should not rise by more.

25. The *Financial Times* (11 November 1994) reports that BS continued to have over 50 per cent of the market.

26. Eurotunnel had gained about a 40 per cent market share of the freight and passenger markets by October 1996 (*Financial Times*, 5 November 1996).

27. Playtex gave several reasons for its exit: it had faced unfavourable publicity associated with toxic shock syndrome, there had been criticism from a competitor over its applicator and no TV advertising of tampons was allowed at the time.

28. There is an apparent parallel here with the salt case, nine years later, and, superficially at least, it is not obvious why price control of Pedigree was not seriously contemplated in

this case. The reason appears to be that Pedigree was not seen to be exercising market power, but merely enjoying the fruits of superior efficiency and superior brands.

7. Predatory Pricing (and Price Discrimination)

7.1 THEORETICAL PERSPECTIVES

7.1.1 Definitional Matters

In this chapter, more than most, we will be especially precise in setting out what is, and what is not, our subject area. *Predatory behaviour* is a term which could be applied to many anti-competitive practices directed towards rivals (either actual or potential): for example, attempts to foreclose a market by vertical integration or by imposing retail exclusivity are obvious candidates. In delineating the subject matter of this chapter, however, we follow usual practice and focus on behaviour designed to discipline or eliminate new entrants and/or rivals from the market. Wider issues of anti-competitive behaviour are discussed elsewhere – notably, in Chapter 8 on vertical restraints.

Second, *price discrimination* involves firms charging different customers different prices which cannot be accounted for by differences in marginal costs. Whilst such discrimination is observed in many markets, our focus in this chapter is on discrimination which has potentially strategic, anti-competitive motives (that is, is directed at rival firms or entrants). Thus we are not concerned with what might be called the standard textbook treatment of price discrimination, in which a monopoly sells directly to consumers, extracting surplus by virtue of charging different prices. Not only are the welfare implications of this potentially very different, but also it belongs more obviously to Chapter 5 on monopoly pricing. Clearly, the two practices may be, but are not necessarily, related. To see this note that (almost by definition) predatory pricing involves price discrimination, since it involves charging a low price now and a high price later (that is, intertemporal price discrimination). However, not all price discrimination is predatory. For example, if a monopolist is found to discriminate between different geographic areas, it may be setting different prices in order to discipline or eliminate a specific rival (that is, engage in predatory pricing). But equally, there may be no strategic motive. Rather it may merely price discriminate because this is the profit maximising policy when faced with two markets with different price elasticities.

The precise definition of predatory pricing is a matter of continuing academic dispute. However, as working definitions, two examples will suffice. The first is a quotation from a classic academic paper by Joskow and Klevorick (1979, pp. 219–20):

> 'Predatory pricing behaviour involves a reduction of price in the short run so as to drive competing firms out of the market or to discourage entry of new firms in an effort to gain larger profits via higher prices in the long run than would have been earned if the price reduction had not occurred.'

The second is what appears to come close to a current 'official' OFT view of predatory *practices*:

> 'The acceptance of losses in a particular market which are deliberately incurred in order to eliminate a specific competitor, so that supra-normal profits can be earned in the future, either in the same or in other markets.' (Myers, 1994, p. 9)

Obviously, one difference between these two is whether pricing or other activities are included. In this chapter we focus mainly on prices but some other predatory actions are also discussed. A second difference is that the latter definition specifies that the purpose of predation is to eliminate a *specific* competitor. Myers explains this by suggesting that 'pricing can be anti-competitive without being predatory, such as limit pricing and selective price cuts. One thing that distinguishes predation from other forms of price-related strategic entry deterrence is that it is targeted at eliminating a specific competitor' (ibid., p. 10). Although this explanation has a somewhat circular feel to it, one can see that it may be operationally easier to employ. In both cases, however, the meaning of predation is reasonably clear in both its price and non-price forms and these definitions form the basis of the discussion in this chapter.

7.1.2 Is Predatory Pricing Credible?

Moving on from matters of definition, there is a much larger question mark attached to predatory pricing; namely, can it actually exist? Consider first a non-rigorous account of what predatory pricing is – as Utton (1995) puts it, the 'classic story' of predatory pricing is as follows:

'A dominant firm operating in a number of regional markets or selling a range of differentiated products will cut prices to a very low level in the short run and sacrifice profits, in order to destroy a rival or deter a potential rival. Once success has been achieved, price is raised again to a monopoly level.' (Utton, 1995, p. 103)

This is, indeed, how the story was traditionally told in textbooks and they very often cited the case of the Standard Oil Company of New Jersey as an example. The empirical arm of this view was provided by the Areeda–Turner rule (Areeda and Turner, 1974/5), which suggested that predatory pricing can be identified whenever a dominant firm reduces its price below short-run marginal cost.

This view has, however, been challenged especially from a theoretical point of view. The main argument (advanced by Chicago writers, in particular) is that the strategy lacks credibility. The essence of the argument is that price-cutting for purely predatory purposes would involve losses for the perpetrator as well as for the victim. Indeed, if, as is often the case, the former has a dominant market share, the absolute magnitude of its lost profits would be considerably larger. In these circumstances, a more plausible response might be for the dominant firm to accommodate an entrant or (perhaps) to merge with it. On the basis of this argument, if a dominant firm is observed to cut price, this cannot be for predatory reasons. In fact, of course, a price cut is hardly surprising since we would expect non-colluding duopolists to charge a lower price/supply a larger quantity than a monopolist – this is the natural consequence of the competitive process, rather than predatory behaviour. This and other arguments were first most forcefully advanced by McGee (1958) (see also McGee, 1980 and Phlips, 1995). The game theoretic justification for them derives from the so-called 'chain store paradox' and Selten's (1978) proof that predation in oligopoly models with a finite time horizon and perfect information is a non-credible threat.

More recently, however, game theorists have shown that, under certain conditions, predatory pricing can still be a credible strategy: specifically, with an infinite time horizon and severe punishment strategies (Abreu, 1986 and Stenbacka, 1990); uncertainty about costs and demand (where a low price can be used as a signal); due to 'deep pocket' possibilities (where a large multi-market firm can threaten to outlast its victim in a war of attrition); and where predatory pricing has a reputation effect to be exploited in an uncertain future. These two latter possibilities have been important, in particular in a number of bus cases one of which is discussed in Section 7.4 below.

7.2 OVERVIEW OF CASES IN THE POPULATION

Although allegations of predatory behaviour or price discrimination surface with a reasonably high frequency in MMC reports, they emerge in a major role in only ten cases (Table 7.1).[1] Superficially at least, these practices are relatively rare, although a number of other cases have been investigated under the Competition Act.[2]

Table 7.1 Discriminatory/predatory pricing in the population

Case	Oligopoly type	Remedy
Footwear machinery (1973)	C	T
Plasterboard (1974, 1990)	A	T
Building bricks (1976)	C	T
Diazo copying materials (1977)	C	None
Credit card services (1980)	B	T
Concrete roofing tiles (1981)	B	T
Animal waste (1985, 1993)	A	T
Steel wire fencing (1987)	A	None
Bus services in Kent (1993)	A	T
Bus services in the north-east (1995)	B	T

Note: Detailed case studies are shown in bold.

The profile of the ten cases reveals three general tendencies. First, five of the ten come from just two sectors: building materials/products and local bus services. The former tended to occur in the early years of our period and usually turned on geographical price discrimination between different regions by a nationally dominant firm. The latter are more recent and relate to specific, very localised markets and are representative of other bus cases in the last ten years.[3] Second, the firms involved were either single dominant firms in an industry (the four A and three C cases in the table),[4] or, in three cases, a pair of dominant firms (the three B cases). As expected, alleged predation and/or price discrimination only occurs in industries in which there is a single dominant firm or several dominant firms. Third, the MMC made an adverse recommendation in eight of the ten cases, which is higher than the overall average for all monopoly references (69 per cent, see Table 3.9). In each case, termination of practices was recommended, and this was often coupled with subsequent price monitoring.

We have selected two industries for detailed investigation in this chapter, building bricks (1976) and bus services in the north-east of England (1995).

Each is meant to be representative of other cases amongst the ten. Bricks is an example of a building material in which there is clear evidence of spatial price discrimination, although this was not necessarily predatory. Buses in the north-east is representative of the two bus cases in this population and the others investigated elsewhere by the MMC (see endnote 3). Here, predation seems to be a more plausible accusation. In contrast to nearly all the other case studies considered in this book, in neither case did we undertake interviews. For bricks, this was because the investigation took place over 20 years ago and we found it impossible to find a sufficient number of people with the required knowledge of the original case. In the bus case, two of the authors were involved in another project (Jones et al., 1996) which included a significant amount of interviewing in other MMC and OFT bus investigations; and we draw on that experience in discussing this particular case. Finally, it should be noted that, unlike all of the other case studies, buses in the north-east is a very recent investigation, from which undertakings have only recently ensued. In this case, we do not know how effective the remedy will be, although it may have important implications for this and other possible bus cases.

7.3 BUILDING BRICKS (1976)

In this case, there was a dominant firm, London Brick Co. (LBC) with an overall market share of about 40 per cent. However, this estimate is an aggregation across the whole country and all types of bricks. More significantly, LBC was (by the time of the report) a virtual monopoly supplier of fletton bricks. These are bricks made from a special type of clay only found in the Peterborough/Bedford area. As the clay has a naturally high carbon content, it is cheaper to burn. Fletton bricks therefore have significantly lower costs of production; and they can thus be transported over much greater distances than other bricks and still remain competitive. So, although this industry is only category C in our structural classification scheme, it bears all the hallmarks of a classic low-cost price leader, able to practise spatial price discrimination and protected by a natural absolute cost barrier to entry.

In fact, in the MMC's judgement, LBC were not making excessive profits, but the Commission was still critical of its pricing policy. In particular, it argued that the company overcharged nearby customers for transport costs and undercharged more distant ones. This price discrimination had potentially predatory motives with respect to smaller regionalised competitors. The undertakings, agreed in June 1978, required that the transport cost component of price should be related to actual cost. The company also agreed to provide the necessary information on costs and prices for the OFT to monitor its subsequent behaviour.

The OFT carried out a review of the case in December 1991 and the company was released from its undertaking to provide actual and forecast transport costs, although still agreeing to provide such details as and when required. The amended undertakings also continued to allow customers to collect bricks directly from LBC's works at ex-works prices. Nevertheless, this was a significant weakening of the original undertakings, and it appears to have been motivated by three developments over the 15 years following the report: (a) a long-term decline in the demand for bricks (there had been no significant new entry for over 10 years); (b) a decrease in the fletton share of that smaller market; and (c) the market had gradually become a national one – not just for LBC, but also for other relatively large firms such as Redland. The first does not seem a very compelling reason for less vigilant monitoring: there are no convincing theoretical reasons for supposing that predatory or discriminatory pricing is less likely when demand is falling. The second and third reasons, however, deserve closer attention. The collapse in demand for flettons was the result of two things. First, it became apparent that flettons, when used for facing purposes, were particular susceptible to frost damage. Second, cost increases as a result of tighter pollution control were more pronounced for fletton bricks (produced in coal-fired kilns) than for other bricks (increasingly produced in gas-fired tunnel kilns). Thus, the fletton brick suffered from a perceived loss in quality and a narrowing of its traditional cost advantage. Both factors, of course, will have undermined LBC's ability to price discriminate. Moreover, the transition of the market from being regional to national was the result of relatively lower transport costs. This had the effect of further narrowing the traditional cost differential between LBC and its medium-sized competitors. In these circumstances, smaller firms might still be susceptible to predatory behaviour, but now, not only by LBC, but also from the other national firms. But, for this reason, competition *amongst* the majors would probably render price discrimination less effective than it was previously, and it would be unfair to single out just LBC for monitoring.

Turning to the direct evidence on LBC's behaviour in the years immediately following the MMC report, it is difficult to form a confident judgement on whether it abandoned price discrimination. There is also insufficient evidence to check for parallel pricing between LBC and the other majors. More indirect statistical evidence certainly confirms that LBC's market share declined, but evidence is thin on who gained at their expense. Was it the other medium-sized firms who were now able to compete nationally? Or was it the smaller, regional firms who would have stood most to gain from the remedy? Without more detailed evidence at our disposal, it is difficult to say. The major problem is that the market had declined drastically with firms exiting before and after the MMC report. How it *might* have changed without MMC intervention is impossible to say without a major further study of the industry. Thus the verdict in this case is that *probably* market power has declined – but largely for reasons unconnected with the remedy.

7.4 BUS SERVICES IN THE NORTH-EAST OF ENGLAND (1995)

This case relates to five separate events which occurred in 1994 in various parts of the north-east of England. Each involved allegations of predatory behaviour by two of the largest national firms against local rivals. In order to explain the specifics of the case, we first need to provide a brief, more general, history of developments in the industry for the UK as a whole.

In 1986, the UK bus industry was deregulated. Prior to this, bus services had been supplied by local authority-owned operators, publicly-owned corporations and by small private operators. The main features of deregulation were: (i) the removal of legal entry barriers, (ii) the privatisation of the nationalised long-distance operators, and (iii) a loosening of the financial and legal ties between local authorities and their bus subsidiaries. In the years which followed, the industry underwent a rapid increase in concentration, as the result of two developments. First, many of the previously municipally-owned and nationalised firms were bought out by their management and/or employees. Second, many of these were, in turn, acquired by fast growing privately-owned firms who were increasingly taking on a national identity. By early 1994, nine of these firms accounted for 56 per cent of the total UK market (their combined market share having been just 13 per cent only five years earlier).[5] Most of these firms should be thought of as multi-market operators, having dominant market shares in a number of separate regions or localities throughout the country. Perhaps only one or two were genuinely national, in the sense of having a leading presence in virtually all regions, but most had leading shares in more than one market – often geographically quite dispersed. Thus, in the 'typical' region, it would not be uncommon to find that two or three of the largest firms dominated, usually faced with a fringe of local competitors. Nevertheless, by 1994, there were still some quite large towns in which there was a local operator with a significant market share.

The other significant feature of the industry was the high incidence of competition investigations, most having a more or less prominent predatory theme.[6] Five of these involved the largest firm on the national scene, Stagecoach Holdings (Stagecoach). Perhaps more than any other, this firm characterises the developments in the industry since 1986. It had grown from quite humble origins in a region in Scotland, by virtue of a series of acquisitions and aggressive entry into many different localities and regions. Although opinions differ on whether this firm behaved in a generally predatory way, few people deny that its success is also based on high efficiency and rapid introduction of new buses and new work practices. Stagecoach is the main actor in the following case.

Turning specifically to the north-east (a fairly wide region including Tyne and Wear, parts of Northumbria, Durham and Cleveland), by the time of the report, three of the national heavyweights had a significant presence: Go Ahead, North-East Buses (NEB)[7] and Stagecoach, although Go Ahead and Stagecoach were rarely direct competitors, the former being more dominant in the north and the latter more dominant in the south of the region. The MMC investigation focused on five separate situations in different parts of the region (two involving Go-Ahead in North Durham and three involving Stagecoach), but it is the Stagecoach in Darlington investigation which attracted most attention, both within the report and in more general debate in the media. Therefore, we concentrate on this part of the report for the sake of brevity.

Following deregulation, the municipal operator, Darlington Transport Co. (DTC), had experienced strong competition from NEB and consistently made losses; there was also considerable local concern about bus congestion as the two rivals escalated the frequency of services. This was aggravated when, in May 1993, a new operator, Your Bus,[8] entered the Darlington market. This affected the patronage of both DTC and NEB, but particularly the latter, which responded by registering additional services, effectively doubling its frequencies on competing routes.[9] Both NEB and DTC reduced the price of their season tickets and offered free passes to concessionary passengers. This bus war resulted in all three operators incurring losses, and, eventually, in December 1994, Your Bus sold out to West Midlands Travel (which had acquired NEB one month earlier). However, more significantly, DTC had been effectively caught in the cross-fire between NEB and Your Bus and its financial plight went from bad to worse. Eventually, in July 1994, its owners, Darlington Borough Council (DBC) announced its intention to sell DTC. It is important to note that, up to this point, Stagecoach had no presence in the Darlington market.

Over the following months, DBC received a number of offers, including one from Busways, a firm which was already established in adjacent areas, being the privatised operations of the municipal Tyne and Wear Passenger Transport Executive. It is at this stage that Stagecoach emerges as a significant player in the market. At the same time as Busways was entering the bidding for DTC, it was itself about to be acquired by Stagecoach – indeed, Stagecoach completed the takeover of Busways on the day following Busway's announced intention to acquire DTC. In other words, Stagecoach wished to enter the Darlington market, via acquisition, using another acquisition in an adjacent area. In the period between July and October, DBC received a number of other bids for DTC and eventually announced its preference to sell to yet another nationally significant firm, Yorkshire Traction.

In the meantime, however (on 8 September), Stagecoach had registered services on four routes in Darlington (to begin operations in December), and announced that it intended to enter the Darlington market in this way, whether or not it was successful with its bid for DTC. Following DTB's announcement that it intended to sell to Yorkshire Traction, Stagecoach (Busways) reacted by advertising in the local press for qualified drivers and announcing a new registration strategy which involved running services on all routes operated by DTC, rather than the very limited entry it had originally planned. At recruitment interviews, Stagecoach offered successful applicants (all of whom were DTC employees) very attractive contracts – basic rates higher than DTC's, three years guaranteed employment and a £1,000 lump sum 'non-training' bonus. By the end of October, 60 of DTC's 90 drivers resigned to join Stagecoach, and Stagecoach announced it would start its services five weeks earlier than originally planned, and, until the date when the registrations became formally operative, it would run 'free services'.

Faced with this strategy, which amounted to a long-term (three year) pre-commitment, coupled with a shorter period of price-cutting (indeed, initially, zero prices), two things happened. First, Yorkshire Traction, and another main bidder, withdrew their bids for DTC. Second, after a short period of trying to compete with a zero-price multi-market rival, DTC exited the industry (on 10 November).

The MMC was scathing of Stagecoach (Busways) in its report: 'It was the combination of Busways' actions in recruiting so many of DTC's drivers so quickly, registering services on all its routes and running free services which caused DTC's final collapse. *We find these actions to be predatory, deplorable and against the public interest'* (our italics). Obviously, the MMC thought there was naked predation in this case. What makes it particularly interesting from a theoretical viewpoint is the use (by Stagecoach) of labour contracts to pre-commit itself (thereby reducing any doubts on credibility) and also setting a zero price (with obviously no doubt that price was below marginal cost).

In this case, the MMC recommended that action be taken to limit Stagecoach's ability to behave in a predatory way in the future. In particular, they required that if entry takes place and Stagecoach retaliates by lowering its fares and/or increasing its frequency of service, and the new firm is forced to exit, Stagecoach should maintain its low fares (subject to increases in line with the RPI) and its frequency of service for a period of three years following the exit. Undertakings to this effect were signed in October 1996.[10] The main problem with this, of course (as in other predation cases involving the bus industry), is that the remedy came too late to offer any protection, either to DTC or other similar firms in other bus markets. This is a major weakness of current law because the OFT has no powers under the FTA to take out an injunction against a predator pending an investigation. This is one of the key areas in which proposed new legislation seeks to change the law, and this is discussed further in Chapter 10.

7.5 OTHER CASES

We now turn more briefly to some of the other cases in which there were significant elements of discriminatory or predatory pricing. First, we consider those cases which display obvious parallels with our two case studies.

In the first plasterboard report (1974) there are marked similarities to the brick case, two years later. British Gypsum (owned by BPB Industries Ltd) had a total monopoly of the supply of plasterboard in the UK. Whilst there were no accusations that it had exploited its position by setting generally high prices and making monopoly profits, its practice of uniform pricing throughout the country, and not allowing customers to collect supplies directly, was judged to be against the public interest. It is difficult to ascertain whether predatory motives were involved, although in the later report (1990) on the same industry, there were suggestions that price was adjusted in parts of Wales to meet the local competition, and, more generally, that there had been strategic loyalty payments. Following the 1974 report, undertakings were given to cease uniform pricing.

Subsequently, there was a major development in industry structure with the entry, in 1988, of a German firm, Knauf. Knauf had multinational operations throughout the EU and was the second largest European firm, behind BPB. Effectively, the industry had become essentially European, rather than merely national (unlike bricks, trade in plasterboard over long distances is quite possible). In the subsequent reinvestigation (in 1990), all remaining undertakings were lifted in the light of this more competitive environment.

Concrete roofing tiles (1981) is a third case in the building materials sector. It differed from bricks and plasterboard in that the market structure was duopolistic: Redland and Marley had market shares of 46 per cent and 36 per cent respectively; a third firm, Sandtoft, had 12 per cent and the remainder of the market was shared by 12 much smaller firms. Here, the Commission was certainly concerned that price competition between the two majors was 'muted'. From a review of the two firms' prices over a period of years, it concluded that 'although there was no evidence to support a suggestion of concerted price parallelism, equally there appears to have been little or no sustained competition in list prices and standard discounts' (1981 report, p. 105). It was also apparent that Redland was far stronger in selling to the public sector, whilst Marley's market share was relatively larger in the private sector. Again, the MMC refrained from explicit accusations of formal market segmentation, but the impression one forms is of very soft competition between the two. This is significant, of course, in assessing the likelihood of predatory behaviour towards third parties, that is, the smaller firms in the industry, and it was on this question that the MMC placed the top priority. The two majors were required to undertake: (i) not to acquire competitors without giving at least four weeks notice, (ii) to notify the DGFT of the discounts it offered to its main customers and (iii) to provide the DGFT with information on profits, costs and so on. In other words, the emphasis was on discouraging predatory behaviour which might constrain the competitive check offered by the smaller concrete tile manufacturers.[11]

Bus services in mid and west Kent (1993), unsurprisingly, share some common features with buses in the north-east, and, more generally, the two cases are fairly representative of the clutch of bus reports undertaken by the MMC and OFT since deregulation. In this instance, Maidstone and District Motor Services,[12] the dominant operator, was accused of a variety of anti-competitive operating and pricing practices and imposing discriminatory access conditions to bus stations which it owned. In addition, alleged predatory pricing was targeted at three very small entrants who had begun to run limited services on certain routes. M&D had responded to their entry by lowering fares selectively on services which competed directly with the entrants' services. M&D's defence was that it did not undercut its competitors but merely matched their prices – in that sense, this was a 'normal competitive response'. The MMC, however, rejected this defence and suggested that the competitive response would involve discounting *all* fares. It recommended undertakings (which were subsequently given) that, in future, there would be no selective fare discounting (either matching or undercutting new entrants) for journeys within 15 minutes of a competing operator. Discounts would only be allowed as part of a generalised fare reduction on all services on that or similar routes. Moreover, in line with buses in the north-east, if M&D were to register a service and a competitor subsequently withdrew, M&D was not subsequently to reduce its own service or increase fares within the following year by more than the rise in the retail price index. This case, then, was similar to buses in the north-east in a number of respects and it seems difficult to argue that M&D's actions were not predatory, at least in intent.

Of the remaining cases in the population as a whole, animal waste (1985) is perhaps most interesting. Here, a monopoly existed in favour of Prosper De Mulder Ltd (PDM) and its various subsidiaries, and the main problem was identified as predatory pricing in order to maintain and exploit the firm's monopoly position. The recommendations, subsequently converted into undertakings, required that the company should not conduct its gut-room activity on a loss-making principle and that there should be no cross-subsidisation from other businesses. It was also required to notify the OFT of any proposed acquisitions of smaller competitors. The firm was subsequently reinvestigated in 1993, partly because it was judged to have breached the earlier undertakings. It was required to give further undertakings which again involved termination of strategic discriminatory pricing.

There were also two other cases at the beginning of our period, on which it is now difficult to gather sufficient information for a detailed analysis. In footwear machinery (1973), the dominant firm, British United Shoe Machinery, was required not to charge customers a higher rate for terminating the lease of a machine if they decided to replace it by a machine supplied by another firm. Librium and valium (1973), in the same year, was primarily a case of monopoly pricing (dealt with in Chapter 5), in which price cuts were recommended. However, the MMC also condemned the investigated firm for supplying tranquillisers free of charge to hospitals; this was interpreted as a strategic device to deter entry in this important part of the market.

Finally, two other cases attracted no recommendations from the

Commission.[13] In diazo copying materials (1977), Ozalid had just over half of the market. The practice under investigation was the use of a discounting system offering incentives to place larger orders with the company, discriminating in favour of larger customers. Similarly, in steel wire fencing (1987), the dominant firm TWILL and its five wholly-owned subsidiaries had 65 per cent of the UK market, and price discrimination was suspected in the form of secondary rebates.

7.6 CONCLUSIONS

There have been ten cases in which predatory pricing, and price discrimination with a potential anti-competitive motive, have been the main focus of attention. Typically, but not always, they have involved a single dominant firm. In spite of the lively debate amongst academics in particular about the likelihood of predatory behaviour, the MMC has revealed, by its decisions, a pronounced tendency to rule against the firms concerned: only two of the ten cases have escaped remedies.

We have concentrated on two cases in particular: bricks, which is representative of a number of other cases in building materials, and bus services in the north-east, which is typical of many other bus references to have been considered by the OFT and the MMC in the last decade. In bricks, the main issue is whether uniform pricing by the national leader throughout the country, which implies a lower mark-up in regions distant from the point of production, amounts to predatory behaviour towards local rivals in those regions. Implicitly, the MMC judged that it did. However, any real chance of evaluating the success of this remedy was effectively ruled out by subsequent (unconnected) developments in the cost structure of the industry.

Bus services in the north-east is more clear-cut in our opinion, in that predatory behaviour was quite nakedly evident. The MMC's remedy in this (and other) bus case(s) was that the predator(s) should be forced to keep their prices low, and their frequency of service high, should price-cutting (or running more buses) have the effect of removing a competitor from the market. This is a novel remedy (in the UK context) and it may well have the desired effect of tipping the balance against predatory action. In the absence of the option of fining firms, it is not clear that the MMC could formulate any other, more punitive, remedy. Unfortunately, for the purposes of the present book, this case is too recent for us to be able to make an informed judgement on whether this remedy is likely to have an effect.

NOTES

1. Another case involving a fairly prominent role for predatory pricing is librium and valium (1973), although this case is, in fact, assigned to Chapter 5.
2. By our reckoning, ten cases have been considered by the MMC under the Competition Act between 1980–95. A number of these involved predation along with other anti-competitive practices: see Utton (1994) for discussion.
3. Other bus cases involving predatory accusations which have been the subject of an MMC investigation are Highland Scottish (1990) and Southdown (1993) (under the Competition Act) and Avon (1989), South Yorkshire (1990), Bognor (1990), Trimdon (1990) and Portsmouth (1990) as mergers references. Beyond this, at least two other cases were investigated by the OFT, but did not get as far as a full MMC investigation (Isle of Wight, 1988 and Fife, 1994). For further details see Jones et al. (1996).
4. Although the leaders in the three C industries did not have market shares which qualified them for inclusion in group A, each was nevertheless very large compared to its closest rivals. See the Appendix for details.
5. By 1996, the big nine had shrunk to four (Stagecoach, First Bus, Cowie (British Bus) and West Midlands Travel (owned by National Express)) mainly as a result of merger activity (see Jones et al., 1996, p. 4).
6. If we include buses in the north-east, there were ten formal competition investigations of bus companies from 1988–95: two FTA cases, three Competition Act cases and five merger cases. An eleventh case, Greater Manchester Buses, was also subject to informal OFT investigation in 1992–94.
7. North-East Buses was a subsidiary of West Midlands Travel, which was subsequently acquired by National Express – both of the latter were among the big nine referred to earlier.
8. This was a new local firm, established by two former senior employees of NEB.
9. In fact, this response by NEB was also investigated by the OFT under the Competition Act and NEB was judged to have acted in a predatory manner towards Your Bus. However, this judgement seems to have been largely overlooked in most commentaries.
10. The undertakings in this case are quite novel in that they seek to limit predation by restricting the *ex-post* behaviour of Stagecoach should it engage in future predatory behaviour. The rationale for this, of course, is that it substantially increases the costs of engaging in predatory action (see Baumol, 1979–80 for a discussion). It remains to be seen, however, whether this will be an effective remedy in preventing predatory action.
11. Apparently, the OFT has not received any complaints from smaller manufacturers since the report, and, although there have been some takeovers of smaller manufacturers, none of these has individually enhanced market shares sufficiently to warrant a reference to the MMC. The undertakings were amended in 1988; Redland and Marley were still required to give four weeks notice to the OFT of a proposed merger, and Redland was required to make roof tile fittings freely available to builders' merchants.
12. Now owned by the British Bus group, one of the four largest national operators.
13. Another case, credit card services (1980, 1989), dealt with a number of quite complex issues. Amongst these, however, was the 'No Discrimination' rule operated by credit card companies which prevented traders from setting different prices for different means of payment (cash or credit card). This rule was finally dropped following the 1989 report.

8. Vertical Restraints

8.1 THEORETICAL PERSPECTIVES

Almost exactly half of the population of MMC reports covered by this book involved some sort of 'vertical relationship' as the main potential problem. This general umbrella term refers to a wide range of different practices and arrangements which can exist between firms at different stages of the production and distribution process. Very often, but not always, they apply to relationships between upstream manufacturers and downstream retailers. It is usually helpful to think in terms of a spectrum, with full-fledged vertical integration (direct ownership of adjacent stages) at one extreme, and various incentives for downstream firms (for example, discounts for reaching sales targets) at the other. In between, there are a variety of other more or less explicit contractual arrangements between firms at the two stages.

Arguably, it is in this broad area of competition policy that economic theory has been at its most equivocal, unable to provide straightforward general rules or guidance to the anti-trust authorities. However, this is not necessarily a weakness of the theory: vertical restraints often involve a (familiar) trade-off between efficiency-enhancing and anti-competitive motives/effects. Which of the two will predominate in any particular model often depends sensitively on the precise assumptions of that model. But this merely underlines the perception of most practitioners of anti-trust policy; namely that any particular vertical restraint may have net welfare-enhancing consequences in some settings, and negative ones in others. Thus, policy can only be applied on a case-by-case basis, taking each particular case on its merits.

In broad terms, the main theoretical issues can be set out as follows. (The specifics will be explained in more detail presently, when we turn to each different type of restraint in turn.) The traditional (loosely speaking, structure–conduct–performance) view was that vertical restraints are largely anti-competitive, and that although they may be in the interests of the firms practising them, they typically impose larger costs (in terms of lost welfare) on society as a whole. This is because they can be employed by incumbent firms, especially at the upstream stage, to foreclose the market to new entrants. Thus, an upstream monopolist may employ vertical ties with its downstream customers in order to deny a potential upstream entrant access to the downstream market. Even where this does not entirely foreclose the downstream market, because the entrant has the option of establishing its own downstream operations, it will necessarily involve a larger scale of entry (in terms of capital outlays and, perhaps, sunk costs) and, at the very least, raise the height of entry barriers. Moreover, restraints may also be motivated by a desire to reduce competition between incumbents. This may happen if they facilitate collusion, or, more generally, reduce the cross-price elasticities of demand between the products of incumbent firms. In terms of recent terminology, the latter is known as 'softening inter-brand competition'.

The traditional counter argument (most strongly argued by economists from the 'Chicago School', for example, Bork, 1978) derived from the central recognition that 'monopoly profits can only be earned once'. If an upstream monopolist sells to final consumers via a competitive downstream market, it is able to extract the full monopoly profit without any formal vertical ties with firms downstream. Moreover, if there is monopoly at both stages, without vertical ties, there is the danger that both monopolists will optimise in a myopic way – each setting its own monopoly price, so that the final price turns out to be higher (and output lower) than would be the case if both stages were under single ownership. In this case, an effective vertical tie will avoid 'double marginalisation', thereby benefiting not only the firms, but also final consumers.

This counter argument was considerably strengthened by developments in the theory of transactions costs, the implications of which were that vertical ties help to minimise transactions costs, reduce uncertainty and help to optimise investment. These benign effects, along with the avoidance of the double mark-up, arise precisely because the tie effectively ensures that the downstream and upstream firms make decisions which are in their joint interests, rather than each optimising merely in their own self-interests. Thus, at the worst, vertical ties are neutral so far as society is concerned, and at the best both cost- and price-reducing.

Not all proponents of this second view would deny that there may be real world markets in which there is both a monopoly problem and vertical restraints, but they would not accept that the restraints are the cause of the problem *per se*. To the extent that policy is required, it should be directed towards removing the source of the horizontal market power, rather than the vertical links.

In more recent years, the debate has matured somewhat, with most economists less inclined to take a doctrinaire stance, one way or the other. One important trend which should be mentioned is an increased emphasis on the distinction between *intra-brand* and *inter-brand* competition. Traditionally, economists focused on inter-brand competition – competition between manufacturers of similar products – and the debate was about whether vertical restraints increased or decreased inter-brand competition. Intra-brand competition, between retailers selling the same brands, was largely ignored. It is clear, however, that in many cases the extent of intra-brand competition is an important determinant of consumer welfare, as well as of the profits of the retailers themselves (Steiner, 1991). Once this is recognised, and one takes into account competition between retailers, the analysis takes on a different slant. On the one hand, vertical ties between manufacturers and retailers may be explained as a device for removing the externality between the two (that is, cost-reducing and joint profit maximising), but they may also be a means of reducing competition between retailers. The welfare implications are not unambiguous in general, and, again, the message for anti-trust authorities is the need for a careful case-by-case approach (see Dobson and Waterson, 1994, 1996).

Against this general background, we now turn to the four broad types of restraint identified in this book: vertical integration, exclusive practices, tie-ins and resale price maintenance (RPM). [1]

8.1.1 Vertical Integration

Most of the discussion above carries over without the need for further elaboration to the case where there is joint ownership of upstream and downstream activities (for example, a manufacturer owns its own retail outlets). The traditional S–C–P competition concerns are that:

(a) integration will extend a monopolist's power to other markets at the upstream or downstream stage, and/or
(b) integration will make entry more difficult either because it is not feasible to enter at the upstream or downstream stage, or because the costs of doing so will be high.

Equally, the benevolent rationale for vertical integration – avoidance of 'double marginalisation'– is easily shown with standard textbook theory (for example, Clarke, 1985): it avoids the outcome under which the manufacturing monopolist (say) charges the retailing monopolist the full monopoly price, who, in turn, adds his own monopoly mark-up when selling to the final consumer. Thus, as Posner (1981) contends, because monopoly power can only be exploited once, it is impossible to use it in one market to gain monopoly power in another.

Vertical integration can, however, extend market power in certain cases. Vernon and Graham (1971) (see also Warren-Boulton, 1974) have shown that a monopolist can extend its monopoly power at the downstream stage if it can prevent downstream customers substituting away from its product. Thus, for example, a manufacturer might choose to own its own retail outlets rather than sell through independent retail firms and this policy could be detrimental to inter-brand competition. In addition, vertical integration can exclude entrants where the number of outlets is limited, and, possibly, if it creates additional entry costs. Several cases discussed further below include such effects.[2]

Transactions costs theory (Williamson, 1975, 1985) shows that integration may simply be a device for avoiding transaction costs in intermediate product markets: gains will often be possible from vertical integration through the avoidance of the small numbers bargaining problem, and through information exchange by agents. A key concept here is *asset specificity*, the extent to which assets are specific to a particular transaction. The major determinant of this, in turn, is the extent to which the costs relating to those assets are sunk. This interacts with two other significant concepts – *uncertainty* and *frequency of exchange* – to determine whether it is more efficient for a particular transaction to be undertaken by two separate firms, or whether it should be internalised within a single integrated firm. (For example, Weiss, 1994, shows that in cases where contracts involve transaction-specific capital, there are significant economies to be made through integration.) For some purposes, this analysis is similar to the contractual rights approach (Grossman and Hart, 1986), which focuses on changes in the bargaining relation that take place over time, as a result of agents acquiring transaction-specific skills. Both approaches acknowledge that the full integration solution is different from that which would occur if 'perfect contracts' were possible, and that vertical integration may be a 'second best' solution to the externality problem. However, they do little to suggest that vertical integration is typically against the public interest.

8.1.2 Exclusive Dealing

This category covers a number of vertical practices, which are described by a variety of different terms in different textbooks, MMC reports and so on. Here, we simplify somewhat by identifying just two broad types: exclusive purchasing and exclusive distribution. Since they both often entail medium to long-term contracts, and are sometimes referred to as quasi-integration, many of the efficiency and competition arguments involved are similar to those just described. Therefore, although there is a substantial recent academic literature on this subject, we shall be brief, referring the interested reader to one or another of the recent summary articles (for example, Kuhn et al., 1992, Dobson and Waterson, 1996, and Rey and Stiglitz, 1995).

(a) Exclusive Purchasing

This refers to agreements in which (usually) the upstream supplier restricts the downstream buyer from stocking the products of rival suppliers; high profile examples found in many countries include ice cream, beer, petrol and new cars. There are a number of variations on this theme, including long-term contracts with onerous termination conditions, contracts requiring specified quantities to be purchased and loyalty bonuses (which are also used to sustain collusion). The common accusation is that this type of arrangement limits the extent of inter-brand competition (competition between manufacturers). On the other hand, the most common efficiency defence is that such contracts ensure that the distributor engages in sufficient promotional effort (see Blair and Lewis, 1994).

(b) Exclusive Distribution

In its most extreme form, this is a contract whereby an upstream supplier (manufacturer) commits to selling to only one downstream buyer (retailer). It is often linked to particular geographic territories, that is, the supplier sells to only one buyer in a particular locality or region, and the buyer agrees not to compete with other retailers in other territories. This is often referred to as 'exclusive distribution rights'. Weaker forms are where the supplier limits the *number* of buyers it will sell to – this is often referred to as 'selective distribution'. We also include 'refusal to sell' under this category: this is where the manufacturer refuses to sell its product through certain retailers, sometimes justified by the claim that the retailer in question does not have the right quality image.[3] The common accusation is that the practice limits the extent of intra-brand competition, because the retailer effectively enjoys a local monopoly. Alternatively, the defence of exclusivity (as in Ornstein, 1989, for instance) is that it avoids free riding by retailers on effort, advertising, brand names and property rights. In addition, exclusivity guarantees a long-term relation between the two parties, such that administrative costs are reduced, and specialised assets can be utilised to the full.

8.1.3 Tie-in Sales

This refers to a practice (usually contractual) whereby an upstream seller of product A requires that its downstream customer should also buy its product B (or products B, C, D, and so on.). Typically, A and B will be complementary products; for example, B might be replacement components/spare parts for A, or B might be maintenance services for A. Extreme forms of this practice are full-line forcing and commodity bundling, in which customers are required to buy an entire product range from the supplier. A milder form is the aggregated rebate scheme, in which the customer is offered discounts for taking the full product range.

The efficiency arguments often invoked in favour of tie-ins include: product reputation (for example, the manufacturer wishes to prevent inferior components from being used with his product), technical efficiency (where products have high maintenance requirements, or are sophisticated enough to warrant specialised complements), and savings in the costs of distribution (where the tied products are delivered at the same time). However, as Utton (1995) points out, distributional efficiency could equally well be achieved by the supplier merely offering a discount to customers who choose to take the full range of products.

The market power interpretation of tie-ins asserts that they restrict competition for tied sales. At one extreme, tie-ins allow a monopoly supplier of one product to extend its monopoly power to the second (complementary) product. More generally, the practice disadvantages rivals who can offer only a limited range of products and/or raises the costs of entry: the market is effectively foreclosed to specialist firms, and, as such, potential entrants may be forced to consider entry in both markets or not at all (see Pittman, 1985 and Shaffer, 1991 for further discussion). It will be clear, however, that, as with other vertical restrictions, tie-in sales can only be anti-competitive if horizontal restrictions exist in the first place.

Full-line forcing, and tie-in sales, were the subject of a special report by the MMC (1981). Its main conclusion was that if tie-ins could be justified in terms of quality assurance or were linked with discounts to retailers, then they would not be anti-competitive, but where used to extend monopoly power, or to discriminate on price, they would be against the public interest. Whilst this distinction is difficult to argue with in principle, the problem lies in distinguishing these effects in practice.

8.1.4 Resale Price Maintenance

This is a practice whereby (typically) manufacturers attempt to fix the price (either a price floor or ceiling) charged by retailers or other distributors.[4] The conventional interpretation is that it facilitates collusion between manufacturers and/or retailers, and, hence it is illegal in a number of countries.

However, there has always been a strong school of thought which has argued in its favour (see Gal-Or, 1991, Mathewson and Winter, 1984, and O'Brien and Shaffer, 1992). The essence of this defence dates back to Telser (1960), who argues that, where product-specific services (such as technical advice) are provided at the retail stage, discounting retailers can free ride on full-service dealers, and offer the product at a lower price. As such, RPM is a device for protecting full-service dealers. Perry and Porter (1990) demonstrate that, in cases where there is a high level of 'service externality' in the downstream industry, RPM can be used, in conjunction with franchising arrangements, to increase the level of service provided by the downstream firm, to the manufacturer's advantage. A similar result is derived by Blair and Lewis (1994), who show that, where the manufacturer faces a moral hazard problem in declining sales, the optimal contract includes some RPM as well as quantity fixing. Blair and Fesmire (1994, 1996) also point out that even if RPM results in higher prices this is not a justification for *per se* illegality, since the enhanced quality/customer service may more than compensate for the increase in price. Undoubtedly, this defence of RPM has had an impact on policy. As Kwoka and White (1989) observe, 'the new economics learning, though, has influenced enforcement policy in the 1980s . . . and the [US] enforcement agencies have not brought any cases challenging RPM' (ibid., p. 268).

The counter argument invariably returns to the common theme: while the restraint itself may not be anti-competitive, RPM is often associated with upstream oligopoly and the possibility of market failure. For instance, Gilligan (1986), in a study of various vertical restraints in the US, concludes that, despite the theoretical ambiguity, any distributional efficiencies that are generated are only temporary, and are exceeded by either monopoly profits upstream or downstream. Recent evidence in the UK suggests that RPM can have anti-competitive effects; most recently, in the domestic electrical products case (MMC report nos 402-3, 1997).

8.2 OVERVIEW OF CASES IN THE POPULATION

There are 31 cases in which we identify vertical restraints as the most important potential problem; they are listed in Table 8.1 along with our assessment of the main type of restraint in each case. As can be seen, exclusive dealing occurs most frequently, in 18 cases, of which nine involved exclusive purchasing, six involved exclusive distribution and three

Table 8.1 Vertical restraints in the population

Case	EXP	EXD	TIE	VI	RPM	Oligopoly	Remedy
Asbestos (1973)	X					B	T
Frozen foods (1976, 1991)	X					D	T
Photocopiers (1976)			X			A	T
Flour and bread (1977)				X		D	None
Petrol (1979, 1990)	X					D	None
Ice cream (1979, 1994)	X		(X)			B	T
Domestic gas appliances (1980)				X		A	D
Liquefied petrol gas (1981)	X		X			A	T
Ready-mixed concrete (1981)				X		D	None
Trading check franchise (1981)	X					A	T
Car parts (1982, 1992)	X	X	(X)			D	T
Films (1983, 1994)		X	X			D	T
Caravan sites (1983)						D	None
Postal franking machines (1986)	X	X				A	T
Greyhound racing (1986)		(X)				D	None
Foreign package holidays (1986)					X	D	T
Marine radio (1987)			X			A	None

Case	EXP	EXD	TIE	VI	RPM	Oligopoly	Remedy
Specialised advertising (1988)		X				D	T
Gas (1988)	X					A	T
Beer (1989)	X					D	D
Artificial lower limbs (1989)				X		A	(D)
Electrical contracting (1990)			X	X		D	T
Cinema advertising (1990)				X		A	None
Carbonated soft drinks (1991)	X		X			C	T
Cars (1992)	X	X				D	T
Contact lens solutions (1993)					X	B	None
Fine fragrances (1993)		X				D	None
Exhaust gas analysers (1993)			X			D	None
National newspapers (1993)		X			X	D	T
On-line databases (1994)		X				B	None
Video games (1995)		X				D	T

Note: Detailed case studies are shown in bold. Other cases in which vertical restraints were (secondary) problems include: pest control (1988, EXD), matches and disposable lighters (1992, EXP, TIE) and contraceptive sheaths (1994, EXP).

Key: EXP – exclusive purchasing; EXD – exclusive distribution; TIE – tie-in sales; VI – vertical integration; RPM – resale price maintenance.

involved a combination of both.[5] We also identify eight cases with tie-ins, six involving vertical integration and 3 involving resale price maintenance.[6]

As noted earlier in Chapter 3, there is some evidence of a systematic link between vertical restraints and industry structure. Most strikingly, there are 11 cases in the population as a whole, in which *only* complex monopoly was involved, and all 11 involved vertical restraints (see Appendix).[7] However, the reverse proposition does not hold, since vertical restraints also occur, albeit less frequently, in seven cases where there was just a single dominant firm. In terms of our own structural classification scheme (Table 3.8), vertical restraints occur in 17 out of 21 'loose oligopoly' (D) cases, as opposed to nine out of 23 dominant firm (A) cases, and only five of the 17 intermediate structures (B and C). In short, there is a bimodal distribution, with vertical referrals tending to occur most often in the less concentrated industries, although they are also quite frequent in markets dominated by a single firm.

In terms of type of vertical restraint, dominant firms are more likely to engage in tie-ins (A and C industries account for five of the eight cases), whilst exclusive distribution occurs primarily in less concentrated cases (eight of nine cases are in D industries). The former tends to confirm the view that tie-ins are often used as a device to extend a dominant firm's monopoly power to adjacent products, whilst the latter points to inter-brand considerations in looser oligopolies.

Table 8.1 also shows the remedies applied. In fact, no remedy was sought in 11 cases (35 per cent), which is slightly more than the corresponding proportion for the population as a whole (31 per cent). Exclusive purchasing is the practice which has been least favourably viewed by the MMC – the probability of no remedies being sought is only 1 in 6 in these cases, whilst vertical integration is the least likely to attract remedies (only 1 in 2). On the other hand, in the three of these cases where the MMC judged against the referred firms (domestic gas appliances, beer and artificial lower limbs), the more drastic divestment remedy was recommended.[8] In the other 17 cases where a remedy was sought, termination of practices was the standard remedy applied.

The six detailed case studies considered in this chapter are highlighted in bold in Table 8.1. There are two examples of exclusive purchasing (frozen foods and ice cream), one exclusive distribution (films), one tie-in sales (postal franking machines), one resale price maintenance (foreign package holidays) and one vertical integration (artificial lower limbs).[9] Two cases relate to dominant firms (A or C), and the other four to looser oligopolies (D or B); termination was the recommended remedy in all cases except for artificial limbs. Thus, our case studies appear to be broadly representative of the population of cases where remedies were applied.

8.3 FROZEN FOODS (1976)

This investigation was concerned primarily with the practices of the largest firm, Unilever (that is, Birds Eye), which was a scale monopolist, having a 31 per cent share of the total frozen foods market in 1974.[10] There were also several other firms with smaller market shares (notably Ross, Findus and supermarket own-brands). We did not undertake interviews in this case since all the key participants in the original investigation had long since left the market. However, we retain the case in our sample because of a number of interesting features and its similarity to the more topical ice cream case discussed below.

Despite the existence of some significant competitors, Birds Eye was the clear market leader, and the suspicion was that it was employing vertical restraints to maintain its dominant position. The main focus of the report was on Birds Eye's price discount system. This entailed giving discounts to supermarket chains (beyond those justified on the basis of cost); target sales discounts to retailers which encouraged them to stock more Birds Eye products; and discounts to retailers who reserved freezer cabinet space exclusively for Birds Eye products. Birds Eye also loaned out freezer cabinets on the understanding that only its products would be stored in such freezers. There appears to have been no strong efficiency argument for these vertical restraints;[11] indeed, there may be significant advantages to the retailer in stocking several manufacturers' brands. In addition, there is no obvious technological explanation for Birds Eye products being stored in a particular type of freezer, as these are standard and available from numerous suppliers. The inevitable conclusion was that the intention was to foreclose the market, thereby dampening the extent of inter-brand competition.

The Commission recommended that Birds Eye's practice of linking cabinet space to price discounts should be discontinued, subject to other manufacturers also dropping this restraint (both Ross and Findus operated similar schemes), and an undertaking to this effect was signed in 1977. However, the Commission made no recommendation on loans of freezers since it understood that this practice was being phased out. It is certainly true that loans of freezers no longer exist in the frozen food sector, but this was probably inevitable anyway given the growth in countervailing power of the larger retailers, for whom freezer cabinets represent relatively insignificant outlays.

It is difficult to gauge the direct effect of the remedy, but it was probably not substantial. Birds Eye introduced a new discount system (in 1976), partly in response to the investigation, which did not include exclusivity in freezer space and which was more closely linked to costs. However, it reserved the right to pay additional discounts to supermarkets, reflecting their growth in importance as large customers.

Table 8.2 Frozen foods, market shares (%)

	1974	1984	% change 1974–84
Birds Eye	31	25	– 19
Own-brands	17	33	+ 94
Others (incl. Ross, Findus)	52	42	– 19

Source: OFT files.

More generally, however, the market was overtaken by other events. These wider developments are described by Sutton (1991, pp. 190-97), who designates the period from the mid-1970s as the 'third phase' in the development of the market: the period of the rise of retailers' own-brands. This resulted from two effects: (i) an increasing share of the retail market cornered by supermarkets at the expense of the smaller retailers (who usually do not have own labels); and (ii) greater penetration of own-brands within the larger retailers. Faced with these developments, branded products produced by Birds Eye (but also other brands) inevitably lost market share. Birds Eye's market share declined in the decade following the report (Table 8.2), and this was matched by a corresponding growth in supermarket own-brand sales. However, the other majors also lost share in similar proportions, and this suggests that Birds Eye's decline had more to do with the growth of own-brands than the removal of the vertical restraint *per se*. Significantly, similar developments were occurring in other countries, in which Unilever was also, more often than not, the market leader and we believe that these changes would have occurred with or without the report.

The conclusion in this case, therefore, is that it is unlikely that the remedy played a decisive role in increasing competition in this market. Rather, it was overshadowed by other events occurring at the same time: notably, the low price entry of supermarket own-brands. This contrasts markedly with the ice cream case considered next where own-brands have not been a significant feature, and where strong competition concerns still remain.

8.4 ICE CREAM (1979, 1994)

8.4.1 Case Summary

This is another example of exclusive practices by, in this case, the manufacturers of 'impulse' ice cream in their relationships with retailers. There were three dimensions to exclusive purchasing in this case:

(i) outlet exclusivity, where manufacturers require that retailers should not stock rival products,

(ii) freezer exclusivity, where manufacturers provide retailers with freezer cabinets on preferential terms, on the condition that the retailer sells only their product from that freezer, and

(iii) exclusive wholesale distribution, where ice cream is distributed to the retailer by carriers who are not allowed to deliver any other make.

The industry was first investigated in 1979, at which time it was an almost classic example of symmetric duopoly, with Birds Eye Wall's (BEW, owned by Unilever) and Lyons Maid (LM, owned by Allied Lyons) each having market shares in the region of 45 per cent, with most of the remaining 10 per cent accounted for by 34 much smaller firms. The MMC report found that competition between BEW and LM was limited, and concluded in particular that the practice of 'outlet exclusivity' should be abandoned. The MMC argued that this practice (which had already, in fact, been discontinued by BEW in 1975) restricted the supply of ice cream to retailers and especially constrained the opportunities for growth by small manufacturers. Significantly, however, the Commission made no recommendations against exclusivity of freezers.[12]

In the 15 years following the report, there were four major developments in market structure:

(i) BEW increased its market share: its share of 'wrapped impulse' ice cream, which accounts for 70 per cent of the reference products, had risen to 67 per cent by the early 1990s.[13]

(ii) LM suffered a major loss of share, having only 11 per cent of 'wrapped impulse' ice cream by the early 1990s.

(iii) LM was acquired by Nestlé in late 1992.[14]

(iv) Mars entered the market in 1989 and achieved a 14 per cent share of 'wrapped impulse' products by 1993.

Significantly then, the market is now dominated by three large multinational firms, who also hold leading positions in many other countries.

The industry was reinvestigated in 1993/4, but this time with the reference limited solely to freezer exclusivity. The Commission came to two important conclusions. First, freezer exclusivity was deemed not to be against the public interest. Second, BEW's 'concessionaire system' (effectively entailing exclusive wholesale distribution) was found to be outside the Commission's terms of reference. The MMC, therefore, made no recommendations for undertakings to be sought from the referred firms. However, exclusive wholesale distribution has remained a contentious issue, as will become apparent below.

Purely in terms of how we were to conduct our investigation, this case posed similar problems to those for films (see below). In both cases, we are considering the effectiveness of a remedy put into place 10–15 years ago, but against the backcloth of a much more recent reinvestigation. While the second MMC report provides valuable new information with which to supplement our interviews, it was difficult to focus the interviewees' attention on the first MMC report. As a result, many of the opinions we received can be found already in print in the 1994 report and/or relate to the controversy since that report concerning exclusive wholesale distribution.

Our primary aim is to examine the efficacy of the 1979 remedy, that is, the banning of exclusive outlets. Nevertheless, *both* reports are relevant: the very fact that there was a second investigation implies some doubts about the efficacy of the original remedy. Had the MMC subsequently decided in 1994 that further remedies *were* called for, this would in itself have constituted a *prima facie* case for dismissing the original remedy as ineffective. In the event, the MMC did not recommend further remedies; but this means that, in making our assessment, we almost inevitably imply a judgement on the Commission's 1994 conclusions. In short, whether or not one believes the original remedy was effective will depend, in part, on whether one believes that the second report came to the 'right' conclusions. For this reason, our interviews were concerned as much with the 1994 report as with the original 1979 report.

8.4.2 Interviews

Since the 1994 report, and indeed during our own investigation, this case has been the subject of public debate.[15] It is also closely linked with complaints made by Mars to the European Commission about BEW's (more correctly, Unilever's) similar practices in Ireland and Germany. The controversial and contested nature of the case is also reflected in the range of alternative opinions we received, although nearly all respondents were critical of the MMC's judgement. Furthermore, in this case more than any other in our sample, the conduct of the investigation itself was criticised in many quarters. In other cases, respondents have invariably complimented the MMC on its thoroughness and fair-mindedness – even when its conclusions have been the 'wrong' ones from the respondents' viewpoint. But in this case, opinion was less favourable. Some criticisms were of a general nature: we were told that the MMC had insufficient awareness of the retailing context, and that it chose to completely ignore some evidence. But others were more specific: it 'showed inconsistency with previous judgements (notably frozen foods, 1976)', 'failed to recognise the significance of exclusivity in distribution', and 'revealed a prior presumption that vertical restrictions were not intrinsically anti-competitive but were always driven by efficiency considerations'.

We sought opinions from customers (retailers and consumer representatives) and rivals. At a trivial level, the 1979 remedy was effective. Clearly, exclusive outlets were abandoned, BEW had already done this prior to the 1979 report anyway, and LM kept to its undertakings to do so subsequently. Casual empiricism is sufficient to establish that many retail outlets now supply more than one make of impulse ice cream, and the 1994 report includes conclusive statistical evidence which confirms this. One respondent suggested that one other, almost immediate, consequence of the remedy was the demise of LM in the marketplace, but the consensus opinion is that this probably reflected more on general mismanagement, a reduction in advertising and a parent which was more interested in its other lines of business.

There was no suggestion, however, that it was the remedy that encouraged Mars' significant entry into the industry. This is also easily confirmed by pointing to Mars' simultaneous entry into the market in other countries: this was obviously entry motivated by product innovation, supported by strong spill-overs in brand loyalty from the adjacent chocolate bar industry and large-scale advertising. Perhaps its entry would have been more difficult had outlet exclusivity remained, but Mars believes (and has claimed publicly) that penetration would have been even greater in the absence of the other vertical restrictions which still remain.

The 1994 MMC report documents (in a rather misleading way, see pp. 19–20) some other new entrants; in fact *de novo* entry has been minimal – even the most conspicuous other firm, Haagen-Dazs, has succeeded in gaining only a small share of the impulse market. In the interviews, we explored at some length the difficulties faced by potential entrants and, equally important, the barriers to growth by existing small independent firms.[16] There is no doubt that entry is difficult, even without outlet exclusivity, given that freezer exclusivity and exclusive wholesale distribution remain. Moreover, there is little doubt that BEW, in particular, enjoys a first mover advantage – it has been the market leader for many years, and is able to reinforce this position with large-scale advertising. It is true that Mars was able to establish a significant place in the market, but only on the back of strong existing brand loyalty, heavy advertising and scale economies emanating from its multinational operations. As was explained to us, Mars is the exception which proves the rule.

Faced then with retail outlets inclined to maintain a first freezer supplied by BEW (and in larger retailers perhaps a second, smaller Mars freezer), smaller manufacturers have little room for manoeuvre. One respondent explained that, in these circumstances, it had decided to concentrate its sales effort on 'second tier shops (that is, not chains) and convenience stores'. He explained that, although his firm also 'puts out' freezers to retailers, it cannot hope to police them. They tend to compete, therefore, by offering retailers larger margins – 'there is no point in having a lower list price – this would just be taken as indicative of lower quality; and anyway the retailers would merely take larger margins'.[17]

The 'concessionaires system' of distribution, introduced by BEW following the first report, was also subject to some fierce criticism. Under this system, individuals or firms (often ex-employees and sometimes ex-wholesale customers of other manufacturers) are contracted to deliver exclusively Walls ice cream to retail outlets. There is some debate (which was reflected in our interviews) on the extent of this exclusivity; indeed, this has spilled over into accusations that BEW may have misled the MMC (in this respect). There is little doubt that these distributors are exclusive to BEW – they do not deliver other makes. Thus other manufacturers are effectively denied access to a large part of the ice cream delivery sector – they must either establish their own distribution network (at substantial capital cost) or, perhaps, use general frozen food wholesalers. Even if this is possible, individual retailers may be disinclined to have multiple deliveries of ice-cream – it is simpler to deal with just one distributor. In any event, a number of firms saw this as a key barrier to entry or expansion by smaller firms. At least two of BEW's rivals believe that the distributors should be allowed to carry products other than Walls'. It was also suggested to us that some foreign importers decided not to enter the impulse market precisely because of this distribution system. The contrast was also made with the case of chocolate, where there is effective competition from smaller makes (for example, from Belgian imports) because of the absence of exclusive purchasing in chocolates.

8.4.3 Conclusions

The remedy of prohibiting outlet exclusivity *per se* has probably helped increase competition at the margin; inter-brand competition within individual retail outlets is now possible – so long as the shops are prepared to operate more than one freezer, although many are not, due to limited space and sales potential. In any event, subsequent experience strongly suggests that more wide-ranging remedies were required following the first report. If competition has increased (due to the entry of Mars), this is in spite of the remaining vertical restrictions, rather than because of the remedy. In effect, we disagree with the conclusion of the 1994 report concerning freezer exclusivity; and we believe it is unfortunate that the Commission was not able to consider exclusive distribution by wholesalers. Exclusivity in both forms has acted as a barrier to entry and softened inter-brand competition, enabling BEW to set high prices and earn high profits. Given the outcome of the 1994 report, this dominance seems likely to continue, at least in the medium term.[18]

8.5 FILMS (1983, 1994)

8.5.1 Case Summary

Competition in this industry has been the subject of concern for many years. At the heart of the problem are the strong vertical linkages which have existed between the three stages of production, distribution and exhibition. These have included a variety of arrangements, notably exclusive or restrictive distribution and tie-ins. On the one hand, those undertaking these practices (in this case, often firms linked to the Hollywood studios) justify them by pointing to the need to spread the risk associated with high demand uncertainty, and to maintain clear vertical information channels in order to coordinate planning.[19] On the other hand, critics complain about potential foreclosure (in this case, the independent film makers, distributors and exhibitors) and possibly collusion between the majors.

The 1983 report[20] found scale monopolies in distribution for Columbia–EMI–Warner Distributors and United International Pictures (UK) – both of which had ownership ties with the Hollywood studios; and, in exhibition, for EMI Cinemas and Rank Leisure. The MMC judged that two vertical restraints practised by these companies were against the public interest: 'alignment' and 'barring'. Alignment was an arrangement under which distributors would always offer the first run of a film to either EMI or Rank, but not both. This restricted competition between both the main exhibitors and the main distributors (that is, both intra- and inter-brand competition). Barring was a system of determining the order in which competing cinemas could obtain access to a copy of a film. First run cinemas would nearly always be either EMI or Rank, and other exhibitors were further disadvantaged when the former obtained runs of unknown duration, depending on the commercial success of the film. This often effectively foreclosed the market to independent exhibitors. The Commission considered recommending divestment of some cinemas by the majors as a remedy for alignment, but decided against this because of the industry's continued decline in sales. However, it did recommend that barring be prohibited, and that popular films should not be exhibited for more than four weeks in a particular cinema unless they were also made available to all other competing cinemas.

In fact, the proposals encountered considerable resistance, with Rank refusing to sign the undertakings. The case was only 'resolved' when the Secretary of State eventually issued an order. This solution was unsatisfactory for two reasons. First, it only emerged six years after the publication of the MMC report, and second it dropped some of the MMC's recommendations: it merely banned barring which excluded exhibitors and/or distributors where they were unwilling to take more than one film, in effect a combination of tie-ins and exclusive distribution.

In the years following the 1983 report, there have been a number of important developments, notably:

(i)   A reversal in the long-run decline in cinema attendances – attendances finally bottomed out in 1984, and since then the market has approximately doubled in size.

(ii) The emergence, and subsequent rapid expansion, of multiplex cinemas.

(iii) Various changes in the structure and ownership of the distribution and exhibition stages.

(iv) A reinvestigation by the MMC in 1994.

8.5.2 Interviews

Our first objective in the interviews was to establish the reasons for the
turnaround in cinema audiences. Various reasons were given. Most argued
that it was due to a combination of better quality films, better equipped
cinemas, greater TV advertising and wider availability of 'blockbuster'
films to the consumer. The improved quality of the cinemas and wider
accessibility of films is undoubtedly a consequence of the appearance and
substantial growth of multiplex cinemas. This was driven by the highly
successful entry of three new firms, UCI, National Amusements and Warner
Theatres, operating multiplex sites. Up to £500 million has been invested
by new entrants in cinemas in the last ten years. By 1994, they had created
45 new multiplex sites and had market shares (by receipts) of 21 per cent, 8
per cent and 5 per cent respectively. UCI had just overtaken Odeon (Rank)
as number two in the market, and was only 6 per cent behind the leader –
MGM Cinemas. The incumbents also moved into multiplex operations, and
so, by 1994, there were 71 multiplexes in total, accounting for about 10 per
cent of all cinemas, but 40 per cent of total admissions.[21]

It was the unanimous view of everyone we spoke to that the emergence of
these modern, comfortable and well-furnished cinemas had transformed
cinema-going into a 'night out' in which the film itself was only one part of
the overall product.[22] However, nobody suggested that this was related to or
activated by the MMC intervention, and, indeed, it is difficult to see how it
could have been. It is evident that the independent cinemas (that is, those
most affected by vertical restrictions) have found it difficult to compete with
the majors in terms of modernisation, comfort and location. Nevertheless,
UCI attracted much praise in the interviews – even from competitors – for
their initiative in developing new cinemas.

This was probably the main change of significance in market structure,
but there have also been various changes in ownership. Since these are
complex and well-documented in the 1994 MMC report (pp. 29–30,
Appendix 4.1), we only highlight three points here. First, there were
changes in the structure of distribution, but it is still true that the five main
distributors are all owned by the Hollywood studios.[23] Truly independent
distributors remain relatively marginal in terms of market share, over-reliant
on the success or otherwise of individual films, and inevitably
disadvantaged by the fact that the Hollywood studios will place their films
with one or another of their own distributors. Second, the major entrant on
the exhibition side, UCI, is, in fact, linked by ownership (as are the other
multiplex specialists) to Hollywood. While this clearly raises their

bargaining potential, it was stressed to us (and not contested by others) that they have been run quite independently as self-standing concerns. Third, until very recently, both MGM Inc. (distributor) and MGM Cinemas were owned by Crédit Lyonnais (by virtue of a loan default). Again, however, it appears that they have been operated as quite separate businesses.[24]

There is no reason to link these changes to the MMC remedy. Indeed, vertical integration remains a bone of contention for many people in the industry. Clearly, this is most obvious in the links between production and distribution, and this attracted adverse comment from some interviewees. It is argued that this gives the leading distributors a first mover advantage over independent distributors; and, in turn, this squeezes out non-US film makers, who most need a thriving independent distribution sector. It has to be said that neither the MMC's 1983 recommendations, nor those in the 1994 report, were really designed to rectify this situation, and one suspects that this issue will remain on the agenda well into the future.

In summary then, none of the broader developments in the industry can be attributed to the MMC remedy. Indeed, amongst our interviewees, the prevailing opinion was that the prohibition of barring had had, at most, a minor beneficial effect on the state of competition. The typical response was either that there was no problem in the first place, or that major vertical restrictions still remained. Of course, complaints to the OFT about restrictions (by independent cinemas, frustrated by their lack of access to new films, and by the British Film Institute) have continued since the 1983 report.

Given that the order was not put in place until 1989, it is a telling comment on the lack of effectiveness of the remedy that a further enquiry by the Commission was considered necessary as early as September 1993. The main reason appears to have been that the DGFT was concerned about complaints from independent cinemas that they were denied access to popular films, and, more generally, about the extent of vertical integration (and alignment) in the industry.

The MMC identified a number of problem areas in this case – notably, alignment, exclusivity, refusal to supply, minimum exhibition periods and restrictions on screen use. Of these, alignment and minimum exhibition periods had been features of the 1983 report and are the subject of prospective undertakings at the time of writing. On alignment, there was general (but not unanimous) agreement amongst respondents that this practice was now less of a problem than it had been. As the MMC reports, there were currently only 20 remaining aligned locations throughout the country. But, more importantly, the main multiplex operators are not victim to this practice;[25] as one explained to us 'the distributors are only too ready to provide us with prints – it is clearly in their own interests'. Nevertheless, the removal of remaining alignments would undoubtedly have beneficial effects for the independent exhibitors.[26]

Turning to minimum exhibition periods, the MMC recommended, in its 1994 report, that these be restricted to no more than two weeks on first release and one week subsequently. This was not popular with some respondents, but it does not appear to have excited much opposition – 'no doubt people can live with it' said one respondent.

In fact, restrictions on screen use attracted more interest. This refers to a commitment by the exhibitor to screen the film at all normal showing times during its 'run'. One respondent suggested that this is something on which the MMC might have intervened, but another defended the MMC's decision to do nothing because, in his view, it was unfair to restrict the commercial judgement of distributors. In fact, this latter remark epitomises the defence of the majors. In a similar vein, one person dismissed the claims of the independent exhibitors in the following terms: 'independents want the right to a print, but they don't want to take the risk. Are they prepared to take it in advance? (that is they expect the West End to take the risk). The countervailing power of the majors can often work to the independents' advantage in bidding down the distributors'. Another argued that 'you can't blame the distributors for not giving them first access. Not only do they offer smaller audiences, but also the quality of their cinemas is not so good – with useless facilities, no car parks, etc.'[27]

8.5.3 Conclusions

There seems to be general agreement that the remedy put into place after the 1983 report had little impact. The prohibitions that were introduced may have been marginally beneficial, but the failure to introduce other orders only led eventually to the need for a further investigation and new recommendations on other vertical restraints. Indeed, the very fact that a second investigation was deemed necessary, and that it judged that further control of the remaining restraints was necessary, is the most powerful testament to the ineffectiveness of the original remedy. If anti-competitive practices have lessened (and we are unconvinced this is so), it is because of innovation and new entry by majors in the exhibition sector; and even this has scarcely benefited independent exhibitors, distributors and film makers.

8.6 POSTAL FRANKING MACHINES (1986)

8.6.1 Case Summary

This case was concerned with the supply, repair and maintenance of postal franking machines in the UK. The market was dominated by two firms: Pitney Bowes (PB) (a subsidiary of the US multinational, Pitney Bowes Inc.), with a share of about 60 per cent of newly installed postal franking machines and 57 per cent of the maintenance and repair market, and Roneo Alcatel (RA) (owned by CIT of France), with a market share of 29 per cent of newly installed machines and 36 per cent of the maintenance and repair market. The MMC found there was a scale monopoly in favour of both firms in both markets and that, in the case of PB, very high profits were being earned. It judged that competition was severely restricted, partly due to rules operated by the Post Office to protect its own revenue, and partly due to various restraints operated by the two leading firms.

The main issues here were tie-ins and the methods of supply. Each manufacturer dealt directly with customers using sales representatives,[28] and there were no independent dealers in machines. In addition, PB only leased its machines and both PB and RA required machines to be returned to them after use. Hence, no second hand market was allowed to develop. Most important for present purposes, the leading producers operated a tie (distinguished as the main problem in this case) between the supply and maintenance of machines. Hence, there was no separate maintenance market. And finally, PB operated its own finance company, PB leasing, which it typically used to finance its sales.

In making its recommendations, the MMC noted that, whilst PB was highly profitable, RA (and the other smaller producers) were not making substantial profits. Hence, it rejected price controls as a remedy, since this was likely to damage PB's rivals more than PB itself. Instead, as the main remedy, it proposed termination of practices along the following lines. First, PB and RA were to allow independent maintenance firms (approved by the Post Office) to provide service and repair cover for their machines. Second, they were not to insist that machines be returned to them after use (thereby preventing the possibility of a second hand market). Third, they were to provide parts for their machines at reasonable prices. Fourth, they were to provide customers with a current price list containing information on the price of machines, terms of their supply, and so on. (In the case of PB, a statement that leases could be obtained from other leasing companies was also required.) And fifth, they were to provide information to the OFT to enable it to monitor compliance. Undertakings to these effects were given in August 1988. In addition (although not part of the undertakings) PB agreed to drop its policy of only leasing machines to customers, now offering customers the alternative option to buy.

8.6.2 Interviews

In reviewing this case, it is important to recognise the central role played by the Post Office[29] in this market. In 1984/5 franked mail raised about £770 million in revenue for the Post Office – about 30 per cent of its total mail revenue. Clearly, the main, and legitimate, concern of the Post Office is to protect its revenue from faults or fraud. In order to do this, it stipulated that all new machines be tested by its own engineers before being brought onto the market, and, once on the market, that they be regularly inspected against faults or fraud. It also required that only registered firms be used to maintain and inspect machines and that all manufacturers, distributors and maintenance firms post a bond with it against risk of fraud or faulty machines. At the time of writing, the value of this bond is set at one quarter of a million pounds for each manufacturer, distributor or maintenance firm.

A consequence of these rules is that there are significant entry costs (in terms of having machines tested, paying bonds, setting up distribution and maintenance networks, and so on) in this market. Perhaps surprisingly, most of the firms we interviewed did not think these requirements were particularly unreasonable. Several commented that 'all suppliers faced the same costs and so were at no special disadvantage in entering the market'. The main reason for this acceptance is that there are very few firms in the world which manufacture postal franking machines and they face regulatory restraints of one sort or another in every market in which they operate. Hence, they are familiar with the need for regulatory compliance and are ready to operate within regulatory rules. However, several firms did comment that the bonds required were quite onerous, although again they accepted that all firms were in the same boat.[30] Hence as far as production and sale is concerned, they felt the restraints acted even-handedly for all firms.

Whilst, in principle, the Post Office rules do not seem to disallow independent maintenance of machines (or the creation of a second hand market), in practice they were interpreted by the Post Office and the leading firms to mean just that. Hence, there were no independent maintenance organisations in the market and producers and distributors simply maintained their own machines. In addition, firms required customers to return used machines to them in line with Post Office requirements that meters (at least) should not go astray. And PB, in particular, by only leasing its machines, ensured that none found their way onto the second hand market.

In its report, the MMC recommended that the Post Office modify its rules to allow more competition. Negotiations on this took place between the Post Office and the OFT following the report and the Post Office agreed to make a number of changes to its rules (OFT Annual Report, 1987). In particular, it agreed to reduce the number of inspection visits required of firms; to allow independent maintenance firms to maintain machines (provided they were approved); and to allow new and second hand machines to be sold through independent office equipment suppliers. These changes are clearly in line with the recommendations of the report and, together with the undertakings by the firms themselves, were expected to introduce more competition into the market.

It is doubtful, however, that these changes have had much effect. As far as industry structure is concerned, there has been, admittedly, some change in shares on the sales side of the market, although PB remains the dominant firm, if with a smaller market share of about 50 per cent of the installed base in 1990 (see Table 8.3). Roneo Alcatel (now Neopost)[31] remains the second ranked firm with about 33 per cent of the market although the third firm, Hasler, has increased its market share to about 13 per cent. Three other small firms currently operate in the market including one new entrant, Addressing Systems International (ASI), which entered in 1990, supplying machines produced by the French company, Secap.

These changes do not appear to be the result of the remedies. At the time of the report, the smaller firms were in a poor financial state – especially RA, which was about to be reorganised following its acquisition by Alcatel, and Scriptomatic and Europak had only recently entered. Therefore, it would be fair to characterise the industry as in disequilibrium at that time, and one might argue that the subsequent strengthening of the smaller firms' positions would have happened regardless of the remedy.[32]

In any event, the main impact of the remedies should have been felt, if anywhere, on the maintenance side of the market. Here, there appears to have been no real change.[33] All firms continue to maintain their own machines and there are still no independent maintenance firms. Most of our respondents felt that the lack of change in the market was mainly due to the unwillingness of the Post Office to change its procedures. This is particularly true in respect of third party maintenance. Moreover, absence

Table 8.3 Postal franking machines, market shares (%)

	1984	1990
Pitney Bowes	60	50
Roneo Alcatel	29	33
Hasler	6	13
Scriptomatic	2	2
Europak	2	2
ASI	-	0

Note: The zero for ASI denotes a market share of less than one half of one per cent.

Source: OFT files.

of entry does not seem to be the result of a shortage of potential entrants – a number of companies (including at least one large one) have expressed an interest, and three of our interviewees confirmed that if independent maintenance was allowed they would enter the market.[34]

The only effective change which the Post Office did allow was the entry of ASI in 1990. Whilst ASI acts as a distributor of Secap machines, it uses some local dealers to service its machines and these are covered by a general maintenance bond paid for by ASI. This means that, for Secap machines, some maintenance is, in fact, done at arm's length. However, ASI is still a very small firm at time of writing, certainly the smallest in the market. Interestingly, one of its local dealers in Scotland (perhaps taking the undertakings at face value) tried to enter the maintenance market for PB's machines in the early 1990s. This led to a court case, which PB eventually lost, although by this time, the firm had already been forced out of the market.

ASI apart, there has been no other progress on third party entry into maintenance. We were told that the Royal Mail was concerned about the possibility that 'cowboys' would enter the maintenance market and that this would lead to an increase in fraud and 'missing' machines. We were also told that they did not really support the sale of machines because this also increased the chances of machines going 'missing' and (possibly) being used fraudulently. Hence (ideally) they would prefer that there was no third party maintenance and no dealers in machines. However, the Royal Mail recognises that there is a competition issue involved here and is currently reviewing its rules on this and related matters – with the encouragement of the OFT.[35]

Turning more briefly to the non-maintenance features of the report, several respondents noted that the undertakings could be circumvented in that they did not apply to refurbished machines. PB, for example, recently engaged in a strategy of selling refurbished machines at very low prices in order to gain customers, who were then required to pay relatively high prices for maintenance.

Another feature of the market prior to the report concerned the activities of salesman. It was alleged that some salesman had engaged in fairly questionable tactics in selling postal franking machines to customers.[36] These tactics have apparently continued (at least to some extent) since the report. Several firms commented that a number of cases had recently come to light involving both PB and Neopost. In one case, in 1993, the Consumer Affairs Section of the OFT had threatened to remove Neopost's consumer credit licence following a number of complaints. In the event, this drastic step was not taken because Neopost was able to convince the OFT that it would take the necessary steps to rectify the problem. These included improved training and discipline of salesman and some salesmen were sacked.

On a slightly more positive note, it appears that the remedies have led to increased availability of information to customers. The leading firms (as well as others) now publish price lists and there is some independent evaluation of franking machines in the relevant trade journal (*What to Buy for Business*, published by Reed International). Several respondents argued that the typical customer now gets a better price and a better quality product than before, and this was in part due to this MMC undertaking. Other respondents, however, were more sceptical and argued that customers still frequently paid excessive prices for machines and service contracts (for example, because they were sold machines which were bigger than they actually required). This seems to come down to a lack of care in spending sometimes considerable sums in buying (or leasing) machines.

Finally, with an eye on the future, we should mention that various respondents anticipated significant change in industry structure as a result of new innovations. One is the remote crediting of meters, which will allow customers to credit machines by computer link (instead of going to the Post Office) – this is being introduced widely at the present time. Even more important, however, for the future structure of the industry is the likely introduction of computer-based systems to actually frank the mail. The Royal Mail told us that they believe this could become a reality in a very short period (possibly as short as a year) and that this would bring dramatic structural changes. The Royal Mail is actively engaged in testing PC-based technology and this is also being tested in the US. Significantly, these machines can be easily produced by firms not already in the market (for example, computer and office machinery manufacturers) and this could lead to a radically different structure within a few years.

8.6.3 Conclusions

The most striking feature in this case is the lack of entry on the maintenance side – arguably, the only real potential indicator that ties have been effectively reduced. The main reason for this absence of entry is that, although the Post Office revised its requirements for maintenance firms, in practice it has not been prepared to allow entry to take place. This highlights a feature common to a number of other cases (for example, opium derivatives, domestic gas appliances, electricity meters) where the real bar to competition lies with barriers created by government and/or public corporations. Faced with this, the remedies following MMC investigation have been virtually impotent in securing effective change in the competitive process.

8.7 FOREIGN PACKAGE HOLIDAYS (1986)

8.7.1 Case Summary

This is a case in which a complex monopoly engaged in a vertical restriction akin to resale price maintenance.[37] The practice was discontinued following the report, but only as a result of orders issued in 1987. Subsequent developments in industry structure have seen increasing vertical integration and this has raised new doubts about anti-competitive behaviour. In November 1996 the industry was referred to the MMC for a second time with vertical integration now the key issue under review.

Foreign package holidays are the product of tour operators. They package together various holiday services (for example, villa rental, air transport, and so on) and sell either directly, or more commonly indirectly, via travel agents, to the general public. In 1985, ABTA (the main trade association which represents both groups) had a membership of about 500 tour operators and five times as many travel agents. The tour operating side was the more concentrated, with the top five firms accounting for over one third of all ATOL (Air Tours Operators Licence) holidays, and the top 20 accounting for about two thirds. The leader was Thomson Travel, with Horizon, British Airways, Intasun and Cosmos also occupying leading positions. The top five travel agents were responsible for about 25 per cent of all foreign package holidays – foreign package holidays accounting for roughly one half of travel agents' business.[38] Agents with multiple branches were becoming increasingly important, and there were five agents who operated more than 100 branches. Leading names at the time were Lunn Poly (owned by Thomson), Thomas Cook, Pickfords and Hogg Robinson.

The case notionally centred around Ilkeston Co-operative Society, which ran a large travel agency. It had devised an innovative and successful scheme in which consumers were given vouchers when they purchased a package holiday. These vouchers could then be exchanged for other, totally unrelated, products elsewhere in that Coop's department stores; in effect, the vouchers were thinly disguised cash discounts. In spite of the fact that other travel agents operated schemes such as free travel insurance or other 'in-kind' travel-related inducements, the main tour operators took exception to Ilkeston's practice. Some reacted by refusing to supply, while others threatened to do so, and it was at this point that the MMC investigation took place.

The Commission ruled against the tour operators and this resulted in the orders being issued in the following year. These orders make it unlawful for operators to prohibit agents from offering inducements, or to refuse to supply where inducements are being offered.

Much was made in the evidence given to the Commission of the right of tour operators to control their own prices. The companies argued that discounting by agents would lead to a price war, the exit of many smaller agents, and possibly price discrimination. Nevertheless, the Commission decided against the operators, arguing that the abolition would encourage more competition at the retail stage, both in terms of price and innovation, and enhance efficiency.

In the decade since the report, demand has continued to grow in the industry, but less rapidly than before (from 4.5 million holidays in 1978, to 9.1 in 1985, to 10.0 in 1995).[39] Thomson has strengthened its position as the leading tour operator and Intasun and Horizon no longer exist.[40] The main operators are now: Thomson, Airtours and First Choice (previously Owners Abroad) and Inspirations. More importantly, there has been significant vertical integration, with the major operators extending their travel agency activities either by acquisition or by opening new sites. Since they have also expanded the scale of these agencies, concentration in the agency part of the industry has increased significantly. Unofficial estimates (provided by one of our interviewees) suggest that Lunn Poly (Thomson) now has about 770 branches, Air Tours (through Going Places) 600 and Thomas Cook about 350.[41]

Thus, increased vertical integration in the industry has become an increasing cause of concern, prompting the DGFT to refer both Thomson and Airtours to the MMC in November 1996. The main issue being investigated by the Commission is whether the leading operators are using their ownership of travel agents to promote their own holidays at the expense of rivals (*Times*, 8 November 1996), to the detriment of consumer choice. It is also suggested that the two leading firms may be able to use their dominant position to set monopoly prices.

8.7.2 Interviews

There is little doubt in this case that the remedy initially worked. The Ilkeston Coop now has the largest single travel agency site in England, with sales in excess of £20 million, and the effect has been to transform it from being a travel agency within a department store to the other way round. Almost immediately following the orders, there was a plethora of price-cutting deals in the industry. These often involved the tour operators doing deals with travel agent chains; but,. especially since 1990, it has been the agents who have (at least superficially) made the running by discounting and chasing market share.

Beyond the immediate consequences of the order, it is difficult to disentangle its effect on subsequent developments in structure and conduct from those accompanying the drive to greater integration by the majors. Smaller agents, unable to match discounts available elsewhere, have been acquired in large numbers by the majors. Likewise, independent operators have been forced into offering integrated agents larger discounts in order to persuade them to stock their brochures. The essential question then, is whether these developments are the consequences of a competitive process, instigated by the order, and now ruthlessly weeding out the inefficient, or whether they are a consequence of the unfair practices of the large integrated majors.

In the interviews, we certainly encountered a variety of criticisms and accusations, some first hand and others not. These varied from general observations about predatory behaviour such as: 'these (vertically integrated) firms can choose where to make their profits, and they operate their agencies as "loss leaders"', to more specific accusations of discriminatory rates of commission against individual firms: 'X can offer bigger discounts to Y than to independent travel agents'; 'Y offers large commission incentives to staff to sell X holidays. The assistants get £5 per X holiday sold'; 'The tour operators with chains of agencies are now abusing their position. X are currently running with a 15% discount'.

We also heard arguments relating to other anti-competitive effects of vertical integration. For example, it was argued that vertically integrated agents demanded high commissions from small tour operators to carry their brochures, compared to in-house brochures. These costs had to be passed on to customers making their holidays look more expensive. Again, it was alleged that integrated firms tended to sell "their own" holidays rather than those of their competitors and would always suggest their holidays (to a particular destination, say) first. Moreover, because customers are typically unaware of the vertical relations within the industry, they do not realise that the advice they might receive is biased to in-house holidays. The result is that the big firms are able to manipulate the market via vertical integration towards their own ends.

Of central theoretical importance here is the condition of entry – for both the independent operators and agents. So long as independent operators are able to enter, possibly with innovative packages (for example, new holiday locations), they should be able to reach the consumer, given a continuing, independent agent sector. At the present time the independent agent sector is still significant (although, arguably, with typically less well-located shops), and independent operators retain a sizeable share of the market. However, under two quite plausible scenarios, the state of competition could change drastically (and quickly) for the worst. The first is a continuing contraction of independent agents. In that case, independent operators would be forced back increasingly on to direct selling, or perhaps downstream entry of their own, acquiring any remaining marginal agencies. The second is reduced opportunity for entry at the operator stage. In this respect, the signs are not good. There seemed to be agreement amongst our interviewees that the total market is near to saturation. Unless consumer tastes can be otherwise manipulated, quite simply, the world is running short of new venues to open up. This is especially worrying for independent operators, as one respondent argued, because the major operators are typically very quick to imitate new locations (often first introduced by the independents) and to colonise them themselves (Mallorca is a classic example historically).

8.7.3 Conclusions

Certainly, it seems fair to suggest that the remedy worked in the short run in this case. However, some of the likely consequences, as predicted at the time, have materialised. There have been increases in both concentration and vertical integration – arguably the obvious (and foreseeable) strategic response of the majors. This now leaves a market which is vulnerable to further strategic behaviour, and strong competition in the future is by no means assured. In this sense, it is difficult to argue that the original remedy has been effective. The fact that a reinvestigation was deemed necessary is an obvious recognition of this, and it is underscored by the fact that conditions have changed not because of some unanticipated exogenous factor, but simply as a result of subsequent behaviour by the investigated firms. Certainly with the benefit of hindsight, one might argue that the Commission should have anticipated this, and widened their recommendations to cover integration as well.[42]

8.8 ARTIFICIAL LOWER LIMBS (1989)

8.8.1 Case Summary

The essential problem in this case was vertical integration between the producers of artificial lower limbs and the service centres where patients are fitted with those limbs, the Artificial Limb and Appliance Centres (ALACs).[43] At the time of the report the two main producers of lower limbs, InterMed and Blatchford, controlled most of the service centres, with InterMed controlling about 70 per cent. This raised two questions; whether the NHS was paying too high a price for prosthetic devices, and whether patients were receiving the highest quality of service possible.

Although it is somewhat unclear who instigated the reference, this appears to be similar to the opium derivatives case (see Chapter 5), in which the government was concerned with the level of spending in certain sectors of the national health service (NHS) – until 1986, all prosthetic services were purchased by the NHS on a cost-plus basis. There were suspicions that InterMed in particular was charging 'high' prices, and that its employees in the treatment centres were favouring InterMed's products over the competition.

In its investigation, the MMC found that both InterMed and Blatchford had scale monopolies, although InterMed was the dominant firm. In the case of Blatchford, it found there were no grounds for public concern. In the case of InterMed, however, the MMC found that the monopoly acted against the public interest: it was shown to have used its market power to set 'high' prices and profits, and it had also used 'refusal to supply' on two occasions as a means of extracting higher prices from the NHS. In addition, it was suggested that the firm had used its dominant interest in the service centres to promote its own products and components, and that the service centres were inefficient and provided a low level of patient care.

In fact, the cost to the NHS of prosthetic services was earlier addressed in the McColl Report, which was published in January 1986. A committee, under the chairmanship of Professor Ian McColl (an eminent surgeon), was set up in May 1984, with a remit to evaluate the adequacy and efficiency of all ALAC services in England.[44] Its main conclusion was that, under the existing system, the DHSS was unable to control costs, prices or profit levels; the main reason being the cost-plus system employed. It also came to the conclusion that the treatment centres were inefficiently managed. It recommended that the cost-plus contracts for prosthetic services (both components, and the management of ALACs) be abolished, and that specific prices should be agreed for these services. It also recommended that all artificial limbs should be available in all centres, irrespective of the company which ran the centre, and that the skills of prosthetists be improved so that the workers at the ALACs be able to act more independently of the manufacturers. This last point is vital, as it led to the division of the industry into the supply of components and the management of the centres.

The other major conclusion of the McColl Report was that an independent body be created to manage artificial limb appliance centre services. In effect, this implied a body to arrange and define the contracts for providing the service at point of delivery in the 80 or so ALACs. This agency came into being on 1 July 1987 as the Disablement Services Authority (DSA), set up by the government to provide prosthetic services, instead of an integrated service being managed by the DHSS. It was created for four years, in order to oversee the changes, at which point the responsibility for the management of these contracts would revert to the NHS.

The DSA was in the process of reporting at the time of the MMC investigation, and indeed would have completed the major changes to the system had InterMed not sought a court injunction. InterMed claimed that the DSA had promised to maintain the status quo in awarding contracts in the first round under the new system. Whilst the case was ultimately rejected by the courts, this action did delay the DSA's changes for two years.

In the meantime, the major recommendation of the MMC report was that InterMed be forced to divest itself of one of its two large operations, Hanger or Vessa, and that Blatchford should not be allowed to purchase the business. This was clearly an attempt to introduce more competition into a small market with only a few players. There were few imports, although in terms of supplying components, a German firm, Otto Bock, has increased sales in recent years. The MMC also noted, however, that the new DSA contracts were shortly to be released, and so it also recommended that no remedies should be introduced until the effect of the new contracts could be assessed.

In the event, the first round of tenders led to dramatic changes in the industry, in that InterMed lost control of most of its service centres and it had to close its Scottish subsidiary, Kellie. In the light of these changes, the government decided it was no longer necessary for InterMed to divest more of its operations and the recommendation was shelved.

8.8.2 Interviews

The crucial change, instigated by the DSA, was to introduce competitive tendering for the management of the prosthetic service centres in the UK. Dividing the artificial lower limb business into component manufacture and service meant that the centres could be run by skilled individuals who were independent of the manufacturers, and able to offer a service to the patient based on individual needs. As just mentioned, in the first round of tenders after this change, InterMed's share of the service centres fell dramatically – from over 70 per cent to around 15 per cent. The reason for this appears to have been that InterMed greatly underestimated the competition and, basically, bid too high. One respondent commented that InterMed did not believe that the government would allow such a dramatic change in the control of the centres and, hence, did not bid low. This respondent also noted that InterMed were genuinely surprised when it lost so many contracts and that, had it bid competitively, it would probably have retained control over many of the centres. Be this as it may, the actual result of this first round of bids was that InterMed was (as one firm put it) 'washed away'. From a position of controlling 25 service centres in 1988 InterMed (now just called Vessa) has just two today. Whilst one of these is its large flagship centre at Roehampton it is clear what a dramatic change happened in this market.

As far as manufacturing is concerned InterMed closed its subsidiary in Scotland, Kellie,[45] due to a lack of demand and Hanger was also effectively closed and merged with Vessa (although some Hanger products are still produced). Industry estimates suggest that Vessa today has only about 10 per cent of the UK market in components, compared to 70 per cent in 1988. The main beneficiary has been Blatchford, which has now grown from being a small family firm in the 1980s to become the dominant supplier in the market today with a market share of about 80 per cent. Most of our respondents argued that the reason for this success has been the superior quality of its products (in particular, its 'endolite' system) which are very popular with the service centres. It has also put considerable effort into training staff in the centres which has made it 'popular with the staff'. The other main manufacturer is Otto Bock with a market share of about 10 per cent. Bock is regarded as having good quality products, although they are seen as expensive and this accounts for its relatively stable market share since 1989. (Vessa is also regarded as having some good products – notably its 'foot' which is often used with Blatchford's 'leg'.)

As far as the service centres are concerned, a number of small independents (including existing managers) were able to enter the market in 1990 whilst Blatchford increased its market share, as did Steeper.[46] Most of our respondents commented that there was fierce competition[47] for new contracts even for the smallest service centres and this has cut NHS costs significantly. One respondent commented that the expertise available in the centres was not as high now as previously, although even he admitted that the centres were now more flexible than they had been in meeting patient needs. Other respondents commented much more favourably on the system emphasising better service, better quality products and lower real prices for limbs. The general feeling seems to be that there have been general all-round improvements in the industry over the last five years.

Whilst, initially, a number of small firms entered the service side of the market, some consolidation has since taken place. One firm suggested that Steeper and Blatchford now dominate the market. Several respondents raised the worry that the vertical tie between production and services through Blatchford's control of service centres has led to a similar situation to that of InterMed although the general view seemed to be that the market is working much more effectively now. The major question as far as vertical integration is concerned is whether Blatchford uses its control of service centres to promote its own products. None of our respondents thought this was the case, however, believing that Blatchford is justifiably the leader due to its superior products. It was noted, however, that in a competitive bidding system Blatchford may have an advantage because it can cross-subsidise its service bids from its sale of products, and this may have happened in some cases.

Most of our respondents thought there had been substantial gains for the public and the NHS from these changes. As far as the NHS is concerned, healthy competition for service contracts has contributed significantly to reducing the cost of the centres. Customers have also gained with better quality products, lower real prices (one respondent suggested they are about 20 per cent lower in real terms compared to 1989) and better service. Currently, contracts for the service centres run for three years, with a roll-over of up to two years, and this seems to have been effective in promoting competition.

Clearly, the crucial change in this case was the introduction of competitive bidding in 1990, and InterMed's failure to win many of the contracts. Since the DSA was set up in July 1987 (that is, prior to the referral to the MMC in December 1987) a question mark arises over whether it was necessary to have an MMC investigation at all. There was some difference of opinion amongst our respondents over this. One firm argued that the MMC had no real effect in this case because the DSA would have introduced the new tendering system anyway. In this respondent's view, the MMC investigation was used as a 'backstop', to be followed if the new tendering system had not brought about change. In the event, this was unnecessary. However, others felt that the intervention did play a useful role in keeping the issue in the public eye, and making it more likely that the DSA would take a firm line on the new system. One firm argued that members of the DSA were the same civil servants who had permitted the situation to develop in the first place, and that the MMC investigation had effectively encouraged the DSA to take firm action. It was also suggested that, without the threat of MMC intervention, the DSA might have become 'bogged down in legal argument with InterMed', resulting in less radical change in the contracts after 1989.[48]

8.8.3 Conclusions

In evaluating this case, there is little doubt that the state of competition has improved since the MMC Report. However, the key judgemental question is how much influence (if any) the MMC had. In our view, there are grounds for believing that the MMC investigation did play a role in maintaining attention on competition problems in the industry and, thereby, supporting the changes introduced by the DSA. It is obviously difficult to quantify the size of such an effect, but the balance of opinion, with which we agree, is that the MMC investigation had a significant, if secondary, influence in the curbing of monopoly power.

8.9 OTHER SIGNIFICANT CASES

Apart from the above, the population includes 25 other cases in which vertical restraints were the main area of concern. Largely for presentational clarity, we have relegated our summaries of most of these cases to the Annex at the end of this chapter, leaving space here to concentrate in more detail on four particularly significant cases. These have been singled out for special attention because of their 'high profile' nature and because they provide further illustrations of some key issues already raised earlier in the chapter.

We start with petrol and beer, and then consider cars and fine fragrances. Both petrol and beer are very large markets (as, of course, is cars), both entailed exclusive purchasing and vertical integration but the MMC came to very different conclusions in each case.

8.9.1 Petrol (1979, 1990)

Petrol supply in the UK is dominated by the major oil companies – a group of 11 multinational firms, the largest being Esso, Shell, BP, Texaco and Mobil. They are responsible for all refining, most of the wholesaling, and a considerable proportion of the retailing of petrol in the UK. Both reports concentrated mainly on the relationship between wholesaling and retailing. Exclusive purchasing was, and still is, the norm: the wholesalers either directly own the petrol stations they supply or they have solus ties with independent retailers, under which the retailer is contracted to sell only one brand of petrol for the duration of the contract (usually five years).

Critics argue that this may unfairly disadvantage independent (that is, non-refining) wholesalers, and independent retailers, and limit inter-brand competition. Entry at the wholesale level obviously requires access to retail outlets, whilst independent retailers depend on equal terms from their suppliers if they are to compete with retail outlets directly owned by those suppliers.

On the other hand, there are clearly tenable efficiency arguments in favour of exclusivity: there are no obvious economies of scope to a retailer in offering more than one brand of petrol, and direct ownership/long-term contracts provide security of supply and encourage a joint interest in investment in petrol station facilities for both parties.

The 1979 report concentrated on these issues, and it also assessed the system of effective price support known as the Selective Retail Price Support scheme. Under this scheme, wholesalers provided their retailers with petrol under favourable terms in areas where they faced competition. The scheme was probably a response to the entry of several small wholesalers who were buying from the Rotterdam market when conditions were favourable. However, the majors successfully argued that price support was employed merely as a response to competitive pressure in different localities. Also, the MMC agreed that the retail market was competitive, with many buyers and sellers. There was no substantive adverse recommendation.

Similar issues surfaced in the second MMC investigation (1990), and again no recommendations were made. In spite of continued growth in the proportion of retail sites owned by the wholesalers, the MMC still believed that the efficiency arguments were persuasive. They were also reassured (i) by the recent entry of a few new wholesalers and significant retailers, and (ii) the apparently low rates of return earned by the majors.

Developments since 1990 have been mixed as far as competition is concerned. On the one hand, a major pro-competitive force has been the rapid inroads made by supermarket chains into the retail market: they have increased their share from about 5 per cent in the late 1980s to over 20 per cent in 1995 – largely as a result of under-cutting prices. On the other hand, wholesale ownership by the majors has continued to grow, the number of independent retail outlets has shrunk rapidly, and, as a result, independent wholesalers have become marginalised. In 1995, Esso introduced its 'Price Watch' scheme; this amounts to targeted local price-cutting, nominally in competition with the supermarkets, but also having the side-effect of forcing many independents out of business. At the time of writing, two of the other majors (BP and Mobil) have merged their UK operations, and further mergers between majors are rumoured. While the supermarket entry has been quite independent of either the MMC investigations or the vertical ties, Esso's (and the other majors) response has clearly been facilitated by their exclusive retail arrangements. In the short run, of course, the consumer has benefited from lower prices, and so long as the majors and supermarkets continue to compete on price, there is perhaps no immediate cause for concern. At the same time, however, the scope for potential competition from independents has shrunk rapidly – in that (admittedly limited) sense, it is debatable whether the MMC's relaxed attitude to exclusivity has been merited.

8.9.2 Beer (1989)

The findings of any MMC report will often attract criticism, but seldom on the scale of the 1989 beer case. This investigation centred around the vertical ties between the brewers and their public houses. Specifically, it involved the number of public houses that were tied to breweries. Vertical ties were either through integration (about 75 per cent of the 60,000 public houses were owned by the brewers) or exclusive purchasing arrangements (about half of the remaining 25 per cent were tied by loans from brewers). The MMC took the view that such extensive exclusivity was against the public interest: any minor efficiency gains (for example, encouraging investment in facilities) being outweighed by the dampening of inter-brand and, in some cases intra-brand, competition. Although this appears to be in direct contrast to its findings in the petrol case, there are significant differences between the two cases. In particular, in contrast to the petrol industry, there are significant local monopolies involved in the supply of beer, and, for this and other reasons, an earlier (1966) report had recommended a 'substantial relaxation' of the tied house system. The essential objective of this was to encourage entry by free houses into the retail market, thereby diluting the effects of the tied system. But, as can be seen in the 1989 report (and an intervening Price Commission report), the 1966 report had had little effect.

The effects of the 1989 case, however, were wide-ranging. Following the MMC's report, there was a concerted publicity campaign by the Brewers Society against its recommendations. Although many commentators argued that these became watered down, no undertakings were agreed, and, ultimately, the Secretary of State issued the so-called Beer Orders. These subsequently received good deal of criticism from many groups involved in the industry, economists and city analysts. There were two major implications of the Beer Orders, first that the 'big five' breweries had to divest themselves of half of their pubs in excess of 2,000, and second, all their tied houses were to be allowed to sell a 'guest beer', that is, one not produced or distributed by their brewery.

It is generally accepted that it was the ruling on divestment that threw the market into chaos with breweries complaining that they were having to conduct a 'fire sale' of their pubs. The initial result of this was that breweries divested themselves of their older inner city pubs, and in some cases small isolated rural ones. Opinion is mixed, however, over whether this increased competition, and, in some cases, it has merely served to reduce competition at a local level – in some localities, one pub now exists where there had been more. Another significant outcome was that several of the smaller breweries purchased pubs from the majors, as a method of increasing their own tied networks.

The other major remedy – the introduction of 'guest beers' in tied pubs – was intended to stimulate inter-brand competition. Again, the results have been mixed: casual empiricism suggests that this has often been effective, but there is also evidence that the major breweries are cooperating on this, supplying guest beers on a reciprocal basis. The net effect, therefore, may have been to increase the horizontal restraints in some cases.

Overall, the industry is now even more concentrated, the top three firms accounting for over 60 per cent of the market, as opposed to 47 per cent prior to the investigation. In addition, prices in pubs have risen well ahead of inflation, even allowing for increases in excise duty and VAT. The main reason for this is that the major companies have had to recoup the cost of implementing the beer orders, which was estimated to be half a billion pounds by the end of 1992. Although the degree of vertical integration may have been reduced, the evidence is that vertical restraints have only been partly diluted. This case appears to be an example of a vertical solution applied to a horizontal problem, with only limited success. However, it would be inappropriate to attribute these effects to the MMC alone, given that the beer orders were significantly different from the MMC's own recommendations.

In the two other cases highlighted in this section, the main focus of attention was exclusive distribution.

8.9.3 New Motor Cars (1992)

Here, the main issue was whether the selective and exclusive distribution (SED) system operated by manufacturers and importers was against the public interest. This was clearly an important case given that about 2 million cars a year were sold in 1990, worth £19 billion (or 3.5 per cent of GDP). In particular, the MMC considered the claim that car prices were higher in the UK than in other countries (especially Holland and Belgium) in the EU.

All the main suppliers in the UK operated (and continue to operate) their own dealership networks. The basic terms under which these operate involve an exclusive distribution agreement with a dealer in a particular area and the refusal to supply cars other than through franchised dealers. In the report, the MMC found some benefits from this system but it also found that a number of agreements were overly restrictive. For example, some agreements limited the total number of cars that could be sold by a dealer in a particular period and/or prevented mergers with dealers in other areas.

The MMC regarded these and other restrictions as unnecessary and recommended that they be dropped. These recommendations were fairly minor, however, and did not affect the basic principle of exclusive distribution. (It has been suggested by some commentators that the MMC may have felt unduly constrained by a desire not to suggest more drastic remedies which had little chance of being enacted, given that they might conflict with the block exemption that cars enjoy under EC legislation.)

The MMC also commissioned a study to consider whether car prices were, in fact, higher in the UK than elsewhere. This found that differentials which appeared to exist were, in part, due to different specifications of cars in the UK and abroad. Also, broad comparisons failed to take account of discounts to list prices often given in the UK. In total, the MMC argued that UK prices were broadly comparable with those in Germany and France, although sometimes higher than those in Belgium and Holland, and it made no recommendation on this issue. It did note, however, that as part of the EU block exemption on SED arrangements (under EU regulation 123/85), parallel importing from other countries in the EU was allowed. This requirement had clearly not worked well for the UK (mainly because of the need to obtain right hand drive cars) and the MMC suggested that the European Commission might look at this. This is an area in which the MMC might have done more, at least in terms of laying down rules under which companies should supply right hand drive cars.[49]

8.9.4 Fine Fragrances (1993)

This is another example of exclusive distribution, in which perfume manufacturers restricted the retail sales of their product to selected outlets. This they justified in terms of quality assurance and the provision of 'expert' information to the customer. In addition, resale price maintenance was employed, to prevent intra-brand competition, and/or to encourage a high quality retail environment for the product.

Perfume is possibly unique, in that the packaging often costs more to produce than does the product itself. Approximately 20 per cent of the retail price accrues to the manufacturer as profit, while 30 per cent is taken by the retailer, 5 per cent covers the cost of the product, and most of the remainder represents fixed costs and tax. The case arose because certain retailers (for example, Superdrug) were proposing to pass on a large proportion of the retailer's 30 per cent share to the consumer in the form of lower prices. This raised obvious opposition from traditional retailers. Similarly, the perfume houses argued that this would allow free riding on the expert advice provided by high cost retailers. (An unusual application of this sort of argument, which is generally associated with the supply of complex machinery, such as cars.) They also argued that, for a luxury product such as perfume, they should be allowed to control the types of outlet stocking their product, and the environment in which it was sold, and, as a luxury item, part of the appeal of perfume was in its reassuringly high price! They claimed that their existing retailers approved of the system of recommended retail prices, and that they threatened a boycott should Superdrug be supplied.

Perhaps surprisingly, the Commission agreed with the perfume houses. While the 'technical efficiency' arguments carried little weight, the MMC accepted the view that much of the appeal of expensive perfume lies in its price, especially when bought as a gift. This decision is doubly surprising when one considers the profit margins on this product. It is difficult to contest the view that the vertical restraints were acting to maintain high profit margins, to the detriment of the customer; and the refusal to supply Superdrug cannot be seen as anything other than a constraint on intra-brand competition.

Again, there was speculation, at the time of the investigation, that the MMC was anxious to avoid possible conflict with EC competition authorities. The EC have granted perfume houses exemption from distribution regulation since 1974, and, had the MMC taken a contrary decision, this might have made a compromise between the two jurisdictions almost impossible. This begs obvious questions, however, about whether such an exemption should continue, or whether steps should be taken to bring it to an end.

Since the investigation, there have been several developments, both in the UK and in Europe, which have led to a fall in prices. Leclerc, a French supermarket chain, challenged the European ruling in 1994, and was subsequently able to reduce its retail prices. By far the most significant development, however, has been the emergence of a 'grey' market immediately after the report. Companies such as Tesco and Superdrug have been able to obtain significant quantities of perfume from European sources, and it is now estimated that up to 25 per cent of all sales by volume pass through this market. Superdrug has continued to offer fine fragrances at prices up to 80 per cent below their RRP. In 1994 'The Perfume Shop' signed dealership arrangements with three of the major houses, and in 1995 Yves Saint Laurent finally agreed to supply Superdrug, prompting claims that many of the restrictive practices were now at an end. This is one of the few examples in our population of the competitive process (via arbitrage) overcoming (at least in part) a vertical restraint.

8.10 CONCLUSIONS

Vertical restraints account for half of all MMC reports on monopoly from 1973–95, and roughly two thirds of this number attracted an adverse judgement from the MMC, and subsequent remedies. In this chapter, we selected six cases for detailed analysis. In three, frozen foods, ice cream and films, exclusivity was the main issue of contention; for postal franking machines, there was a variety of practices including tying of contracts for maintenance and repair; foreign package holidays involved a practice akin to RPM; and artificial lower limbs revolved around vertical integration between producers and service centres. In three of these cases, the three firm concentration ratio exceeded 90 per cent, indicative of dominant firms; but, in the other three, concentration was much lower – below 60 per cent – revealing the existence of complex monopoly, which is often involved when a number of firms pursue a particular common vertical practice in a given market. This dichotomy is representative of a general pattern in the population as a whole: most vertical restraint cases involve either groups of firms pursuing a given practice or (less frequently) a dominant firm.

The arguments for and against the restraints in each of these case studies provide specific illustrations of the issues raised in the voluminous academic literature on vertical restraints summarised in Section 8.1. The defence invariably rests on the claim that the restraint in question helped to reduce the, potentially costly, externality which would otherwise have existed between vertically related firms. The accusation that there are anti-competitive consequences usually entails a foreclosure dimension and/or the softening of inter-brand and/or intra-brand competition.

Of course, in one obvious sense, our cases are not a random sample, and that is that each attracted adverse judgements by the MMC, following which a remedy was put in place. In five of the six cases, that remedy was termination of a practice, the exception being artificial lower limbs, for which divestment was recommended. Overall, however, we have not found that the remedies have typically had much effect.

Certainly, in frozen foods, there was at most a negligible effect. The remedy was to prohibit a form of freezer exclusivity, and some price discounting practices. These were fairly minor changes, but even more important, the market was about to undergo a major development which soon overshadowed the remedy itself. This was the widespread introduction and growth of the supermarkets' 'own labels', reinforced by the general increase in market shares of supermarkets at the expense of smaller retailers. Whatever the likely impact of restraints on inter-brand competition between the heavily advertised products of the majors, the emergence of low-priced alternatives made major inroads into the market shares of all the majors, including Unilever – the main actor in this case.

Unilever was also the dominant firm in the (impulse) ice cream case, but, in this instance, there is no equivalent to the supermarket own label. The remedy again entailed prohibition of exclusivity, but this was restricted only to outlet exclusivity, whilst the manufacturers were allowed to continue with their practice of freezer exclusivity. Although this possibly increased competition at the margin (in retail outlets with more than one freezer), subsequent experience strongly suggests that more wide-ranging remedies were required. If competition has increased (due to the entry of Mars, with an innovatory product), this is in spite of the remaining vertical restrictions, rather than because the remedy was effective. In our opinion, the MMC simply failed in its 1994 report to recognise that, precisely because of the impulse nature of ice cream purchase at the point of sale, exclusive freezers effectively remove most inter-brand competition. We also believe that it is very unfortunate that the Commission was handed terms of reference which did not also include exclusive wholesale distribution.

A second investigation was also deemed necessary in the films case, in which the majors were found to be operating a range of vertical restraints. Following the first report, there was a long delay before an order was put into place (six years later). The delay seems to have been due partly to continuing resistance to the MMC's recommendations by the majors, and partly to lengthy deliberations by the OFT as various alternative remedies were contemplated. Moreover, when the order did materialise, it was limited to just one practice – prohibition of barring (a form of exclusive distribution). In this case, there was significant entry (unrelated to the remedy), but the industry continued to attract adverse comment concerning remaining vertical restraints. The fact that it was deemed necessary to have a second investigation, which advocated further control of other vertical restrictions, is probably the strongest testament to the ineffectiveness of the original remedy.

In postal franking machines, the two leading firms controlled about 90 per cent of the market, for both new machines, and their repair and maintenance. Their practice of tying supply and maintenance services amounted to a very effective entry barrier, especially on the maintenance side. In spite of the remedy (to end this tie), there has been no independent entry into maintenance, and the main reason for this has been the continuation of restrictive rules operated by the Post Office. The Post Office has been very sluggish in following MMC suggestions for change in its practices and this has prevented new entry even ten years after the report was published.

On the other hand, in foreign package holidays, the remedy, permitting agents to offer discounts and special offers on tour operators' holidays, was undoubtedly successful in the short run. Following the remedy, there was a period of intense price competition. However, there has also been significant structural change in the industry, which we believe was, at least in part, the direct result of the remedy used. In particular, the major firms have integrated forward extensively into the travel agent business, and this has led to accusations that this strategy has had the effect of foreclosing the market to independents, as well as potentially softening both intra- and inter-brand competition. Yet again, this is a case which was re-referred to the Commission.

Artificial lower limbs differs from the other cases in that it was the only case for which the MMC recommended divestment as opposed to termination of practices. But, equally, it was the only case in which the remedy was not in fact implemented. This is because a major change in the system of tendering for service centres under the NHS had more or less the same effect as that intended of the remedy; namely, a reduction in the domination of Intermed in this case. There is little doubt that the change in NHS practice (which was instigated as the result of a separate inquiry) has led to more competition in this market. However, and perhaps ironically, although the MMC remedy was no longer necessary, we believe that the MMC investigation (and threat of a remedy) played an important role in reinforcing these changes in competitive tendering.

We have also examined four other significant cases in this chapter. Petrol and beer offer an interesting contrast: both involved extensive exclusive purchasing by retailers (either through direct manufacturer/retailer integration or solus ties between independent retailers and major manufacturers/wholesalers). However, whilst the MMC made no recommendations for petrol, it concluded that extensive divestment was necessary in beer. These findings are not inconsistent, however, because beer retailing (through pubs) is more likely than petrol retailing (through service stations) to entail localised monopoly. As such, exclusive purchasing/vertical integration may be a major threat to inter-brand (and perhaps intra-brand) competition in beer. Beyond this comparison, however, these two cases also provide further examples of issues raised in our main case studies: for example, as with films, the beer case resulted in orders being made, which were (arguably) weaker than the MMC's original recommendations, and both cases remain controversial. As in frozen foods, the emergence of strong competition from the major supermarkets has dominated the retail petrol market, although fears remain in the latter concerning the effects of vertical ties on independent retailers and wholesalers.

Turning finally to our other two featured cases, new cars and fine fragrances, neither attracted very significant MMC intervention. For new cars, only minor remedies were recommended, and for fine fragrances, none. In both cases, there was a potential conflict with EC legislation, and for fine fragrances, at least, questions arise over the conclusions reached by the MMC.

ANNEX TO CHAPTER 8

This annex summarises all other cases in our population in which the principal problem was one of vertical integration/vertical restraints. The 21 cases are classified by type of restraint and brief details are given for each case.

8.A.1 Exclusive Purchasing

Six cases involved exclusive purchasing as the main type of vertical restraint. In car parts (1982, 1992) attention focused on exclusive purchasing in wholesale supply. In its 1982 report the MMC found that a complex monopoly existed in favour of manufacturers and importers of cars, who required their franchised dealers to buy parts exclusively through them, or through sources approved by them. This restricted competition as well as producing other adverse effects such as less speedy delivery of parts; the restrictions tended to raise prices and were found to be against the public interest. The MMC recommended that exclusive purchasing of car parts be removed from car suppliers' contracts with their franchisees and an order to this effect was introduced in 1982. However, it recognised that other types of restraint might also be used to similar effect, and, if this should happen, it recommended that another enquiry should take place.

At the time of the 1982 report, independent suppliers of car parts argued that removal of exclusive purchasing for car franchisees would allow gradual entry into that part of the market. However, evidence in the 1992 report shows that progress had been very slow, with the vast majority of components used by franchised car dealers still being supplied by car manufacturers and importers. The 1992 report looked at both the supply to franchised car dealers (about 55 per cent of the market) and the independent aftermarket (for example, independent garages, autocentres and retail outlets, accounting for about 45 per cent). Concern was expressed that car manufacturers and importers still dominated the market for spare parts. However, in its report the MMC took a much less critical line and concluded that, whilst there were a number of vertical restraints, none acted against the public interest. These restraints included refusal to supply parts except to franchised dealers, restrictions on the ability of component makers to supply the independent aftermarket, and withholding information needed for the use of diagnostic equipment. The MMC ruled that these restrictions were insufficiently important to be judged against the public interest, but they might be in the future, in which case a further investigation might be required.

In carbonated soft drinks (1991), two firms dominated the market: Coca-Cola and Schweppes Beverage Ltd (CCSB), a joint venture of Coca-Cola and Cadbury Schweppes, with a 43 per cent market share in 1989; and Britvic Soft Drinks Ltd (Britvic), a joint venture of PepsiCola and three brewers (Bass, Allied-Lyons and Whitbread), which had 22 per cent of the market. A third firm, Coca-Cola Bottlers (Ulster) Ltd (CCBU), which had a franchising agreement with Coca-Cola, was also involved. The MMC argued that the 'take home' market (that is, sales via grocery outlets, confectioners, and so on) was fairly competitive and there were no public interest concerns. In the 'leisure' market (that is, sales to pubs, clubs, fast food chains, and so on), however, the leading two firms had a combined market share of 90 per cent and this did give cause for concern. These firms, the MMC argued, had monopolised the market and used a number of vertical restraints to restrict competition and limit new entry. These included restrictions (by CCSB) requiring distributors not to sell its products on to other wholesalers and distributors, restrictions on the range of products to be carried and on the sale of rival products. The MMC found these measures to be against the public interest and recommended that they be terminated.[50] It also found that CCSB had been buying up a number of dispense operations[51] in the public house sector of the market and recommended that it should seek OFT approval before any more acquisitions were made.

All three firms used exclusive purchasing agreements with downstream firms. These accounted for 30 per cent by volume of CCSB's sales to the leisure trade, 15 per cent of Britvic's (including 6.5 per cent under an agreement with Allied Breweries) and 2.5 per cent of CCBU. These had the effect of preventing entry by other suppliers and of dividing available outlets between the leading firms and the MMC recommended that they be terminated.[52] CCSB and some other smaller manufacturers also complained of the link between the brewers in the Britvic joint venture and sales to their downstream pubs. This effectively foreclosed their managed pubs and restaurants to outside firms and made it difficult to gain access to tenanted estates. The MMC considered the possibility of divestment in this case but concluded that it would be disproportionate and no specific recommendation was made. The MMC also suggested that changes going on in the tenanted estate resulting from the 1989 beer report would ease access in future years.

In the gas (1988) case, the MMC considered the monopoly position of British Gas (BG) in the supply of gas in the UK. BG had recently been privatised but at the time of the report was still the only significant supplier both to the retail and the non-tariff markets. The report focused on the latter[53] and sought to introduce measures which would lead to more competition in the supply of gas. It argued that British Gas should not be allowed to contract for more than 90 per cent of the output of any new gas field, thereby enabling other firms to break into the market. It also argued that British Gas should be required to speed up its arrangements for allowing other suppliers to use its pipe network and undertakings to this effect were signed in 1990. The report also discussed a number of other issues such as BG's use of price discrimination and the non-transparency of its prices to downstream users, but no undertakings on these issues were actually put in place.

In liquefied petroleum gas (1981), attention focused on the Calor Group which had over 70 per cent of the LPG market, as well as being the major supplier of appliances using this fuel. It operated an exclusive purchasing agreement with its distributors which required them to buy all their LPG from it,[54] and it also used a 'binding out' condition which prevented distributors from handling supplies from other firms for various periods after ceasing to handle its supplies. Calor argued that the latter condition was no longer employed and an undertaking that it not be used in future was given in 1981. On the broader issue, however, the MMC found that exclusive purchasing was not against the public interest and no other recommendation was made. This was, in part, due to the ease of entry at the downstream stage. The MMC also considered Calor's practice of requiring its distributors to buy appliances through it. This, it claimed, was to monitor likely future demand for LPG; nevertheless, Calor told the MMC that it had now given up the practice and the MMC recommended that it not be introduced. This was also part of the undertakings in 1981.

Asbestos (1973) was the first case in the time period considered in this book. It was actually referred under the 1948 Monopolies and Restrictive Practices Act (the predecessor of the FTA). It involved Turner and Newall which supplied well over one third (43 per cent in sales value) of all asbestos products in the UK. Although a variety of problems were considered in the report, the main one (in our view) involved exclusive purchasing arrangements between Turner and Newall and its customers. Concern was also expressed about the firm's horizontal and downstream acquisitions and various agreements – some excluding former competitors from re-entering the market. Undertakings were given by Turner and Newall to terminate these agreements, and it was required to request the consent of the Secretary of State before acquiring any further customers or competitors. It was finally released from these undertakings in January 1985.

Finally, trading check franchise and financial services (1981) was a relatively small case which focused on credit arrangements made available to individuals which could then be used to buy goods in selected retail stores. Typically, credit was supplied by a specialist finance company which then collected repayments, using a weekly payment scheme. The main provider of these services was the Provident Financial Group which had 66 per cent of the market and which used exclusive purchasing contracts with its 'signed up' firms. The MMC found that these arrangements were against the public interest and recommended that they be dropped. An undertaking to this effect was given in 1982.

8.A.2 Exclusive Distribution

Apart from the cases already described in the main text, we identified four other cases in which exclusive distribution was the main problem. In national newspapers (1993) it operated at both the wholesale and the retail stages.[55] At the former level, publishers gave exclusive rights to wholesalers to supply newspapers in a given area. The main argument for this was that it was an efficient system of distribution which ensured the widest possible availability of titles over a given geographic area. The main argument against it was that it might lead to inefficiencies in distribution. The MMC considered the benefits of introducing alternative arrangements in this case, but was unconvinced that they would be an improvement; hence, it made no recommendations for change. At the retailing stage, distributors operated a system of exclusive (or, at least, restricted) distribution to retail outlets. This resulted in as many as 60 per cent of applications to sell newspapers being rejected. Not surprisingly there were many complaints, especially given that newspapers are a relatively risk-free product (being provided on the basis of sale or return) and are a useful way of generating cashflow. The wholesalers argued that this policy avoided sales becoming too fragmented which might jeopardise home deliveries and the early morning opening services offered by newsagents. This, they argued, could actually reduce sales of newspapers. Whilst the MMC was sceptical about this argument, it was not prepared to suggest that a completely free system should be introduced. Instead, it recommended that a code of practice be used to bring about a 'fairer' system of regulating entry, and that retailers be allowed to sell newspapers on to other retailers satisfying this code (for example, to shops that might open later). Undertakings to this effect were given in 1994.

In video games (1995) the leading firms, Nintendo and Sega, dominated the market for games consoles and maintained tight control over software games that could be played on their machines. In particular, both firms limited the number of games that could be produced by outside companies, required that games should be subject to their approval, and controlled the packaging and presentation of such games. They also insisted on manufacturing software cartridges (although Sega allowed some large software firms to manufacture their own). The MMC found that these restrictions were against the public interest and recommended they be removed. In on-line databases (1994) there were two scale monopolists: the Financial Times (FT) group which supplied nearly 40 per cent of reference services[56] and Knight-Ridder Inc. and its subsidiaries, which supplied about a third. The central issue was the FT's policy of not licensing its database information to outside service providers. In addition, it imposed a 10 per cent surcharge on its data to information brokers, thereby 'exploiting' its monopoly position. The MMC argued that the market was competitive (and likely to become more so) and that the FT's policies were not against the public interest. Finally, in greyhound racing (1986) concern was expressed over rules which tied trainers to particular tracks and prevented licensed trainers and owners from racing at 'independent' tracks. This was a very small case, and since the racing authorities agreed to modify their rules voluntarily, no undertakings were required.

8.A.3 Tie-in Sales

Tie-in sales were an important factor in five cases. In the photocopiers[57] (1976, 1991) case, concern was expressed (in the first report) about the dominant firm, Rank Xerox, which (largely through patents) had 89 per cent of the market in 1975. Rank Xerox operated a policy of leasing its photocopiers and required customers to buy everything that photocopiers use (except paper) directly from it. This tie included servicing, the supply of components and the supply of toner. This was a case where a first-mover had been able to dominate a market by developing a new product and monopolising its sales. The MMC noted, however, that new competition was a real possibility and did not find that Rank Xerox's dominance itself was against the public interest. The Commission decided that the company was within its rights to tie servicing and components to its leases because the photocopiers were its own property. It did, however, recommend that Rank Xerox allow customers to purchase toner separately. This was clearly a very minor recommendation which was unlikely to have had any major effect on competition. By the time of the 1991 report, market conditions had changed radically. In particular, Rank Xerox, whilst still the largest firm, had only 31 per cent of the market, with Cannon having 14 per cent and ten other firms having between 3 per cent and 7 per cent. There were also major changes in distribution, with machines now being sold as well as leased, and sales/leases taking place through dealers rather than directly from the manufacturers themselves. The investigation took place, in part, because Rank Xerox wanted the toner undertaking relaxed, but the MMC also considered claims that some manufacturers were refusing to supply spare parts to third parties involved in maintenance. In its report, the MMC concluded that the market was competitive and that no practices acted against the public interest. The toner undertaking was dropped following the report.

Tie-in sales were also important in exhaust gas analysers (1993). EGAs had become necessary following the introduction of tests for exhaust gas omissions in the 1991 Ministry of Transport (MOT) tests. The leading firms not only supplied machines but also operated ties which included the calibration and servicing of machines. Each company (or its nominee) undertook its own servicing and calibration and refused to supply manuals and, in some cases, software to others. Firms also declined to offer training programmes. The companies argued that, nevertheless, the market was competitive, with 30 independent firms, and that customers looked at the whole package including costs of servicing, and so on, in making their choice of machine. Since there were no complaints over services offered and profits were not 'too high', the MMC concluded that the ties were not against the public interest.

Three other cases (all of which were very small) involved tie-in sales. In holiday caravan sites (1983), a complex monopoly existed whereby a number of firms owning caravan sites in Northern Ireland linked the provision of pitches at those sites to the sale of caravans. It was suggested that up to 70 per cent of capacity on sites was tied to caravan sales. In fact, however, there was very little evidence that this restriction had any effect, merely that site owners also tended to sell caravans, and the MMC found no public interest problem in this case. In electrical contracting (1990), a number of large exhibition halls in Greater London tied provision of electrical contract work to the hire of a hall. This created a complex monopoly in which five major contractors undertook about 75 per cent of the electrical work for the reference halls in 1988. In addition, there was evidence that contractors paid owners a commission of up to 20 per cent for the contract work. The MMC argued that the tie and the commissions were against the public interest and recommended that they be removed. An order to this effect was eventually made in December 1995. Finally, marine radio (1987) was a somewhat different case in which a dominant firm, Racal Electronics, supplied marine radio equipment to be operated using a proprietary navigation system, DNS.[58] The company set 'high' prices for its equipment in part to cross-subsidise the navigation system which has the properties of a public good. During the investigation, however, the company was able to negotiate a contract with the general lighthouse authorities for them to take over financial responsibility for the system and, in light of this, it agreed to remove most of the anti-competitive practices identified by the MMC. The MMC, therefore, recommended no further action in this case.

8.A.4 Vertical Integration

In domestic gas appliances (1980) the main focus of attention was the dominant position of British Gas (BG) which as well as being the monopoly supplier of domestic gas in the UK was also the dominant buyer and retailer of gas appliances. The case involved five scale monopolies, three relating to the manufacture of gas appliances[59] and two involving BG both as a buyer and seller of appliances. In addition, the MMC found that a complex monopoly existed involving all firms which were either members of the Society of British Gas Industries or the Gas Stove Makers' Panel.

It was clear in this report that this market was not working competitively, and this was primarily due to the dominant position of BG. BG was the main buyer of gas appliances accounting for 93 per cent of cookers, 88 per cent of space heaters and 67 per cent of water heaters in 1977–78, and it was the main retailer with 97 per cent of cookers, 92 per cent of space heaters and 97 per cent of water heaters in the same year.[60] Given its market dominance, BG was able to exert pressure on its suppliers to extract favourable terms and at the same time dictate the types of product available to customers. In the absence of competition at the retail stage, it was not clear whether its policies were cost-effective and whether it was providing the range of appliances consumers wanted at the right price. In addition, because manufacturers relied on it almost exclusively, it was able to impose its views on product design rather than let the market decide. The MMC argued that the monopoly was against the public interest and considered three options for change. First, BG should withdraw from retailing entirely and allow the private sector to take over. Second, BG should keep its retail arm but operate it at arm's length with separate accounts. And third, that BG should continue as it was but provide a clearer statement of cost allocations in its accounts. The Commission was divided over which option to choose. The Secretary of State, however, chose the first option and divestment which took place over a period of five years.

Flour and bread (1977) involved vertical integration between the major flour producers and their bread-making subsidiaries. All the companies involved required their baking subsidiaries to buy as much flour as possible in-house and this suggested that there might be an anti-competitive effect. However, the MMC found that there were important efficiency gains from doing this, including savings on storage and transportation costs, and by enabling the companies to supply particular types of flour on demand. Given that there was no major horizontal problem in this case, the MMC concluded that vertical integration was not a problem and no recommendation was made.

Two other cases involved vertical integration. In ready-mixed concrete (1981), Ready Mixed Concrete (UK) Ltd (the scale monopolist) and other major producers had integrated backward into the supply of aggregates (particularly, sand and gravel) which were thought to be in limited supply. This, in turn, raised the possibility that producers without access to these supplies could be prevented from entering the market. In fact, however, the MMC found that there was no real evidence that aggregates were in limited supply. It therefore concluded that no adverse effects from integration were likely to arise. Finally, in cinema advertising (1990), two firms, Rank Screen Advertising and Pearl & Dean, dominated the market with the former having a 78 per cent market share in 1987[61] and the latter a 22 per cent market share. The case arose because of a complaint by Pearl & Dean that Rank had used unfair competition in gaining its market share, and, in particular, that it had a captive market in that it owned the Odeon cinema chain. The MMC found, however, that the Odeon link accounted for only 14 per cent of all available screens and hence was not a major issue in this case. Moreover, it found that Rank had not acted unfairly in winning contracts and hence there were no grounds for public policy concern.

8.A.5 Resale Price Maintenance

Finally, three cases involved some element of resale price maintenance. In contact lens solutions (1993), monopolies existed at both the manufacturing and the retail stage. Two scale monopolies, in favour of Allergan and CIBA-Vision (a wholly-owned subsidiary of CIBA-GEIGY), existed in manufacturing; whilst Boots had a scale monopoly, with a 36 per cent market share, at the retail stage. The Commission also identified four complex monopolies amongst producers, retailers and opticians in this case. The market was subject to a number of government controls. First, all companies producing contact lens solutions had to be licensed by the Medicines Control Agency (MCA) or the Department of Health and this tended to create a barrier to entry (or, at least, an extra cost of entry to the industry). Second, at the retail stage, contact lens solutions could only be sold by recognised opticians or pharmacists.[62] This also restricted competition. The measures were designed to protect the consumer from a health and safety point of view. From the competition viewpoint, however, their effect was to limit competition and this created a rather cosy relationship between manufacturers and retail firms. Boots, the biggest single retailer, was found to use recommended retail prices (RRPs) on branded products and to sell its own-brand products at a discount of only about 6 per cent. Other retailers also tended to use RRPs. The result was that both manufacturers and retailers were able to earn significant monopoly profits. The MMC argued that the best remedy in this case was to relax government restrictions on entry to allow more competition to develop. Failing that, the government should consider using price controls both at the production (Allergan) and retail (Boots) stage.[63]

In specialised advertising (1988), attention focused on advertising in specialist magazines for campers, climbers and walkers. The problem in this case was that magazine owners refused to carry advertisements which included prices. The main reason for this was that it would favour mail order firms who tended to compete on price, against other more traditional, 'high service' sellers. However, the MMC found that there was no real free rider issue in this case. It recommended that the magazines drop this policy and an order to this effect was implemented in 1988.

Finally in national newspapers (1993) (already described above under exclusive distribution), publishers also engaged in RPM, in that they set both retail margins and the cover price at which newspapers were sold. As far as retail margins were concerned, the practice existed mainly for historical reasons and the MMC concluded that it probably did introduce some distortions and that, under an unrestricted system, some variation of margins might result. It noted, however, that the maintenance of margins tended to protect smaller retailers, and retailers at more remote sites, and it found no compelling case for change. As far as retail prices were concerned, it felt the current practice of selling newspapers at the price on the paper was fairly innocuous, and that to remove it would be unlikely to bring any tangible gains. Hence, in this case, resale maintenance was not viewed as against the public interest.

NOTES

1. By categorizing all restraints under these four headings, we necessarily simplify. Moreover, our typology may differ slightly from that used in other sources – not all terms have universal unambiguous definitions. Nevertheless, we believe that our typology comes as close as possible to 'common practice'.
2. Notably, foreign package holidays, artificial lower limbs, petrol and beer.
3. Related practices are exclusive franchising and restrictive licensing policies.
4. However, Marvel and McCafferty (1985) report that in some US cases RPM has also arisen at the instigation of powerful retailer associations forcing it on manufacturers.
5. The totals (given below) include some double counting because some cases involve several types of restraint. However, they exclude the bracketed entries in Table 8.1 as these are regarded as secondary to the main problem(s) involved.
6. Resale price maintenance is prohibited in the UK under the 1976 Resale Prices Act, although firms can seek exemption from the Restrictive Practices Court (in the case of a single, but not collective, RPM). The three cases here represent informal attempts to apply RPM by refusal to supply. For a similar case, under the Competition Act, see the 1981 Raleigh bicycles case (discussed in Utton, 1994).
7. To some extent this relationship is tautological, in that complex monopolies have sometimes been defined as complex precisely because of a common vertical restraint.
8. As discussed further below, the remedy was not actually used in artificial lower limbs.
9. Note, a number of these cases also involve other vertical practices.
10. The reference market in this case covered a wide range of products including fish, vegetables, meat and confectionery and fruit, but excluding, in particular, ice cream and water ices. It also included both retail and non-retail sales. Birds Eye specialised in retail sales for which its 1974 market share was 47 per cent in aggregate; it was considerably higher than this, however, for some specific products; for example, frozen vegetables.
11. Arguably, there were efficiencies in the distribution of Birds Eye's products if it could guarantee that sizeable quantities of its goods were stocked by retailers. This was clearly not the main intent of the restraints, however.
12. Except that retailers should be allowed to stock rival manufacturers' products in the same freezer, in the short term, if the firm was unable to supply due to temporary factors.
13. It is difficult to derive exactly comparable market share figures for the majors from the 1979, and subsequent 1994, MMC reports. Rather strangely (perhaps due to worries of disclosure), the 1994 report fails to report precise figures for the majors' shares of the *total* impulse market. We are merely told that the three leading firms accounted for 88 per cent of 'wrapped impulse' and 'a lesser but still very large share of the market for all reference products'. But it seems safe to conclude that BEW's share of total reference products did increase significantly between the two reports.
14. LM were first sold by Allied Lyons (the parent in 1979) to a small family firm, which went into receivership soon after. Nestlé bought LM from the receiver.
15. Examples include: Robertson and Williams (1995) and 'Was the MMC misled?', *The Economist*, 6 May 1995, p. 36. The former is an academic analysis, suggesting that freezer exclusivity should, in fact, be prohibited; the latter reports the claims (which we also

frequently encountered in our interviews) that BEW may have misled the MMC concerning wholesaler exclusivity (see below).

16. We should mention one other unrelated disadvantage faced by small independent firms when competing with large multinationals. This concerns the MMC investigations themselves. One third party suggested to us that the smaller manufacturers had a very muted voice in the evidence collection and subsequent debate. They have neither the time nor the resources to lobby or respond comprehensively to the MMC. Certainly, there is evidence that both Mars and Unilever spent a lot on this investigation and this is one obvious consequence of their large multinational status – none of the other impulse manufacturers is of any significant corporate size, apart from Nestlé.

17. Most of our interview discussions centred on the potential role of freezer exclusivity as an entry barrier. In addition, however, it has a fairly obvious softening impact on price competition. One suspects that price is not a major influence on which shop a consumer chooses to buy her ice cream from – the very term 'impulse' is entirely appropriate. If so, the real prospect for price competition depends on there being a choice once the consumer is in the shop. Quite obviously, this will be absent within a given cabinet stocking only one brand.

18. Mars is very concerned that these practices are limiting its ability to expand, both in the UK and other EU markets where similar restraints exist. It is currently pursuing its case with the European Commission arguing that these restraints violate article 86 of the Treaty of Rome. At the time of writing, cases in Germany and Ireland (both involving Unilever subsidiaries) are going ahead. A recent decision in the Court of First Instance (in the German case) suggests that Unilever will eventually have to drop 'freezer exclusivity', although it may take some time before the legal process works itself out.

19. There is no doubt of the high-risk nature of the film industry – films are typically costly to make, and it is difficult to anticipate in advance which will be profitable. In fact, most turn out to be unprofitable, but a few become very big earners.

20. The industry was also referred to the MMC in 1966, following which a number of undertakings were given. This report, however, comes before our period of enquiry and hence is not discussed here.

21. These and other figures are taken from the 1994 report. All other 'independent' cinemas accounted for only about 20 per cent of box office receipts.

22. This is not to deny that some cinemas had already moved in this direction. It was explained to us that, even prior to the entry of the multiplexes, some independent cinemas, whilst not being able to compete by showing current films, did try to make the experience a 'night out' with themed showings, drinks in your seat, and so on. The 1983 report was critical of the lack of marketing initiative shown by the major chains, and it suggested the use of discounted seats to attract customers on weekday nights. It was suggested to us that the removal of barring may have had the effect of stimulating the cinema chains to be a bit more proactive, rather than relying solely on having the first showing of a film for as long as they wished.

23. There were only two main distributors in 1983: a joint venture of Columbia–EMI–Warner, and UIP. By 1994 only UIP remained, as the leader; Buena Vista (linked to Disney), Warner, Columbia and Rank/Fox each operated separately.

24. At the time of writing, MGM Cinemas has been acquired by an independent consortium.

25. Interestingly, one interviewee referred to Rank earlier trying to freeze out the multiplexes by encouraging restrictive agreements with distributors.

26. One other effect was mentioned by another respondent: 'what will go is the talking about when the films are to be released'. This refers to the prior discussions between aligned distributors and exhibitors concerning release dates and sequencing. From the point of view of competition, this may be no bad thing.

27. This is an obvious example of the 'efficiency' defence of exclusivity: the upstream firm can control the conditions (quality) under which the downstream firm sells the product.
28. As discussed further below, another important issue in this case was the methods used by salesmen to make a sale. Some of these methods were, at the least, very questionable indeed.
29. Since a major reorganisation of the Post Office in 1992, postal franking machines have become the responsibility of the Royal Mail. We use the terms 'Post Office' and 'Royal Mail' interchangeably in this section.
30. Interestingly, we were told that the UK is the only country where firms are required to post bonds. In our discussion with the Royal Mail it appears that one of the changes that might be made in the future is to drop this requirement.
31. Neopost was formed as part of a world-wide leveraged buyout in 1992.
32. In addition, PB continued to be a highly profitable company and its rate of return showed no tendency to fall in the four years after the report.
33. As noted below, a small service firm in Scotland tried to enter the business repairing PB's machines in the early 1990s, but was met with legal action by PB which, effectively, forced it out of the market.
34. One firm told us that it had tried to enter the market following the report but had only met with a blank wall from the Post Office. This respondent seemed to think the Post Office did not know its own rules and any attempt to get it to clarify its position only led to obfuscation. Eventually, it told us, it gave up.
35. Part of the problem seems to be that the Post Office gave postal franking machines a very low priority prior to 1992, and it is only since its reorganisation in 1992 that these issues have been seriously addressed. Whilst some control of 'cowboys' may be necessary, there are many reputable firms interested in entering the maintenance market and it is difficult to see why such firms should be excluded.
36. Stories of this are legion in the industry. In the case of leased machines, for example, it was alleged that salesmen sometimes claimed that a lease had expired when, in fact, it still had considerable time to run and office staff (who, quite surprisingly, often sign invoices or leases for postal franking machines rather than refer decisions to managers) would duly sign up for a new lease. Even more apocryphal, some salesmen would apparently recover old machines which had been 'leased' when, in fact, they had actually been sold to the firms involved!
37. However, it was not judged at the time to be literally RPM, otherwise it would have been covered by the 1976 Resale Prices Act (see above).
38. Other activities include arranging business travel and independent holidays.
39. The 1995 figure is an estimate from Lunn Poly of the number of holidays as reported in The *Observer* (June 1995); the two earlier figures are given in the MMC Report.
40. Intasun was bankrupted and Horizon was acquired by Thomson (cf. MMC report no. .234, *Thomson Travel Group and Horizon Travel Ltd: A Report on the Merger*, London: HMSO, Cmnd 550, 1989).
41. However, since ABTA claims to represent 7,500 travel agents (owned by 2,000 firms), it is clear that, in terms of numbers, there are still many (typically) small travel agents surviving in the market.
42. The most recent MMC report was published on 19 December 1997. Whilst it found evidence of some abuse of monopoly power, it stopped short of suggesting that a structural remedy was required. Rather it suggested that firms be required not to link the sale of travel insurance to holiday discounts, that they not impose most favoured customer agreements on travel agents and that links between travel agents and tour operators be made clear to customers (*Times*, 20 December 1997).
43. There are two types of *prosthetic* services provided by the NHS, dealing with lower and upper limbs. It is generally agreed that the latter is the more specialised area.

44. This was, therefore, a somewhat wider brief than that of the MMC, as the services covered by the Artificial Limb and Appliance Centres (ALACs) include wheelchairs, vehicles and artificial eyes, as well as artificial upper and lower limbs.
45. Kellie had supplied over 70 per cent of all the prosthetic services in Scotland, with Blatchford being its major competitor. However, with the new contracts, InterMed decided that rationalisation was necessary and Kellie was closed. This option appears to have been considered prior to intervention by the DSA, but there is little hard evidence on this.
46. Steeper specialised in upper limbs which are also dealt with through the ALACs.
47. Indeed, several firms suggested that the market was too competitive, with firms bidding prices that were not sustainable in the long run.
48. One other suggestion made to us (if correct) would imply an even greater indirect effect of the MMC's proposed remedies. This was that the OFT had made it clear that it would implement the divestment remedy if the review of the first round of tenders showed no, or insufficient, change. This may, or may not, have influenced some InterMed staff in the service centres to split away from InterMed.
49. The MMC noted (quite rightly) that there were other distortions in the UK market. The most important of these were the voluntary export restraints operated by Japanese manufacturers and distortions created by company cars in the UK.
50. More precisely, CCSB announced during the investigation that it was terminating these restrictions voluntarily and the MMC recommended that they not be reintroduced.
51. These are where a product is diluted and carbonated at the point of sale.
52. Undertakings were given in 1993.
53. The reference specifically excluded the retail market for gas. This latter is to be opened up to competition in 1998.
54. The distributors were also required to fill only calor containers, not those of competitors.
55. There is also a resale price maintenance element in this case; see Section 8.A.5 for details.
56. The market in this case involves provision of mainly financial and business information in on-line form.
57. Referred to as indirect electrostatic reprographic equipment in the 1976 report and indirect electrostatic photocopiers in 1991.
58. DNS stands for the Decca Navigation System which had been developed during the war. Racal acquired Decca in 1980.
59. Thorn Gas Appliances had scale monopolies of cookers (with a 40 per cent market share) and instantaneous water heaters (with a 52 per cent market share), whilst Chaffoteaux had a scale monopoly of water heaters (with a 26 per cent market share).
60. The only other significant retailer was Comet with about 4 per cent of the cooker market (although less for the reference products as a whole).
61. Rank had only recently obtained such a dominant market share; it had a 40 per cent market share prior to winning two Cannon contracts in 1987.
62. This is one of the relatively few cases that highlighted retailer power in the market.
63. After initial price-cutting following entry by Tesco and others, the producers have found a way around this by producing 'optician only' brands. This raises the question of whether stronger measures are, in fact, needed in this case.

PART III

Conclusions

9. An Overall Assessment of the Effectiveness of Policy

9.1 INTRODUCTION

So how effective have the remedies been? This simple question can be posed and answered on a number of different levels. Perhaps most fundamentally, do our case studies confirm that anti-trust intervention in this area is preferable to leaving the market free to find its own solutions to market imperfections? Alternatively, accepting that intervention *will* be broadly necessary in certain circumstances, do our case studies show that some types of remedy turn out to be more successful than others? Or yet again, on a more institutional and practical level, are there lessons to be learned about how the institutional framework and actual practice of MMC investigations constrain (or enhance) the effectiveness of remedies? Does the MMC have sufficient 'power'? Are the 'right' industries investigated? Do investigations take too long? In this chapter, we draw together the findings of the case studies described in Part II in the search for answers to at least some of these questions.

The chapter is structured as follows. Section 9.2 introduces the broad theoretical battle-lines by discussing the relative stances of different schools of thought on the need for anti-trust intervention, and what can be hoped of it. Section 9.3 recalls, in an initially abbreviated form, our reading of the outcomes in each of the case studies described in the chapters of Part II. Section 9.4 summarises the changes observed in market structure in those industries. On a negative level, this confirms an assertion that we have noted at various points in the book, namely that a more statistically based methodology would probably have not proved fruitful in this study. Section 9.5 presents our main conclusions through a simple typology for assessing effectiveness, whilst also taking a broader view on whether the underlying monopoly problems have ceased to remain a cause for concern. This proves a useful device for distinguishing effectiveness in the narrower and broader senses. Finally, Section 9.5 summarises the main lessons to be learned.

9.2 THEORETICAL PERSPECTIVES ON THE EFFECTIVENESS OF MONOPOLY POLICY

A good place to start on the 'fundamental issue' of the effectiveness of anti-trust intervention versus laissez-faire, is to recall the familiar debate between structure–conduct–performance (S–C–P) economists and the Austrian and Chicago schools (summarised, for example, in Clarke, 1985, Chapter 1 and Davies et al., 1989, Chapter 1). At the core of S–C–P paradigm is the belief that high market concentration, protected by entry barriers, will lead to monopolistic/collusive behaviour and high prices and profits. From this perspective, monopoly policy will be deemed effective if it manages to reduce concentration and/or the market shares of the dominant firms, thereby intensifying competitive pressures, with resulting lower prices and profits. This tends to point to remedies which ease the condition of entry, or, more extremely, break up large firms (divestment). Quantifiable evidence of effectiveness would be post-remedy declines in concentration, prices and profits.

Alternatively, the Austrian/Chicago view is that the market, if left to its own devices, will ultimately provide its own solution to horizontal market imperfections. If high profits are observed as anything other than a transitory phenomenon in a given market, then this will provide an incentive for other firms to enter, and compete away those super-normal profits. There is, however, one exception to this story, and this concerns barriers to entry (market imperfections) resulting from state intervention. Such barriers might include controls and regulations on price, quality and entry, state ownership, patents, and so on. Whilst they may or may not be justified in the pursuit of other government objectives, they tend to operate in an anti-competitive way, and crucially, such barriers may not necessarily be brushed aside by the forces of competition. It is in these instances that there may be a role for intervention – but only to remove these impediments. Given this view then, when appraising the effectiveness of any particular remedy in any particular case, one should compare outcomes with what *would* have happened absent the intervention – the counterfactual. One might also look for evidence that the market was working anyway, alongside (or in spite of) the remedy, towards its own solution. Alternatively, in those cases where there is a state-imposed barrier, a successful remedy would be the removal of the impediment.

Of course, other perspectives are also possible, and these are not necessarily just compromises of the two above extremes. In particular, the game theoretic revolution of recent years has provided considerable insights. (Tirole, 1988, is the classic textbook exposition, and his Chapter 8 on vertical controls is a perfect illustration.) Another example, which turns out to be especially pertinent for some of our case studies, is contemporary game theoretic research on the evolution of market structure. Notably, Sutton (1991) alerts us to the existence of 'natural oligopoly' and 'endogenous sunk costs' in certain types of industry. These occur in markets in which firms compete mainly by increasing the quality (actual or imagined) of products, and thus consumers' willingness to pay. This, they do through escalating advertising and/or R&D expenditures. Whilst these expenditures may not necessarily deliberately create entry barriers, the effect is the same as if they did – small-scale entry is difficult, given the enormous advertising/R&D outlays needed to join the oligopoly game. Looked at from this perspective, neither S–C–P nor Chicago policy prescriptions seem appropriate. On the one hand, the underlying logic of the competitive process (the market solution) cannot be relied upon to produce creative destruction – market dominance may be a long-term self-perpetuating phenomenon. But, equally, simple attempts to break down barriers, or introduce divestment may be Canute-type gestures, which simply fail to recognise that firms are forced to compete by scale-enhancing investment in sunk costs. Although the anti-trust policy prescriptions of these sorts of models have yet to be analysed in any detail, we suggest that they may not be so very different from those for natural monopoly: 'effective' intervention may dictate more emphasis on price regulation – and not just in the short run.

The upshot of this debate is not, in our opinion, merely an *impasse*. Whilst it is true that a simplistic application of S–C–P analysis – in particular, using mechanical statistical tests, based on *ex ante* and *ex post* data on market shares, and so on – can be very misleading, we hope to show below that each of the above approaches provides some important insights into the competitive process and the outcomes of remedies in our various cases.

9.3 SUMMARY OF THE CASE STUDY FINDINGS IN PART II

Our findings on each of the 14 case studies discussed in Part II are reproduced in abbreviated form in Table 9.1. It should be recalled that this sample was taken from a full population of 61 markets investigated by the MMC (some, on more than one occasion) between 1973 and 1995. In the population as a whole, roughly two thirds of the cases attracted some sort of adverse finding, and subsequent remedies. We have argued above that our

Table 9.1 Brief summary of findings in Part II

Remedy: price control/monitoring (4)	
Breakfast cereals (1973)	Effective into the medium term, but should it have been removed? Are own-brands a sufficient discipline?
Contraceptive sheaths (1975, 1982, 1994)	Effective in the short run, whilst prices were controlled, but should it have been removed? Are the entrants strong enough?
White salt (1986)	Effective, benefits small customers in particular.
Opium derivatives (1989)	Effective in the short run: reduced price at the time and after; but longer-term effects unclear – depends on import controls.
Divestment (2)	
Roadside advertising (1981)	Dramatic short-run structural effects, but has market power merely regrouped?
Artificial lower limbs (1989)	Not applied in the event, but almost certainly an important supporting role.
Termination of practices/agreements (8)	
Building bricks (1976)	Possibly positive short-run effects, but overtaken by events.
Frozen foodstuffs (1976)	Negligible effect, and overtaken by events.
Ice cream (1979, 1994)	Limited short-run effect, but remedies too narrow.
Electricity meters (1979)	Ineffective, and later overtaken by events.
Films (1983, 1994)	Little effect, remedies too narrow.
Postal franking machines (1986)	No effect, constrained by Post Office practices.
Foreign package holidays (1986, 1996)	Very effective in short run, but dominance re-emerging and other restraints now in place.
Bus services in the north-east (1995)	Not effective at the time, but too early to judge wider effectiveness.

sample is broadly representative of the population as a whole, in terms of market structure, remedies and monopoly problems. It is, of course, biased in one obvious respect, namely that in all 14 cases[1] remedies were put in place.

In Chapters 5–8, the case studies were organised and described according to type of monopoly problem, but it now proves presentationally more convenient to arrange them in Table 9.1 according to type of remedy used. At this point in the chapter, we merely summarise our earlier judgements in 'bullet point' form.

As can be seen from the table, we find that in eight of the 14 cases the remedies had *some* effect, whilst in the other six the effect was *minimal* or *non-existent*. When arranged, as here, by type of remedy, it is very evident that the success rate is much higher for price control/monitoring and divestment (6 out of 6) than for termination (only 2 out of 8). However, these simple statistics take no account of short versus long-run effects and various extenuating circumstances and other qualifications. We return to a deeper investigation of them in Section 9.4.

9.4 CHANGES IN MARKET STRUCTURE

We have suggested, both earlier in this chapter and elsewhere in the book, that a simple analysis of pre- and post-investigation market shares, prices, and so on would be of limited value in an overall assessment of the effectiveness of *remedies*. In fact, we formed this opinion at an early stage in our research, and the reasons are discussed in Chapter 4. Especially for prices and profits, it proves very difficult to unearth truly comparable data at a sufficiently low level of aggregation when investigated firms are large multinationals or conglomerates, and post-investigation data on the relevant individual subsidiaries of such firms are simply not available. Whilst data on market shares and concentration are usually more accessible, we have explained in Chapter 4 why we believe that they provide ambiguous messages: for example, the effective removal of a vertical restraint might facilitate entry and lower concentration, effective price control will not. Moreover, meaningful statistical controls for the counterfactual (how *would* market structure have evolved had the market been left to its own devices?) are difficult to specify when confronted with a heterogeneous sample.

To illustrate, Table 9.2 gathers together the information on changes in market structure which was reported earlier within the individual case studies. Whilst the data concerned were collected in a largely ad hoc way[2] the summaries shown in the table are sufficiently robust and accurate for present purposes. It appears from this table that concentration and/or market dominance have not changed by very much in the majority of cases (10) following the remedy; and there is a rough balance between increases and decreases. In some of the cases we have assessed to be effective, there was

Table 9.2 Changes in market structure

Dramatic Change in Market Shares (2)	
Roadside advertising	Considerable turbulence and merger activity, although CR3 largely unchanged in aggregate.
Artificial lower limbs	Drastic reversal of market shares for numbers one and two firms.
Some Decline in Market Dominance (3)	
Contraceptive sheaths	LRC remains the leader, but has lost some share to entrants.
Building bricks	LBC remains the leader, but some loss in market share.
Frozen foodstuffs	Birds Eye lost market share to own-brands, but so did the other majors.
Little or No Change (6)	
Breakfast cereals	Kellogg remains the leader, with largely unchanged market share.
Electricity meters	The top four firms still dominate as a group.
Films	Distribution still largely dominated by firms linked to Hollywood.
Postal franking machines	No entry in maintenance, and Pitney Bowes is still the market leader (but with loss of some share in supply).
White salt	Remains a stable duopoly.
Opium derivatives	MSL remains a monopoly firm.
Increased Dominance (2)	
Ice cream	Unilever increased its market share, but there has been significant entry by Mars.
Foreign package holidays	Increasing dominance by Thomson, but the identities of other majors has changed.
Too Soon to Say (1)	
Bus services in the north-east	Stagecoach remains the dominant firm in this market - unlikely to change.

little or no change in structure (for example, salt and opium derivatives), but the same is also true for cases in which we judge the remedy to have been ineffective (for example, postal franking machines and films).   In both roadside advertising and artificial lower limbs, there were dramatic subsequent changes in structure which were due, at least in part, to the remedy; but then there were also fairly significant changes in other cases (for example, contraceptive sheaths, building bricks, frozen foodstuffs) which were largely independent of the remedy. In foreign package holidays, a case where we judge the remedy to have been effective in the short run, concentration actually increased (as, indeed, it did in ice cream). Overall, it is difficult to argue, from the evidence of this table, that intertemporal comparisons of summary statistics on market structure add much to the analysis.

9.5   ARE THERE STILL CAUSES FOR CONCERN?

Returning then to a more qualitative mode of analysis, can we go any further than the bullet form summaries in Table 9.1? In particular, can we distinguish between short-run and long-run effectiveness, and can we assess the impact of remedies *vis-à-vis* other developments in the marketplace (referred to in Table 9.1, using the catch-all 'overtaken by events')?

This is the purpose of the typology used in Table 9.3,[3] which cross-classifies the 14 cases by (a) effectiveness of remedy, and (b) whether the case still remains a 'cause for competition concern'. We refer to each of the four possible combinations as 'outcomes', and list the alternative scenarios which could, in principle, have accounted for each outcome. Thus, outcomes A and B cover the eight cases we have previously defined as 'effective'. But we now distinguish between those where there is no longer cause for competition concern (A) and those in which concerns still remain, in spite of the effectiveness of the remedy in its own terms (B). In turn, we suggest three possible scenarios which could account for outcome A: this could arise, *in principle*, either because the remedy was permanently effective (I), or because, whether it was permanently effective or only effective in the short run, other developments have so changed the market that no concerns remain. These other developments might have been an endogenous reaction within the market which has removed the market power problem (II), or, more generally, exogenous events (III).

In fact, we find only two cases under the most favourable outcome A. One is building bricks, in which exogenous events – changed relative transport costs, pollution concerns, and doubts about product quality – effectively removed the specific advantages historically enjoyed by the products of the leader (LBC). Although we are not entirely convinced that the MMC remedy was especially effective *per se* in this case, these other developments (scenario III) made it largely irrelevant. The other case is artificial lower limbs. This is a singular case within our sample, in that the remedy was not actually put into place because competitive tendering, introduced as the result of an NHS review, had the effect that was intended of the remedy itself. We categorise this under scenario II because, with the removal of a quasi-state imposed impediment, the natural forces of competition were sufficient to break the vertical link between manufacturing and prosthetic services. It is, perhaps, a moot point as to whether the remedy can really be defined as effective, since it was not actually enacted. However, in Chapter 8, we concluded that the MMC investigation, and the threat of the impending remedy, were important contributory factors in forcing through the changed procedures in this market.

Outcome B is far more common. Here, although we have deemed the remedy to be effective in its own terms, a question mark remains about the state of competition over the longer term. Significantly, this outcome includes all four cases in which the remedy was price control/monitoring; and, in each case, our worry is that the remedy worked in the short run whilst in place, without changing the underlying cause of the problem (monopoly or duopoly). This diagnosis fits all four price control cases to a lesser or greater extent. In white salt, the only one of the four where price control remains in place, the remedy has had the effect of reducing price, particularly to smaller firms: but question marks exist over whether removal of the price control would simply re-establish the previous status quo.[4] In opium derivatives, MSL (the monopolist) followed the price control voluntarily for three years, but subsequently did not. In this case, government restrictions on imports of narcotic drugs have been the main factor in protecting MSL's monopoly position, and this is a problem which still remains at the present time. Below, we shall encounter other cases where the MMC's ability to encourage competition has been constrained by market imperfections outside of its own direct control.

The other two cases involving price control are breakfast cereals and contraceptive sheaths. In both cases, we believe that the nature of the product dictates that the competitive process will emphasise perceived vertical product quality, achieved via 'high' advertising expenditures.[5] In these circumstances, even with market growth, the opportunity for new entry remains constrained because of the need to match the high and increasing advertising outlays of the incumbent firms. Because of this, we suggest that actual/potential entry may be insufficient as a market discipline since price controls were lifted. On this issue we disagree, implicitly, with the OFT's (for cereals) and the MMC's (for

Table 9.3 Is there still cause for concern?

A: Remedy effective, and no remaining concerns about competition (2)
possible explanations:
I: remedy effective in achieving a permanently more competitive market.
II: remedy effective and overtaken by competitive functioning of market.
III: remedy effective and overtaken by exogenous changes.

Building bricks	III
Artificial lower limbs	II

B: Remedy effective, but concerns remain about future competition (6)
possible explanations:
IV: remedy worked while in place, but problem may resurface if (or did resurface when) remedy is (was) relaxed (natural monopoly/duopoly).
V: remedy removed initial problem, but other potentially anti-competitive factors emerged.

White salt	IV
Breakfast cereals	IV
Contraceptive sheaths	IV*
Opium derivatives	IV
Foreign package holidays	V*
Roadside advertising	V*

C: Remedy ineffective, but no remaining competition concerns (1)
possible explanations:
II: in spite of ineffective remedy, overtaken by competitive functioning of the market.
III: in spite of ineffective remedy, overtaken by exogenous changes.

Frozen foods	II

D: Remedy ineffective, and concerns remain (5)
possible explanations:
VI: MMC analysis wrong, referral too limited and/or remedies too narrow.
VII: Secretary of State did not adopt all recommendations.
VIII: remedy thwarted by inaction by crucial third parties.
IX: remedy ineffective in penalising past predatory behaviour; it remains to be seen whether it deters future predation.

Ice cream	VI*
Films	VI*,VII
Electricity meters	VI, VIII
Postal franking machines	VIII
Buses in the north-east	IX

Note: * indicates a case which was reinvestigated.

sheaths) understandings of the significance of the entry which did occur in the two markets. In cereals, whilst the emergence of supermarket own-brands proved attractive to those consumers without pronounced brand loyalty, Kellogg's ability subsequently to retain a dominant market share suggests that most consumers continue to be willing to pay premiums for the higher quality (either actual or perceived) offered by Kellogg. We are, therefore, not persuaded that the presence of supermarket own-brands was sufficient reason for lifting the price controls/price monitoring in this case. Similarly, although the entry of Mates and others in contraceptive sheaths undoubtedly initially reduced LRC's market share, its subsequent advertising has reversed the trend and confirmed its role as market leader. In this case, the MMC's (1994) decision to lift controls may prove to have been misplaced.

The two other cases, which we previously designated 'effective', foreign package holidays and roadside advertising, are listed under outcome B, but for a different reason. In these cases, we accept that the remedies were initially successful – the former in introducing price competition and the latter in breaking a collusive selling arrangement – but subsequent action by the firms concerned has raised concerns about long-run effectiveness (scenario V). Indeed, the OFT must have shared these worries since both cases have been referred back for further MMC investigations. In the case of foreign package holidays, there was a monopoly re-referral to the MMC in 1996, but this time with the focus changed to vertical integration as the potential source of anti-competitive practices.[6] In the case of roadside advertising, in the years following the monopoly report itself, there was a series of mergers some of which were referred under the mergers legislation. The common theme in these two cases is the subsequent attempts by the firms involved to re-establish control of the market using an alternative strategy to that terminated under the remedy. In the case of roadside advertising, intervention by the OFT and MMC has had the effect of maintaining a (precarious) balance between the roadside advertisers themselves and the 'outdoor specialists'.

Turning to the six cases where the remedy was judged 'ineffective', we believe that in only one case, frozen foods, is there no particular cause for concern (outcome C). This is because of the emergence of effective competition from supermarket own-brands, which appear to have been more successful in contesting a wider part of the market than is the case in breakfast cereals. Here, although the remedy was relatively minor, market forces were relatively strong (probably because frozen vegetables, in particular, are more of a homogeneous good thus attracting less brand loyalty and advertising by the majors) than breakfast cereals. Along with artificial lower limbs, this is a relatively rare case when market forces have effectively solved the monopoly problem.

However, in the five other 'ineffective' cases, very real concerns remain about the state of competition (outcome D). Indeed, in two of the cases, ice cream and films, further MMC investigations were undertaken; and, in a third, buses in the north-east, the MMC was largely unable, under UK law, to rectify the initial problem – predatory behaviour in the particular local market concerned. In our reading of these cases, there are a number of reasons for these unsatisfactory outcomes. In ice cream, initially (1979), the Commission framed its remedy too narrowly by excluding exclusive freezer contracts. Also, in its second report, the MMC's hands were tied by the referral from the OFT which turned out to be too narrow, in excluding exclusive wholesale distribution from the terms of reference. At time of writing, it is rumoured in the national press that a further investigation may be imminent on just this matter (*Sunday Times*, 20 July 1997).[7] In films, again we believe the recommendations of the earlier report (1983) were too narrow, and this problem was exacerbated by a further narrowing of the remedy before it appeared as an order from the Secretary of State. In the buses case, the fault lies not with the OFT or the MMC, but with the inadequate nature of existing UK law concerning predatory behaviour.

Finally, the two other cases listed under this outcome, postal franking machines and electricity meters, also share a common feature. For the remedy to have been effective in both cases, it was necessary for a third party to change its own practices. In the former, the main reason why new entry of maintenance firms has not occurred is that the Post Office has failed effectively to change its over-cautious requirements concerning the maintenance of machines. In the latter, the area electricity boards, for a number of years after the MMC report, apparently continued not to negotiate aggressively with the meter manufacturers on price. In these circumstances, the removal of an information sharing agreement by the manufacturers had little practical effect. It is only more recently, following privatisation, that price competition appears to have tightened. In fact, in this case greater competition has developed in the 1990s due, in part, to the recession of the early 1990s and, in part, to the more aggressive buying behaviour of the RECs since privatisation. Electricity meters might, therefore, be seen as a borderline case (between outcomes C and D).

In summary, the conclusion to be drawn from this section is less favourable than might have been supposed from the brief check list provided in Section 9.3 and Table 9.1. On our assessment, in only three of the 14 case studies (outcomes A and C) can we say that competition concerns no longer remain, and in two of these, this is largely the result of other developments in the marketplace, as opposed to the remedy itself. Although some success can be claimed for the remedies in six other cases (outcome B), there are continuing worries – either because the effectiveness of price controls may have been only a short-term phenomenon, or because the monopoly problem has resurfaced in another form. In five other cases (outcome D), remedies have been largely ineffective and concerns remain, although in the case of bus services in the north-east it is too early to say whether the longer-term remedies will have an effect .

9.6 CONCLUSIONS

We should preface our conclusions by acknowledging that sweeping generalisations about monopoly cases are dangerous. Each case is different, and no matter how carefully one conducts the research, there is inevitably a strong element of opinion in any conclusions drawn. In this book we have not tried to hide this fact. Indeed, by downplaying the use of formal econometric analysis and emphasising interviews which concentrate on opinion and qualitative information, we have deliberately highlighted the 'subjective' element. To do otherwise on such a heterogeneous (and relatively small) group of cases would have been misleading and pointless in our opinion. With this 'health warning' acknowledged, we turn to the lessons we have learned.

9.6.1 Intervention Versus Market Solutions

We begin by recalling the conclusions of Shaw and Simpson from their study of 1959–73 (1989, p. 23):

> 'any assessment of whether the Commission has a useful role to play should attempt to discover how effective its interventions have been in eliminating market power relative to the competitive process. Clearly if the Commission fails to eliminate market power any faster than normal competition between firms, its justification is weakened. The evidence from both the background sample and the case-study suggests that the Monopolies Commission had only a minor impact on the competitive process.'

Our own study has come to a broadly similar conclusion for 1973–95: on balance, *remedies have had a limited impact in the cases with which we were concerned.* However, we do not find much evidence, either, of 'normal competition between firms eliminating market power'. So, although the effectiveness of remedies was limited in practice, *we do not infer from this that there is no need for active intervention in principle.* Thus, our dissatisfaction does not derive from a Chicago or Austrian perspective that the market can be relied upon ultimately to provide the solution to the monopoly problem.

On the contrary, most of the evidence we have uncovered concerning the subsequent reactions of firms in investigated markets relates to efforts they have made either to have remedies removed, or to install alternative means of market control. In some cases, this is the major reason why the remedy has eventually proved to be (at best) only partially successful. This suggests the need for clear-cut rules in the application of remedies, and foresight on behalf of the anti-trust authorities in anticipating strategic responses by the investigated firms.

9.6.2 Comparisons of Different Types of Remedy

In our judgement, the success rate for remedies involving either price control or divestment was significantly higher than for those involving termination of practices.

However, we are unconvinced that even price control remedies provided long-term solutions to market power problems in markets which we have characterised as 'natural oligopolies'. In such cases, price control, once introduced, should not be readily relaxed until there is strong evidence that new entry has effectively transformed the long-run market structure of the industry. Where such entry does not occur, the implication is that price control might have to be used for longer periods of time.

Although divestment appears to have worked well in one of our case studies (artificial lower limbs), and had some effect in another (roadside advertising), we are cautious about drawing strong general conclusions regarding the efficacy of this remedy on the basis of just two cases. In particular, one consequence of divestment which appeared in roadside advertising is worth underlining, because it was also apparent in another, high profile, case not in our sample – beer. This is the tendency for a dramatic structural remedy to provoke a lively bout of subsequent restructuring amongst the divested firms, in the form of mergers. Clearly, this implies that the initial divestment may be only the first stage in a period of subsequent anti-trust interventions (for example, merger referrals) if concentration is not to emerge in a different form.

There are various reasons why termination has not typically proved effective, and since they are not necessarily peculiar to termination *per se*, they have already been enumerated at various places in this chapter. Also, the issues raised in the next sub-section have been particularly relevant in cases where termination has been the chosen remedy.

9.6.3 The Allocation of Responsibilities between the OFT, MMC and DTI and the Secretary of State

The main purpose of this book has been to evaluate the effectiveness of UK monopoly policy at a micro level: how effective have specific remedies been in specific cases? We have not devoted much attention to wider institutional issues. Nevertheless, some of our cases have provided examples where one might question the efficiency of the present four stage system, in which the OFT first makes a referral, the MMC undertakes an investigation, the Secretary of State takes a decision on whether to implement a remedy and the OFT attempts to secure undertakings.

For example, there was at least one case (ice cream) where the MMC was effectively constrained by inappropriately restrictive terms of reference from the OFT. In other cases (most notably films), there were clearly difficulties in converting recommendations in full into practicable remedies – leading to sometimes long delays between the MMC report and remedies being put into place. There are also instances where the Secretary of State effectively watered down the recommendations – arguably to no good effect (for example, films and beer).

Another issue relating to the effective 'power', or rather the absence of it, enjoyed by the MMC concerns cases where for a termination remedy to be effective, the compliance of third parties (such as the Post Office and the area electricity boards in two of our cases) is necessary and this is not always subsequently forthcoming.

Whilst it would be inappropriate for us to form strong conclusions on these issues on the basis of a few examples, it is fair to point out that the effectiveness of the MMC must be judged in the context of the constraints within which it must operate.

9.6.4 Conduct of Investigations

Finally, in the course of our own interviewing, we frequently encountered opinions on the manner in which the MMC conducted its investigations. In the main, there were favourable comments on its fairness and thoroughness.[8] However, many respondents also wondered whether certain very small markets (opium derivatives is perhaps the best example) really merited the high costs (for all parties) that a full-fledged MMC investigation entails. Given that any welfare gains are likely to be limited in such cases, simple cost–benefit calculations might suggest that only briefer and lower cost investigations might have been justified.

On a related issue, the sheer cost to the firms themselves in the investigated markets perhaps leaves smaller firms at a disadvantage: whilst large multinationals are often able to consult panels of skilled lawyers, accountants (and even economists), this option may be beyond the reach of their smaller rivals. We noted some comments on this in our interviews although we recognise that the MMC does make considerable efforts to obtain the views of smaller firms and other parties.

NOTES

1. This is not true in artificial lower limbs where we have argued that the investigation had a 'shining a light' effect in encouraging change in this case.
2. Obviously, more rigorous tests would require standardisation across cases – for example, observations might be taken uniformly, say five years after the remedy was enacted, to compare with market shares and concentration at the time of the investigation, as typically recorded in the MMC report.
3. We should acknowledge our debt to David Elliott for suggesting this typology as a useful summary device.
4. Arguably, foreign imports could curb the market power of the leading firm, British Salt, in this case although in its 1992 review of the case the OFT presumably felt this would not be so.
5. Breakfast cereals has been interpreted in this way by other writers (see Sutton, 1991). For contraceptive sheaths, this characterisation may not always have been appropriate. However, as described in Chapter 5, the market was transformed following the AIDS epidemic, which made advertising more socially acceptable. As a result, LRC has been able to use advertising to exploit its strong brand name and first mover advantage.
6. As noted in Section 8.7.3, the MMC decided in its most recent report against a structural remedy in this case, recommending instead that vertically integrated firms make clear their links with travel agents.
7. A further reference was, in fact, made on 22 December 1997.
8. As academic teachers ourselves, we might add that in some cases MMC reports make admirable teaching resources for precisely these reasons.

10. The Case for Reform

In this final chapter, we consider the case for reform of UK monopoly policy. Whilst this is a broader topic than that discussed in the book as a whole, our findings are clearly relevant to it. In particular, our analysis enables us to consider what 'might have happened' if a different policy framework had been in place during the period we have examined. This, in turn, provides a useful background to the current policy debate in this area.[1]

We outline the basic case for reform in Section 10.1. Section 10.2 considers a counterfactual experiment which examines which cases might, and might not, have been considered under an alternative EU-type framework, and Section 10.3 concludes.

10.1 THE CASE FOR REFORM

As noted in Chapter 2, there has been considerable debate in recent years over reform of UK competition policy. Whilst this has focused, in particular, on reform of restrictive trade practices policy, monopoly policy has also been considered. As far as monopoly policy is concerned, the last Conservative government issued a Green Paper in 1992 which set out various options for reform. This was followed in April 1993 by a Ministerial statement setting out the (Conservative) government's point of view and this was followed by a consultative document (DTI 1996) which was published in March 1996. A draft bill dealing mainly with restrictive agreements was published in August 1996 but then dropped from the government's legislative programme in October 1996 due to lack of parliamentary time. Finally, the Labour Government published its draft competition bill in August 1997 and this is currently being considered in Parliament.

As with restrictive trade practices, a central theme in the policy debate has been whether the UK should adopt an EU-type prohibition approach to monopoly policy in line with article 86 of the Treaty of Rome. In contrast

190

to restrictive trade practices policy, however, where the broad consensus appears to be in favour of prohibition, the case for reform of monopoly policy is less clear. In its 1993 Ministerial statement, the Conservative government took the view that it was *not* desirable to move towards a prohibition approach at that time and opted instead for reform of the present system. However, the new Labour Government has taken a different view and has moved swiftly to introduce policy change. In its draft bill (DTI, 1997a; see also DTI, 1997b) it proposes that the UK adopt a prohibition approach in line with article 86 of the Treaty of Rome. This would imply stronger powers for the OFT to investigate cases, as well as introducing fines. It would also allow private parties to sue for damages when abuse of a dominant position was found. The government also proposes[2] at the present time to keep some parts of the FTA to enable investigations by the MMC (now to be called the Competition Commission) in cases of complex monopoly or where structural remedies might be required in a scale monopoly case. The proposal is, therefore, for a hybrid system with prohibition the usual rule but with scope for MMC (CC) investigation of some individual cases.

The arguments in favour of a prohibition are as follows.[3] First, it would bring UK policy into line with that in the EU (and several other European countries) and thus provide a more consistent approach to monopoly policy in Europe. Given that an article 85-type approach is likely to be adopted in respect of restrictive trade practices, the UK would then face similar policies under both jurisdictions. Second, prohibition would strengthen the law by providing tougher penalties for anti-competitive behaviour and by creating precedents for other cases of abuse. The law would be strengthened in that the competition authority (like the Commission) would have strong powers to investigate cases and the ability to prohibit certain practices and to impose fines. Moreover, over time, a body of evidence would develop which would indicate which types of conduct the competition authority would view as anti-competitive and thereby create precedents for other firms thinking of pursuing such conduct. This contrasts with the current policy where, since each case is dealt with on its merits (often after a long and detailed investigation), no precedents are created. Third, in cases where evidence of anti-competitive behaviour is found, third parties would be able to sue for damages and seek injunctive relief. This might also thereby strengthen the law, by providing further penalties for engaging in such behaviour. It would also remove an important weakness of the current legislation, under which the Secretary of State can ban a particular practice in an individual case but no compensation is available to any injured parties. As we have noted elsewhere in this book, this problem features, in particular, in cases of predatory pricing but would (presumably) also apply in other cases.

On the other hand, there are several disadvantages of an EU-type approach. First, whilst article 86 in principle deals with abuse of market power by one *or more* firms, in practice it has been interpreted in the European courts to apply to only *single* dominant firms (Green Paper, 1992, p. 9). Cases where no one firm is dominant may only be covered under (the equivalent of) article 85, and even then only when evidence of *concerted practices* is found. Moreover, EU policy typically deals with cases where dominant firms have at least a 40 per cent market share, considerably higher than the 25 per cent share used for jurisdictional purposes in the UK (ibid., p. 13). Both features suggest that fewer cases would be considered under an EU-type approach, and this is confirmed in Section 10.2 below. Another feature of EU policy is that it focuses more on *anti-competitive* behaviour than *exploitative* conduct, and this is reflected in the fact that few cases of outright monopoly pricing have been pursued by the Commission (ibid., p. 9). Moreover, the main 'remedies' used by the Commission are prohibition and fines, whilst there are no provisions for the use of divestment or price control in monopoly cases. In our opinion, these are significant weaknesses of EU law, particularly in respect of monopoly pricing. Of course, it would be possible for the UK to adopt a wider policy,[4] but this would obviously deviate from that operating in the EU. Hence, there may be a fine balance between harmonisation with the EU, on the one hand, and a weakening of current UK law on the other.

Overall then, arguments exist for moving to a prohibition system, but the case is by no means clear-cut. The current UK system provides a wide remit for investigations under the FTA and the Competition Act, and strong powers exist to impose remedies, but there is little or no protection for injured parties and the MMC deals with only a limited number of cases. A prohibition system, on the other hand, might better deter certain types of practice and deal with more cases, albeit with less breadth in terms of issues considered and remedies used. There is no overwhelming case in favour of either approach.

10.2 COUNTERFACTUAL ANALYSIS

In this section we consider how an EU-type policy might have operated over the past quarter century in the UK. First, we examine the effects of switching to alternative definitions of market dominance. Table 10.1 provides some evidence on this for the population of 61 cases covered in this book. In the first column, we show how many cases might have been investigated using a 40 per cent market share rule for the largest firm: an indicator typically associated with article 86 investigations (Green Paper, 1992, p. 13). As can be seen, 25 cases (41 per cent) involved no such dominant firm, and, using this criterion, they 'might' not have been pursued under an EU approach. Whilst the MMC made no adverse recommendation in 12 of these cases, the other 13 include some of the more important (and interesting) cases in the period.[5] Similarly (Table 10.2) shows that amongst our own sample of 14 cases, six[6] involved a dominant firm with less than a 40 per cent market share, in all of which, of course, remedies were put in place.

Table 10.1 Analysis of population by firm dominance

	Dominant firm MS1 > 40%	Dominant firm MS1 > 25%	More than one scale monopoly
Yes	36	50	15
No	25	11	46
Total	61	61	61

Note: Market share data are not available in five cases. We have assumed in these cases that the dominant firm has a market share of less than 25 per cent.

On this basis then, we would argue that a 40 per cent criterion is too high, and would have represented an undesirable weakening in the coverage of UK monopoly policy. However, it may be misleading to compare the 40 per cent EU *indicator* with the 25 per cent UK yardstick, which is a *jurisdictional* figure. In fact, there would seem to be no reason why the UK should be restricted to a 40 per cent jurisdictional criterion under any new policy.

If, instead, a 25 per cent market share criterion was retained – but only for the single most dominant firm – the difference between the two systems would have been much smaller. In effect, the only change compared to actual UK practice from 1973–95, would have been that cases *only* involving a complex monopoly (that is, no scale monopoly) would have escaped the net. This amounts to only 11 cases (column 2 of Table 10.1) of which, in turn, only five attracted remedies. In terms of our sample of 14 case studies, only one, foreign package holidays, would have been missed.

There is a second possible way in which an EU-type approach might have narrowed the range of cases actually covered. This is if cases involved more than one scale monopoly and were, therefore, not interpreted as instances of a single dominant firm. Over the period 1973–95, there were 15 instances considered by the MMC where this was the case (column 3 in Table 10.1). Of these, 10 involved a single firm with more than a 40 per cent market share. Clearly such cases *could* be investigated under an EU-type law, but there is a danger that they might be ignored because of the absence of a *single* dominant firm. If so, there is a worry that cases involving tight oligopoly might escape the regulatory net:[7] significantly, only three[8] of these cases involved no remedy.

Table 10.2 Analysis of sample by firm dominance

	Dominant firm MS1 > 40%	Dominant firm MS1 > 25%	More than one scale monopoly
Yes	8	13	6
No	6	1	8
Total	14	14	14

Similarly, Table 10.2, column 3 shows that six of the cases in our sample involved two or more scale monopolies. Of these, two nevertheless also involved a dominant firm (postal franking machines and artificial lower limbs) whilst the remaining four[9] were either B or D category cases (that is, dominant group or loose oligopoly group). It is less certain that these latter four cases would have been investigated under an EU-type approach. Again, an EU-type approach might restrict the scope of the law.

We now turn to the implication of switching to alternative remedies. Recall that in about one third of all UK cases (19 out of 61), in 1973–95, no remedy was applied. In the remaining 42 cases, termination was used in 30 (over two thirds of cases where a remedy was used), price control/price monitoring in seven, and divestment in five. The effects of an EU-type approach would probably have been twofold. First, in the absence of price controls and termination, policy would obviously have been weakened to a considerable extent. In some cases, of course, it would have been possible to apply alternative policies (for example, prohibition of price discrimination might have been used in white salt or opium derivatives) but, in others, particularly where price controls were used, policy effectiveness would have been reduced. The key question is whether these cases were sufficiently important to warrant retaining this policy option in any move to a prohibition approach.

Turning to those cases where termination was involved, arguably, policy might have been *strengthened* in that fines might have been applied. Certainly, we have found in the previous chapter that termination was the least effective of the remedies in general. In only two cases (building bricks and foreign package holidays) did the remedies have some effect, and in one of these, foreign package holidays, this was later undermined by the strategic response of the leading firms. If we put buses in the north-east to one side as being too recent, this leaves five cases where termination had no or little effect. In two of these, one suspects, things would have been little different under an EU-type of approach: frozen foodstuffs, where the problem was overtaken by events, and electricity meters where firms simply chose not to compete. This leaves three other cases. In postal franking machines, it is likely that fines might have worked to some extent, at least in curbing the excesses of some of the salesmen in this case. Similarly, in ice cream and films, fines might also have had some effect – in each case assuming that the competition authority had taken a stronger line. Moreover, arguably, fines in the case of foreign package holidays and buses in the north-east might have proved more effective than the remedies actually put into place.

Clearly, these conclusions are speculative, although they may give some guide to the operation of a prohibition approach. In practice, of course, the effect of policy will depend as much on the way in which the competition authority chooses to operate it, as on the policy itself.

10.3 CONCLUSIONS

It can be argued from the above that a move towards an EU-type prohibition approach, coupled with fines, is required. Certainly some of the case evidence under article 86 (see, for example, Goyder, 1993, Chapter 18) suggests that the Commission and the European Court have taken a firmer line on some cases of monopoly abuse. However, there is nothing in current UK law which precludes the MMC and OFT from adopting a more proactive approach; for example, by anticipating likely responses to remedies introduced. Arguably, increased investigatory powers and new powers to accept undertakings at an early stage, would equally well achieve the same result.

However, there is a residual case for switching to a prohibition approach particularly as it seems likely that UK policy on restrictive trade practices will be brought into line with article 85 of EU competition policy. Our analysis in Section 10.2 suggests that such an approach should use the lower 25 per cent criterion for monopoly cases rather than the implicit 40 per cent used in the EU, and that powers be retained to deal with oligopoly cases where no single firm has a dominant position (category B or D cases on our classification of oligopoly). Attention should also be given to 'complex monopolies' where no individual firm has a 25 per cent market share; such cases could easily fall through the net, especially if no evidence of concerted practices or anti-competitive conduct can be found. Whilst these points suggests some flexibility in the criteria for identifying a monopoly, they could still be regarded as within the spirit of an EU-type approach.

One other factor might also be brought into line: namely, the remedies used in cases of monopoly abuse. Whilst, in principle, article 86 deals with both 'exploitative' and 'anti-competitive' behaviour, in practice policy has been aimed more at the latter than the former. In particular, the Commission has not generally used price controls or divestment as remedies in cases of monopoly abuse. We believe that the UK should retain such powers, even though it would fit less with EU policy: this would be a price worth paying in order to maintain control over certain cases of significant monopoly abuse. On the other hand, introduction of fines would in our view strengthen UK policy, as would the ability of private parties to sue for damages and seek injunctive relief.

NOTES

1. At time of writing, the Labour government has introduced its new competition bill into Parliament. This seeks to reform both restrictive trade practices policy and monopoly policy in the UK. Its latter provisions are discussed briefly in Section 10.1
2. In its consultative document (DTI, 1997b), the government asked for comments on its proposals in this (and other) areas. It is possible that it will introduce some changes to the bill in the committee stage as it goes through Parliament.

3. For more detailed arguments see Green Paper (1992).
4. As, indeed, is proposed in the new competition bill.
5. The cases are: frozen foodstuffs, electricity meters, roadside advertising, car parts, films, foreign package holidays, specialised advertising, beer, electrical contracting, cars, national newspapers, video games and bus services in the north-east.
6. The cases are: frozen foodstuffs, electricity meters, roadside advertising, films, foreign package holidays and buses in the north-east.
7. This would appear to be a real possibility if evidence of collusive behaviour could not be found and if no evidence of anti-competitive tactics was also found.
8. The cases are cat and dog foods, contact lens solutions and on-line databases.
9. Ice cream, films, white salt and buses in the north-east.

Appendix: The Population of Cases: 1973–95[1]

No.	MMC Case	MMC Report	Main Problem[2]	Scale/ Complex	MS1	MS2	MS3	CR3	Structure Type[3]	Remedy[4]
66	Asbestos	1973	EXP	S	44	25	11	80	B	T
67	**Breakfast cereals**	1973	MP	S	55	22	12	89	A	PC/PM
68	Librium & valium	1973	MP	S	100	0	0	100	A	PC
69	Footwear machinery	1973	DP/PRED	S	51	11	5	67	C	T
73	Wire & fibre ropes	1973	MP	S	54	6	4	64	C	T
74	Plasterboard	1974	DP	S	100	0	0	100	A	T
75	Cross-Channel car ferries	1974	C	2S,C	45	35	8	88	B	T
81	Primary batteries	1974	MP	S	75	12	6	93	A	PC/PM
82	**Contraceptive sheaths**	1975	MP	S	90	10	0	100	A	PC/PM
88	**Building bricks**	1976	DP/PRED	S	41	11	8	60	C	T
99	**Frozen foods**	1976	EXP	S	31	11	11	53	D	T
100	Photocopiers	1976	TIE	S	89	11	0	100	A	T
102	Diazo copying materials	1977	DP	S	52	6	4	62	C	None
105	Flour & bread	1977	VI	C	31	19	11	61	D	None
106	Cat & dog foods	1977	C	2S	49	29	5	83	B	None
113	Ceramic sanitaryware	1978	C	S,C	31	21	19	71	D	None
114	Petrol	1979	EXP/DP	C	20	19	15	54	D	None
116	Insulated wires & cables	1979	MP	S,C	37	16	10	63	D	None
119	**Ice cream**	1979	EXP/(TIE)	2S,C	45	45	4	94	B	T
120	**Electricity meters**	1979	C	S,C	27	25	25	77	B	T
124	Domestic gas appliances	1980	VI	5S,C	97	3	0	100	A	D

127	Credit card services	1980	DP	2S,C	39	36	17	92	B	T
130	Tampons	1980	C	2S	61	39	0	100	A	PM
132	Liquefied petroleum gas	1981	EXP/TIE	S	73	8	6	87	A	T
140	**Roadside advertising**	1981	C	S,2C	25	24	10	59	D	D
142	Ready-mixed concrete	1981	VI	S	33	13	10	56	D	None
145	Concrete roofing tiles	1981	DP	2S	46	36	12	94	B	T
148	Trading check franchise	1981	EXP	S,C	66	10	7	83	A	T
151	Car parts	1982	EXP/EXD	C	14	8	5	27	D	T
158	*Contraceptive sheaths*	1982	MP	S	92	4	n.a.	96	A	PC/PM
165	**Films**	1983	EXD/(TIE)	4S,C	32	26	n.a.	58	D	T
168	Caravan sites	1983	TIE	C	17	10	7	34	D	None
187	Animal waste	1985	PRED	S	69	7	3	79	A	T
195	*Tampons*	1986	MP	2S	59	38	n.a.	97	B	None
197	**Postal franking machines**	1986	TIE	2S	60	29	6	95	A	T
200	**White salt**	1986	C	2S	50	45	3	98	B	PC
201	Greyhound racing	1986	EXP/EXD	C	n.a.	n.a.	n.a.	n.a.	u	None
205	**Foreign package holidays**	1986	RPM/(EXD)	C	n.a.	n.a.	n.a.	n.a.	D	T
209	Steel wire fencing	1987	DP	S	65	10	5	80	A	None
215	Marine radio	1987	TIE	S	79	15	6	100	A	None
222	Specialised advertising	1988	EXD/DP	C	n.a.	n.a.	n.a.	n.a.	u	T
225	Pest control	1988	MP	S	61	3	2	66	C	T
232	Gas	1988	EXP	S	100	0	0	100	A	T
245	Beer	1989	EXP/VI	C	23	13	11	47	D	D
249	**Opium derivatives**	1989	MP	S	88	11	1	100	A	PM
251	**Artificial lower limbs**	1989	VI/MP	2S	71	26	1	98	A	(D)
255	*Credit card services*	1989	DP/TIE	S	39	17	13	69	D	T

No.	MMC Case	MMC Report	Main Problem	Scale/ Complex	MS1	MS2	MS 3	CR3	Structure Type	Remedy
261	*Cross-Channel car ferries*	1989	MP/C	2S	54	36	10	100	B	None
265	*Petrol*	1990	EXP/DP	C	19	16	13	48	D	None
269	Electrical contracting	1990	TIE	C	n.a.	n.a.	n.a.	n.a.	u	T
273	Cinema advertising	1990	VI	S,C	78	22	0	100	A	None
286	Plasterboard	1990	MP	S	65	18	10	93	A	None
300	Coffee	1991	MP	S	56	25	8	89	A	None
302	Razors & razor blades	1991	MP	S	60	20	15	95	A	None
309	Carbonated soft drinks	1991	EXP/TIE	S,C	43	22	6	71	C	D
310	*Photocopiers*	1991	TIE	S,3C	31	14	7	52	D	T
313	Cars	1992	EXP/EXD	S,C	26	17	14	57	D	T
314	*Motor car parts*	1992	EXP/EXD	C	14	8	5	27	D	None
315	Cross Solent ferries	1992	MP	S	77	19	4	100	A	None
317	Matches & disp. lighters	1992	MP	S	86	5	5	96	A	T
332	Contact lens solutions	1993	RPM	3S,4C	38	34	9	81	B	None
336	Bus services in Kent	1993	PRED/VI	S	95	5	0	100	A	T
339	*Animal waste*	1993	DP/PRED	S	50	4	n.a.	54	C	T
342	Fine fragrances	1993	EXD	C	n.a	n.a.	n.a.	n.a	D	None
343	Exhaust gas analysers	1993	TIE	C	24	16	14	54	D	None
345	National newspapers	1993	EXD/RPM	2S,2C	28	17	12	57	D	T
351	*Ice cream*	1994	EXP	S	67	11	10	88	A	None
352	*Contraceptive sheaths*	1994	EXP	S	80	16	3	99	A	T
354	On-line databases	1994	EXD	2S	40	30	10	80	B	None
356	Compact discs	1994	MP	S,C	24	21	10	55	D	None

357	*Films*	1994	EXD/TIE	S,C	27	21	20	68	D	T
359	Video games	1995	EXD/DP	S,C	38	24	10	72	D	T
371	**Bus services in the north-east**	1995	PRED	2S	33	33	11	77	B	T

1. This table lists 73 cases for the period 1973–95 omitting 17 cases which dealt with the supply of professional services or other issues not of direct relevance to this study. Twelve cases (shown in italics) involved repeat referrals leaving a net population of 61. The 14 detailed case studies considered in this book are shown in bold.

2. This is the main problem identified in this book and, in some cases, an element of judgement is involved in this classification. The problems are: MP – monopoly pricing; DP – discriminatory pricing; PRED – predatory behaviour; C – collusive behaviour; EXD – exclusive distribution; EXP – exclusive purchasing; TIE – tie-in sale; VI – vertical integration; RPM – resale price maintenance.

3. The categories are: A – dominant firm; B – dominant group; C – partial dominance; D – loose oligopoly.

4. Remedies are PC/PM – price control/price monitoring, D – divestment; T – termination of practices.

n.a. denotes not available; u denotes unclassified.

201

References

Abreu, D. (1986), 'Extremal equilibria of oligopolistic supergames', *Journal of Economic Theory*, **39**, 191–225.

Areeda, P. and D.F. Turner (1974/5), 'Predatory pricing and related practices under section 2 of the Sherman Act', *Harvard Law Review*, **88**, 697–733.

Banerjee, A. and L. Summers (1987), 'On frequent flyer programs and other loyalty-inducing economic arrangements', Harvard University Working Paper.

Baumol, W.J. (1979–80), 'Quasi-permanence of price reductions: a policy for prevention of predatory pricing', *Yale Law Journal*, **89**, 1–26.

Baumol, W.J. (1982), 'Contestable markets: an uprising in the theory of industry structure', *American Economic Review*, **72**, 1–15.

Baumol, W.J., J.C. Panzar and R.D. Willig (1982), *Contestable Markets and the Theory of Industry Structure*, New York: Harcourt.

Blair, R.D. and J.M. Fesmire (1994), 'The resale price maintenance policy dilemma', *Southern Economic Journal*, **60**, 1043–7.

Blair, R.D. and J.M. Fesmire (1996), 'The resale price maintenance policy dilemma – reply', *Southern Economic Journal*, **62**, 1087–9.

Blair, R.D. and T.R. Lewis (1994), 'Optimal retail contracts with asymmetric information and moral hazard', *Rand Journal of Economics*, **25**, 284–96.

Bork, R. (1978), *The Antitrust Paradox*, New York: Basic Books.

Caminal, R. and C. Matutes (1990), 'Endogenous switching costs in a duopoly model', *International Journal of Industrial Organisation*, **8**, 335–73.

Carlton, D.W. and J.M. Perloff (1994), *Modern Industrial Organization*, 2nd edn. New York: Harper Collins.

Clarke, R. (1985), *Industrial Economics*, Oxford: Basil Blackwell.

Clarke, R. and N.L. Driffield (1995), 'European merger policy: past, present, future', *Cardiff Business School Discussion Paper*, no. 95: 041.

Clarke, R., S.W. Davies and N.L. Driffield (1995), 'Remedies to monopoly abuse – stage 2', Report to the Office of Fair Trading, London, September 1995.

Clarke, R., S.W. Davies and M. Waterson (1984), 'The profitability–concentration relation: market power or efficiency?', *Journal of Industrial Economics*, **32**, 435–50.

Clarke, R., S.W. Davies, N.L. Driffield and M. Lund (1994) 'Remedies to monopoly abuse: the effectiveness of measures implemented after MMC monopoly investigations', Report to the Office of Fair Trading, London, September 1994.

Cooper, T.E. (1986), 'Most-favored-customer pricing and tacit collusion', *Rand Journal of Economics*, **17**, 377–88.

202

Davies, S.W. (1996), 'Competition and competition policy in the UK', in *OECD Surveys: United Kingdom*, Paris: OECD.

Davies, S.W. and P. Geroski (1997), 'Changes in concentration, turbulence and the dynamics of market shares', *Review of Economics and Statistics*, 79, 383-91.

Davies, S.W., P. Geroski, M. Lund and A. Vlassopoulos (1991), *The Dynamics of Market Leadership in UK Manufacturing Industry, 1979-86*, London: Centre for Business Strategy, London Business School.

Davies, S.W., B.R. Lyons, H. Dixon and P. Geroski (1989), *Economics of Industrial Organisation*, London: Longman.

Demsetz, H. (1973), 'Industry structure, market rivalry and public policy', *Journal of Law and Economics*, 16, 1-9.

Dobson, P.W. and M. Waterson (1994), 'The effects of exclusive purchasing on inter-brand and intra-brand rivalry', University of Warwick, Economics Working Paper.

Dobson, P.W. and M. Waterson (1996), 'Vertical restraints and competition policy', *OFT Research Papers*, no. 12.

Dobson, P.W. and M. Waterson (1997), 'Countervailing power and consumer prices', *Economic Journal*, 107, 418-30.

DTI (1996), *Tackling Cartels and the Abuse of Market Power: Implementing the Government's Policy for Competition Law Reform*, London: DTI.

DTI (1997a), *Competition Bill*, London: DTI.

DTI (1997b), *A Prohibition Approach to Anti-Competitive Agreements and Abuse of Dominant Position: Draft Bill*, London: DTI.

Gal-Or, E. (1991), 'Duopolistic vertical restraints', *European Economic Review*, 35, 1237-53.

Geroski, P. (1989), 'Competition policy and the structure–performance paradigm', in S.W. Davies, B.R. Lyons, H. Dixon and P. Geroski, *Economics of Industrial Organisation*, London: Longman.

Gilligan, T.W. (1986), 'The competitive effects of retail price maintenance', *Rand Journal of Economics*, 17, 544-56.

Goyder, D.G. (1993), *EC Competition Law*, Oxford: Oxford University Press.

Green Paper (1992), *Abuse of Market Power: a Consultative Document on Possible Legislative Options*, London: HMSO.

Green Paper (1997), *Vertical Restraints in EC Competition Policy*, Brussels: European Commission.

Grossman, S.J. and O.D. Hart (1986), 'The costs and benefits of ownership: a theory of vertical and lateral integration', *Journal of Political Economy*, 94, 691-719.

Hart, P.E. and R. Clarke (1980), *Concentration in British Industry: 1935-75*, Cambridge: Cambridge University Press.

Jones, I., C. Willis, J. Jorge, S.W. Davies and R. Clarke (1996), 'The effectiveness of undertakings in the bus industry', Report to the Office of Fair Trading, London, July 1996.

Joskow, P. and A. Klevorick (1979), 'A framework for analyzing predatory pricing policy', *Yale Law Journal*, 89, 213-70.

Klemperer, P. (1992), 'Competition in the presence of switching costs: an overview', CEPR Discussion Paper, no. 704.

Korah, V. (1994), *An Introductory Guide to EC Competition Law and Practice*, 5th edn. London: Sweet and Maxwell.

Kuhn, K-U., P. Seabright and A. Smith (1992), *Competition policy research: where do we stand?*, London: CEPR Occasional Paper no. 8.

Kwoka, J.E. and L.J. White (1989), *The Antitrust Revolution*, Chicago: Scott Foreman and Co.

Marvel, H.P. and S. McCafferty (1985), 'The welfare effects of resale price maintenance', *Journal of Law and Economics*, **28**, 363–79.

Mathewson, G.F. and R.A. Winter (1984), 'An economic theory of vertical restraints', *Rand Journal of Economics*, **15**, 27–38.

McGee, J.S. (1958), 'Predatory price cutting: the Standard Oil (NJ) case', *Journal of Law and Economics*, **1**, 137–69.

McGee, J.S. (1980), 'Predatory pricing revisited', *Journal of Law and Economics*, **23**, 289–330.

Monopolies and Mergers Commission (1981), *Full Line Forcing and Tie in Sales*, London: HMSO.

Morrison, E., A. Sewell, D. Matthew, D. Elliott and M. Parr (1996), 'Cost benefit assessment of competition inquiries and *de minimus* thresholds', London: Office of Fair Trading.

Myers, G. (1994), 'Predatory behaviour in UK competition policy', *OFT Research Papers*, no. 5.

Nuttall, R. and J. Vickers (1996), 'Competition policy for regulated utility industries in Britain', mimeo.

O'Brien, D.P. and G. Shaffer (1992), 'Vertical control with bilateral contracts', *Rand Journal of Economics*, **23**, 299–308.

Office of Fair Trading (1995), 'Monopolies and anti-competitive practices: a guide to the provisions of the Fair Trading Act 1973 and the Competition Act 1980', London: HMSO.

Office of Fair Trading (1996), 'Register of undertakings and orders under the Competition Act 1980 and the monopoly provisions of the Fair Trading Act 1973', London: Office of Fair Trading.

Ornstein, S.I. (1989), 'Exclusive dealing and antitrust', *Antitrust Bulletin*, **34**, 65–98.

Padilla, J. (1991), 'Dynamic duopoly with customer switching costs: an overlapping generations model', CEMFI Working Paper, Madrid.

Perry, M.K. and R.H. Porter (1990), 'Can resale price maintenance and franchise fees correct sub-optimal levels of retail service?', *International Journal of Industrial Organization*, **8**, 115–41.

Phlips, L. (1995), *Competition Policy: a Game Theoretic Perspective*, Cambridge: Cambridge University Press.

Pittman, R. (1985), 'Tying without exclusive dealing', *Antitrust Bulletin*, **30**, 279–97.

Porter, R. and J.D. Zona (1993), 'Detection of bid-rigging in procurement auctions', *Journal of Political Economy*, **101**, 518–38.

Posner, R. (1981), 'The next step in the antitrust treatment of restricted distribution – per se legality', *University of Chicago Law Review*, **48**, 6–26.

Rees, R. (1993a), 'Tacit collusion', *Oxford Review of Economic Policy*, 9, 27–40.

Rees, R. (1993b), 'Collusive equilibrium in the great salt duopoly', *Economic Journal*, 103, 833–48.

Rey, P. and J. Stiglitz (1995), 'The role of exclusive territories in producers' competition', *Rand Journal of Economics*, 26, 431–51.

Robertson, A. and M. Williams (1995), 'An ice-cream war: the law and economics of freezer exclusivity', *European Competition Law Review*, 16.7-20.

Salop, S.C. (1986), 'Practices that (credibly) facilitate oligopolistic coordination', in J.E. Stiglitz, and G.F. Mathewson (eds), *New Developments in the Analysis of Market Structure*, London: Macmillan.

Scherer, F.M. and D. Ross (1990), *Industrial Market Structure and Economic Performance*, 3rd edn. Boston: Houghton Mifflin.

Schmalensee, R. (1978), 'Entry deterrence in the ready-to-eat breakfast cereal industry', *Bell Journal of Economics*, 9, 305–27.

Selten, R. (1978), 'The chain store paradox', *Theory and Decision*, 9, 127–59.

Shaffer, G. (1991), 'Capturing strategic rent: full line forcing, brand discounts, aggregate rebates and maximum resale price maintenance', *Journal of Industrial Economics*, 39, 557–76.

Shaw, R. and P. Simpson (1986), 'The persistence of monopoly: an investigation of the effectiveness of the UK Monopolies Commission', *Journal of Industrial Economics*, 34, 355–72.

Shaw, R. and P. Simpson (1989), *The Monopolies Commission and the Market Process*, London: Institute of Fiscal Studies.

Spengler, J. (1950), 'Vertical integration and anti-trust policy', *Journal of Political Economy*, 58, 347–52.

Steiner, R.L. (1991), 'Intrabrand competition – stepchild of antitrust', *Antitrust Bulletin*, 36, 155–200.

Stenbacka, L.R. (1990), 'Collusion in dynamic oligopolies in the presence of entry threats', *Journal of Industrial Economics*, 39, 147–54.

Sutherland, A. (1970), *The Monopolies Commission in Action*, Cambridge: Cambridge University Press.

Sutton, J. (1991), *Sunk Costs and Market Structure*, Cambridge, Mass.: MIT Press.

Telser, L.G. (1960), 'Why should manufacturers want fair trade?', *Journal of Law and Economics*, 3, 86–105.

Tirole, J. (1988), *The Theory of Industrial Organization*, Cambridge, Mass.: MIT Press.

Utton, M.A. (1986), *Profits and the Stability of Monopoly*, London: NIESR Occasional Papers.

Utton, M.A. (1994), 'Anti-competitive practices and the UK Competition Act 1980', *Antitrust Bulletin*, 39, 485–539.

Utton, M.A. (1995), *Market Dominance and Antitrust Policy*, Aldershot: Edward Elgar.

Vernon, J. and D. Graham (1971), 'Profitability of monopolisation by vertical integration', *Journal of Political Economy*, 79, 924–5.

Vickers, J. (1996), 'Market power and inefficiency: a contracts perspective', *Oxford Review of Economic Policy*, 12, 11–26.

Warren-Boulton, F.R. (1974), 'Vertical control with variable proportions', *Journal of Political Economy*, **82**, 783–802.

Weiss, A. (1994), 'Vertical mergers and firm-specific physical capital', *Journal of Industrial Economics*, **42**, 395–417.

Williamson, O.E. (1975), *Markets and Hierarchies*, London: Macmillan.

Williamson, O.E. (1985), *The Economic Institutions of Capitalism*, New York: Free Press.

Index

Abreu, D., 95, 104
Abreu/Lambson model, 95
advertising, 6, 31, 63, 64, 65, 66, 67,
    72, 80, 89, 90, 92, 98, 100, 130,
    131, 134, 177, 182, 189
advertising agencies, 89, 90, 91
aggregated rebates, 121
AIDS, 66, 67, 72, 78, 80, 189
Airport Act (1986), 17
alignment, 133, 135–6, 170
Alternative Investment Market (AIM),
    73
animal waste, 105, 113, 199, 201
anti-competitive agreements, 16, 18,
    21, 82, 170, 190
anti-competitive behaviour, 11, 15, 18,
    24, 61, 71, 142, 191, 192, 196,
    197
anti-competitive practices, 11, 16, 18,
    21, 25, 39, 42, 102, 112, 115, 116,
    121, 145, 156, 167, 184, 190, 191
anti-trust authorities, 116, 118, 187
anti-trust policy, 1, 32, 52, 62, 79, 116,
    175, 176, 177, 187
    see also UK competition policy
Area Electricity Boards (AEBs), 85, 86,
    88, 99, 185, 188
Areeda, P., 104
Artificial Limbs and Appliance
    Centres, 146, 147, 148, 149, 150,
    172
artificial lower limbs, 3, 44, 49, 54, 55,
    62, 124, 125, 146–51, 157, 159,
    169, 178, 180, 181, 182, 183, 184,
    189, 194, 200
asbestos, 123, 162–3, 198

asset specificity, 119
Austrian school of thought, 176, 187
Avon bus case (1989), 115

Banerjee, A., 99
barriers to entry, 6, 12, 52, 61, 68, 71,
    76–7, 78, 80, 83, 94, 106, 108,
    113, 117, 118, 119, 121, 131, 132,
    138, 142, 145, 161, 164, 168, 170,
    176, 177
barring, 133, 135, 158, 170
basing point pricing, 99
Baumol, W.J., 61, 115
beer, 25, 41, 49, 70, 120, 124, 125,
    151, 153–4, 159, 162, 169, 187,
    188, 197, 200
Blair, R.D., 120, 122
Bognor bus case (1990), 115
books RPM case, 26
Bork, R., 117
brand proliferation, 63, 80, 98
breakfast cereals, 11, 25, 42, 54,
    55, 62, 63–5, 78, 79, 80, 178,
    180, 182, 183, 184, 189, 198
Brewers Society, 153
Broadcasting Act (1990), 17, 18
building bricks, 11, 54, 55, 105,
    106–8, 111, 114, 178, 180,
    181, 183, 195, 198
bus cases, 104, 105, 106
    and deregulation, 108, 109, 112
bus services in the Isle of Arran, 27
bus services in Kent, 105, 112–13,
    201
bus services in the north-east, 3,
    49, 54, 55, 105, 106, 108–11,

112, 113, 114, 115, 178, 180,
183, 185, 186, 195, 197, 202
buying power,
  see monopsony power

Caminal, R., 99
caravan sites in Northern Ireland, 49,
  123, 165, 199
carbonated soft drinks, 124, 161–2,
  201
Carlton, D.W., 49
car parts, 41, 123, 160–61, 197,
  199, 201
cars, 120, 124, 151, 154–5, 160,
  197, 201
cartels, 22, 82, 98
cat and dog foods, 84, 98, 99, 197,
  198
Celler-Kefauver Act (1950), 21
ceramic sanitaryware, 84, 98, 198
Chicago school, 104, 117, 176,
  177, 187
cinema advertising, 124, 167, 200
Clarke, R., 6, 11, 23, 49, 52, 54, 56,
  118, 176
Clayton Act (1914), 21, 24
coffee, 62, 78, 200
collusion, 5, 7, 11, 21, 35, 40, 46,
  80, 82, 83, 94, 98, 99, 117,
  120, 132, 184
  see also collusive behaviour,
  collusive practices
collusive behaviour, 7, 39, 40, 41,
  49, 54, 55, 176, 197, 198–202
collusive practices, 10, 40–41, 43,
  48, 55, 82–101
commodity building, 121
Common Market, 72
compact discs, 62, 77, 79, 99, 201
Companies Act (1989), 17, 26
Competition Act (1980), 16, 17,
  18, 19, 20, 21, 24, 27, 50, 105,
  115, 169, 192
Competition bill, 1, 4, 11, 25, 27,
  190, 196, 197
Competition Commission, 191

competition policy,
  see antitrust policy, UK competition
  policy
complementary products, 121
complex monopoly, 7, 16, 22, 28, 34,
  39, 46, 47, 55, 89, 98, 122, 142,
  157, 160, 165, 166, 168, 169, 191,
  196, 198–202
concentration, 28, 30, 34–9, 46, 48, 49,
  51, 66, 91, 92, 108, 125, 143–4,
  145, 154, 176, 179, 187, 189
concentration ratio, 35–8, 47, 92,
  157, 180, 198–202
concerted action, 23, 99, 192, 196
concrete roofing tiles, 105, 112,
  199
condition of entry
  see barriers to entry
conglomerate firms, 32, 33, 179
contact lens solutions, 49, 124,
  167–8, 197, 201
contestable market, 61
contraceptive sheaths, 11, 25, 42, 55,
  62, 63, 65–72, 78, 79, 124, 178,
  180, 181, 182, 183, 189, 198,
  199, 201
Cooper, T.E., 99
countervailing power, 91, 126, 136
Courts and Legal Services Act
  (1990), 17
credit card services, 41, 105, 115,
  199, 200
Cross-Channel ferries, 84, 96–7, 98,
  99, 198, 200
Cross-Solent ferries, 62, 78, 201

Davies, S.W., 6, 11, 26, 49, 52, 54, 56,
  57, 176
Demsetz, H., 52
Department of Health and Social
  Security, 80, 147, 168
Department of Justice,
  see US Department of Justice
Department of Trade and Industry, 1, 3,
  16, 188, 190, 191, 196
Deregulation and Contracting Out

Act (1994), 16, 17, 24, 26
diazo copying materials, 105, 114, 198
Director General of Fair Trading, 11, 15, 17, 24, 26, 41, 97, 112, 135, 144
Disablement Services Authority, 147–8, 150–51, 172
diversified firms,
  see conglomerate firms
divestment, 3, 5, 25, 42, 43, 44, 48, 54, 55, 62, 77, 84, 89, 91, 93, 98, 99, 123–4, 125, 133, 148, 153–4, 157, 159, 162, 167, 172, 176, 177, 178, 179, 187, 192, 194, 196, 198–202
Dobson, P.W., 8, 11, 118, 120
domestic electrical products case (1997), 77, 81, 122
domestic gas appliances, 38, 44, 123, 125, 142, 166–7, 199
dominant firm, 5, 22, 34, 35–8, 40–41, 44, 47, 48, 49, 51, 54, 55, 57, 62, 63, 65, 68, 70, 76, 77, 78, 79, 84, 92, 99, 104, 105, 106, 108, 113, 114, 123–4, 125, 139, 146, 157, 158, 162, 164–5, 166, 172, 176, 180, 184, 192, 193, 194, 198–202
dominant group, 36–7, 40–41, 44, 47, 48, 49, 54, 55, 62, 84, 105, 123–4, 125, 180, 194, 196, 198–202
double marginalisation, 117, 118
Driffield, N.L., 11, 23, 54, 56
dumping, 74
duopoly, 84, 93–4, 97, 98, 104, 112, 128, 180, 182, 183

EC Green Paper on Vertical Restraints (1997), 26
economies of scale, 6, 92
economies of scope, 151
efficiency, 52, 53, 78, 82, 83, 98, 99, 101, 109, 116, 119, 120, 121, 130, 143, 151, 152, 153,

163, 167, 169, 171
electrical contracting, 38, 49, 124, 165–6, 197, 200
Electricity Act (1989), 17
Electricity Council, 86
electricity meters, 11, 55, 84, 85–8, 96, 98, 99, 142, 178, 180, 183, 185, 195, 197, 199
Elliot, D., 27, 189
endogenous sunk costs, 6, 77, 79, 80, 177
EU competition policy, 3, 4, 10, 15, 20–23, 24, 25, 26, 27, 99, 155, 191, 192, 193, 194, 195, 196
EU industrial policy, 23
EU merger regulation, 20, 21, 22
European Commission, 11, 20, 22, 23, 74, 88, 129, 155, 170, 191, 192, 195
  and DG IV, 21, 22, 23
European Community,
  see European Union
European Court, 22, 75, 170, 192, 195
European Union, 73, 74, 88, 92, 112, 154, 155, 156, 160, 170, 190, 192
exclusive dealing,
  see exclusive purchasing
exclusive distribution, 9, 11, 26, 39, 40, 55, 119–20, 122–4, 125, 132, 133, 154–5, 155–6, 158, 163–4, 168, 198–202
exclusive practices, 40, 41, 42, 43, 48, 49, 57, 102, 118, 128, 135, 157, 158, 171
exclusive purchasing, 8, 9, 11, 23, 24, 26, 39, 40, 55, 67, 71, 119–20, 122–4, 125, 128, 132, 151–2, 153, 159, 160–63, 198–202
exclusive wholesale distribution, 128, 129, 130, 131, 132, 158, 170, 185
exhaust gas analysers, 124, 165, 201

Fair Trading Act (1973), 1, 3, 15,
    16, 17, 18, 19, 21, 22, 24–5,
    26, 27, 28, 29, 34, 37, 41, 64,
    111, 115, 162, 191, 192
Federal Trade Commission,
    see US Federal Trade Commission
Fesmire, J.M., 122
Fife bus case (1994), 115
films, 11, 25, 41, 49, 55, 57, 123,
    125, 129, 132–7, 157, 158,
    159, 170, 178, 180, 181, 183,
    185, 188, 195, 197, 199, 202
Financial Services Act (1986), 17
fine fragrances, 124, 151, 155–6,
    160, 201
fines, 18, 21, 22, 24, 27, 191, 192,
    195, 196
first mover advantage, 131, 135,
    164, 189
flour and bread, 123, 167, 198
footwear machinery, 105, 113, 198
foreclosure, 9, 89, 102, 117, 126,
    132, 133, 157, 161–2
foreign package holidays, 3, 41, 54,
    55, 123, 125, 142–6, 157, 159,
    169, 178, 180, 181, 183, 184,
    194, 197, 200
franchising, 70, 122, 154, 160–61,
    169
free entry, 62
free riding, 155–6, 168
free trade, 75
freezer exclusivity, 126–7, 128,
    129, 131, 132, 157, 158, 169,
    170, 185
frequency of exchange, 119
frozen foodstuffs, 11, 54, 55, 57, 123,
    125, 126–7, 157, 159, 178, 180,
    197, 198 181, 183, 184, 195,
full-line forcing, 9, 39, 121

Gal-Or, E., 121
game theory, 2, 7, 39, 95, 104, 176,
    177
gas, 124, 162, 172, 200
Gas Act (1986), 17
gas case (1993), 27

gateways, 16
Geroski, P., 57
Gilligan, T.W., 122
Goyder, D.G., 26, 195
Graham, D., 119
Greater Manchester bus case
    (1992–4), 115
Green Paper, *Abuse of Market
    Power* (1992), 27, 190, 192,
    193, 196
greyhound racing, 38, 49, 123,
    164, 200
Grossman, S.J., 119

harmonisation conference, 97
Hart, O.D., 119
Hart, P.E., 49
Highland Scottish bus case (1990),
    115
Home Office, 72, 73, 74

ice cream, 3, 11, 54, 55, 57, 120,
    123, 126, 128–32, 157, 178,
    180, 181, 183, 185, 188, 195,
    197, 199, 201
import competition, 30–31, 62, 72,
    74, 75, 76, 85, 88, 95, 96, 100,
    148, 178, 182, 189
index-x formula, 80, 94, 100
industry structure, 34–9, 40–41, 44,
    51, 53, 54, 57, 89, 90, 92, 96–
    7, 122, 139, 141, 142, 148–9
inefficient allocation of resources, 6, 8
inequality index, 35–8
information sharing agreements,
    49, 83, 84, 96, 98, 99, 185
insulated wires and cables, 62, 77,
    79, 199
intellectual property rights, 26
inter-brand competition, 9, 117,
    118, 119, 120, 125, 126, 132,
    133, 151, 153, 154, 157, 158,
    159
intra-brand competition, 9, 118,
    120, 133, 153, 155, 156, 157,
    159
Isle of Wight bus case (1988), 115

joint selling agency, 84, 89, 90
joint ventures, 23
Jones, I., 11, 57, 106, 115
Joskow, P., 103

Klemperer, P., 99
Klevorick, A., 103
Korah, V., 22, 26
Kuhn, K-U., 83, 120
Kwoka, J.E., 122

Lewis, T.R., 120, 122
liberalisation of electricity supply,
    87–8, 100
librium and valium, 62, 76, 113,
    115, 198
limit pricing, 103
liquefied petroleum gas, 123, 162,
    199
literal monopoly, 36–7, 61–2, 111
lobbying, 63, 64, 66, 70, 79, 99,
    170
local monopolies, 153, 159
loose oligopoly, 36–8, 40–41, 44,
    47, 48, 49, 54, 55, 62, 84, 123–
    4, 125, 194, 196, 198–202
'loyalty clause' policies, 83, 120
Lund, M., 11, 54

marine radio, 38, 123, 166, 200
market concentration,
    see concentration
market definition, 93
market dominance, 177, 179, 180,
    193
market power,
    see monopoly power
market shares, 4, 5, 18, 26, 27, 35,
    37, 38, 51, 52, 53, 57, 63, 64,
    65, 67, 70, 77, 78, 79, 80, 86,
    93, 100, 107, 108, 109, 115,
    127, 128, 134, 140, 149, 152,
    157–8, 167, 169, 172, 176,
    177, 179, 180, 184, 189, 192,
    194, 198–20
market structure, 10, 28, 47, 55, 175,
    177, 178, 179–81, 187, 198–202

Marvel, H.P., 169
matches and disposable lighters,
    62, 77, 124, 201
Mathewson, G.F., 121
Matutes, C., 99
McCafferty, S., 169
McColl Report, 147
McGee, J.S., 11, 114
medicaments case, 26
Medicines Control Agency, 168
'meet the competition' policy, 83
merger guidelines, 21
mergers, 16, 17, 18, 19, 20, 21, 22,
    26, 83–4, 90, 91–2, 93, 97, 99,
    100, 115, 152, 180, 184, 187
    see also takeovers
minimum exhibition period, 135,
    136
Ministry of International Trade and
    Industry, 23
Monopolies Commission, 4, 186
Monopolies and Mergers
    Commission, *passim*
Monopolies and Restrictive
    Practices Commission, 10, 15
Monopolies and Restrictive
    Practices (Inquiry and Control)
    Act (1948), 15, 162
monopoly power, 9, 11, 16, 17, 22,
    27, 34, 35, 44, 47, 52–3, 63, 64,
    65, 70, 72, 74, 76, 77, 92, 93, 98,
    99, 101, 118, 119, 121, 125, 147,
    151, 171, 178, 186, 187, 189
monopoly pricing, 6–7, 10, 21, 39,
    40, 41, 43, 48, 54, 55, 61–81, 89,
    94, 99, 113, 144, 146, 147, 154,
    166, 176, 192, 198–202
monopoly problems, 5–9, 10, 28,
    39–41, 43, 48, 53, 54, 55, 57, 117,
    175, 176, 178, 186, 198–202
monopoly profits, 6, 61, 63, 65, 70,
    72, 76, 77, 89, 91, 117, 122,
    132, 147, 168, 176
monopoly rents,
    see monopoly profits
monopsony power, 8, 11, 71, 89,
    90, 91, 95, 108

Morrison, E., 50
'most favoured customer' practice,
    39, 83, 171
multinational firms, 31, 33, 129,
    131, 151, 170, 179, 189
Myers, G., 11, 103

National Board for Prices and
    Income, 11
National Health Service, 75, 76,
    80, 146, 147, 149, 150, 159,
    182
nationalised industries, 19, 20, 50,
    97, 99, 108
national newspapers, 124, 163–4,
    168–9, 197, 201
natural monopoly, 6, 61, 79, 177,
    183
natural oligopoly, 32, 79, 177, 187
new entry, 65, 66, 67, 68, 70, 71,
    72, 75, 76, 78, 79, 80, 86, 92,
    97–8, 99, 102, 103, 107, 112,
    128, 130–31, 134, 137, 139,
    142, 152, 153, 158, 160, 171,
    172, 178, 180, 182, 185, 187
new technology, 82, 86, 87
Nuttall, R., 69

O'Brien, D.P., 122
Office of Fair Trading, 3, 11, 15,
    16, 17, 18, 20, 24, 26, 27, 47,
    49, 54, 61, 63, 64, 65, 73, 75,
    76, 78, 79, 80, 89, 91, 92, 93,
    94, 100, 103, 106, 107, 111,
    112, 113, 114, 115, 135, 138,
    139, 141, 158, 161, 172, 182,
    184, 185, 188, 189, 191, 196
oligopolistic markets, 7, 34
oligopoly, 39, 41, 62, 93, 98, 122,
    194, 196
oligopoly power, 35
oligopoly theory, 82, 114
on-line databases, 124, 164, 197,
    201
opium derivatives, 11, 49, 55, 62,
    63, 72–5, 79, 142, 146, 178,
    180, 182, 183, 188, 195, 200

orders, 3, 17, 18, 24, 25, 41, 45,
    56, 133, 136, 142, 143, 153–4,
    158, 159, 166, 168, 185
Ornstein, S.I., 120
outdoor specialists, 90, 91, 93, 99,
    100, 184
outlet exclusivity, 128, 129, 130,
    131, 132, 158
    see also exclusive practices
own-brands, 64, 65, 78, 79, 80,
    126–7, 152, 157–8, 159–60,
    168, 178, 180, 184

Padillo, J., 99
parallel pricing, 83, 84, 99, 107,
    112
partial dominance, 36–8, 40–41, 44,
    45, 54, 55, 62, 105, 106, 115,
    123–4, 125, 198–202
patents, 6, 76, 87, 164, 176
Perloff, J.M., 49
Perry, M.K., 122
pest control, 62, 76, 124, 200
petrol, 25, 49, 84, 120, 123, 151–2,
    153, 159, 169, 200
Phlips, L., 11, 104
photocopiers, 123, 164–5, 172, 198,
    201
Pittman, R., 121
plasterboard, 105, 111–12, 198, 200
policy reform, 190–97
Porter, R.H., 83, 122
Portsmouth bus case (1990), 115
Posner, R., 118
postal franking machines, 11, 55,
    123, 125, 137–42, 157, 158,
    171, 178, 180, 181, 183, 185,
    194, 195, 200
Post Office, 137, 138, 139, 140,
    141, 142, 158, 171, 178, 185,
    188
predatory behaviour, 11, 49, 100,
    102, 103, 106, 108, 109, 110–
    11, 114, 115, 144–5, 183, 185
predatory pricing, 7–8, 10, 11, 21,
    23–4, 39, 40, 41, 42, 43, 48,
    54, 55, 102–15, 192, 198–202

Price Commission, 63, 64, 80, 153
price controls, 3, 5, 11, 22, 25, 42,
   43, 44, 46, 48, 49, 52, 54, 55,
   62, 63–4, 65, 66, 67, 68, 69,
   70, 72, 73, 76, 77, 78, 79, 80,
   84, 94, 95–6, 98–9, 100–101,
   137, 168, 177, 178, 179, 182,
   184, 186, 187, 192, 194, 195,
   196, 198–202
price discounts, 8, 72, 76, 87, 98,
   100, 112, 114, 116, 121, 126–
   7, 143, 144, 145, 155, 157,
   159
price discrimination, 8–9, 10, 21,
   24, 39, 40, 41, 42, 43, 48, 49,
   54, 55, 65, 69, 72, 76, 82, 95,
   102–15, 121, 143, 162, 195,
   198–202
price leadership, 10, 35, 39, 40, 41,
   43, 48, 54, 55, 61–81, 98
price monitoring, 11, 42, 43, 44,
   45, 48, 49, 54, 55, 62, 63, 64,
   73, 75, 76, 78, 84, 97, 98, 105,
   107, 178, 179, 182, 184,
   194, 198–202
price notification agreement, 85,
   86–7, 94, 98
primary batteries, 38, 42, 62, 76,
   198
privatisation, 1, 16, 17, 19, 20, 88, 99,
   108, 110, 162, 185
product innovation, 130, 141–2,
   158
product proliferation,
   see brand proliferation
product quality, 85, 87, 99, 131,
   149, 150, 177, 181, 182
profitability, 4, 5, 51–3, 63, 64, 65,
   67, 69, 73, 74, 78, 80, 94, 96,
   98, 137, 152, 156, 165, 170,
   171
prohibition approach, 190–91, 192,
   195
Public Utility Procurement
   Directive, 88

Railways Act (1993), 17

Raleigh bicycles case (1981), 169
razors and razor blades, 44, 49, 62,
   77, 200
ready-mixed concrete, 123, 167,
   199
Rees, R., 11, 83, 95
refusal to supply, 39, 120, 135,
   143, 147, 154, 156, 161, 165,
   168, 169
Regional Electricity Companies,
   87, 88, 185
Registrar of Restrictive Trading
   Agreements, 15–16
remedies to monopoly abuse, 1, 2,
   5, 10, 32, 42–5, 48, 53, 54, 55,
   57, 84, 135, 148, 157, 175,
   178, 179, 181, 187, 188, 189,
   192, 194–5, 196, 198–202
reputation effect, 7–8, 104
resale price maintenance, 16, 18,
   26, 39, 55, 99, 118, 121–4, 125,
   142, 155, 157, 167–9, 171, 172,
   198–202
Resale Prices Act (1976), 16, 17,
   21, 26, 169, 171
research and development, 6, 22,
   23, 27, 31, 83, 177
restrictive agreements,
   see anti-competitive agreements
Restrictive Practices Court, 15, 16,
   18, 26, 169
restrictive trade practices,
   see anti-competitive practices
Restrictive Trade Practices Act (1976),
   16, 17, 21, 82, 98
Rey, P., 120
roadside advertising, 11, 49, 55,
   83, 84, 89–93, 97, 98, 99, 178,
   180, 181, 183, 184, 197, 199
Robertson, A., 169
Robinson-Patman Act (1936), 21,
   24
Ross, D., 11, 26
Royal Mail
   see Post Office

Salop, S.C., 99

scale monopoly, 16, 22, 25, 28, 34,
    37, 39, 46, 47, 55, 61, 65, 78,
    81, 89, 98, 126, 132, 137, 146,
    164, 166, 167, 168, 172, 191,
    193, 194, 198–202
Scherer, F.M., 11, 26
Schmalensee, R., 80
schools of thought, 175
Secretary of State, 3, 16, 17, 18,
    24, 25, 27, 41, 45, 49, 97, 153,
    163, 167, 183, 185, 188, 191–2
selective distribution, 120
selective price cuts, 103
Selective Retail Price Support, 152
Selten, R., 104
Shaffer, G., 121, 122
Shaw, R., 1, 4–5, 11, 29, 48, 51,
    186
Sherman Act (1890), 20, 21, 23, 24
Simpson, P., 1, 4–5, 11, 29, 48, 51,
    186
size of firm, 189
size inequalities, 35–8
    see also concentration
size of the market, 32, 33, 49, 72,
    75, 77, 79, 83, 85–6, 188
Southdown bus case (1993), 115
South Yorkshire bus case (1990),
    115
spatial price discrimination, 8–9,
    105, 106
specialised advertising, 38, 41, 49,
    124, 168, 197, 200
Spengler, J., 9
statutory orders,
    see orders
steel wire fencing, 105, 114
Steiner, R.L., 118
Stenbacka, L.R., 104
Stiglitz, J., 120
strategic responses, 187, 195
structure-conduct-performance
    approach, 116, 118, 176–7
Summers, L., 99
sunk costs, 31, 119, 177
    see also endogenous sunk
    costs

supermarket own-brands,
    see own-brands
survey method, 56
Sutherland, A., 10
Sutton, J., 6, 31, 80, 127, 177, 189

tacit collusion, 7, 11, 77, 82, 83,
    84, 85, 94, 98, 99, 100
takeovers, 76, 94, 99, 108, 109,
    110, 113, 115, 161, 163
    see also mergers
tampons, 84, 97–8, 99, 199
technological agreements, 83
Telecommunications Act (1984),
    17
Telser, L.G., 122
termination of practices, 3, 24, 25,
    42, 43, 44, 45, 48, 54, 55, 62,
    76, 83, 84, 85, 97, 98, 99, 105,
    107, 111, 112, 123–4, 125,
    133, 136, 137, 157, 159, 161,
    163, 172, 178, 179, 184, 187,
    194, 195, 198–202
third party benefits, 191–2, 196
tie-in sales, 9, 23, 24, 39, 49, 55,
    118, 120–21, 122–4, 125, 132,
    133, 137, 142, 157, 158, 164–
    6, 198–202
Tirole, J., 11, 49, 176
trading check franchise and financial
    services, 123, 163, 199
transaction costs, 117, 119
Treaty of Rome, 11, 20
    article 85, 20, 21–2, 23, 26, 191,
    192, 196
    article 86, 11, 20, 21, 22, 23,
    170, 190, 192, 195, 196
Trimdon bus case (1990), 115
Turner, D.F., 104
tying,
    see tie-in sales

UK competition policy, 4, 10, 15–
    20, 26, 82, 190, 192
UK monopoly policy, 15, 24–6, 28,
    185, 188, 190, 191, 192, 193,
    195–6

uncertainty, 119
undertakings, 3, 17, 18, 24, 26, 28,
    41, 44–5, 49, 56, 63, 67, 85,
    86, 94, 97, 100, 106–7, 111,
    113, 115, 126, 133, 135, 138, 139,
    140, 141, 153, 162, 163, 164,
    165, 170, 172, 188, 196
    see also orders
uniform pricing, 111, 114
US competition policy, 10, 15, 20,
    21, 23–4, 26, 99
US Department of Justice, 24
US Federal Trade Commission, 24,
    27
Utton, M.A., 10, 26, 27, 49, 51,
    103–4, 115, 121, 169

Vernon, J., 119
vertical controls, 176
vertical disintegration, 44
vertical integration, 9, 55, 102,
    116, 118–19, 122–4, 125, 135,
    142, 143, 144, 145, 146, 149–
    50, 151, 153–4, 157, 159, 160,
    166–7, 184, 189, 198–202
vertical problems, 46, 48
vertical restraints, 9, 10, 11, 21,
    22, 26, 39, 40, 41, 42, 43, 48,
    49, 52, 53, 54, 55, 82, 102,
    116–72, 179
Vickers, J., 69, 99
video games, 124, 164, 197, 202
voluntary export restraints, 172

Warren-Boulton, F.R., 119
Water Industry Act (1991), 17
Waterson, M., 6, 8, 11, 52, 118,
    120
Weiss, A., 119
White, L.J., 122
white salt, 11, 25, 49, 55, 57, 84,
    93–6, 98–9, 100, 178, 180, 182,
    183, 195, 197, 200
Williams, H., 169
Williamson, O.E., 119
Winter, R.A., 121

wire and fibre ropes, 38, 62, 76,
    198

Zona, J.D., 83